RESEARCH HIGHLIGHTS IN SOCIAL WORK 47

Residential Child Care

RESEARCH HIGHLIGHTS IN SOCIAL WORK 47

Residential Child Care
Prospects and Challenges

Edited by Andrew Kendrick

Jessica Kingsley Publishers
London and Philadelphia

First published in 2008
by Jessica Kingsley Publishers
116 Pentonville Road
London N1 9JB, UK
and
400 Market Street, Suite 400
Philadelphia, PA 19106, USA
www.jkp.com

Library of Congress Cataloging in Publication Data
A CIP catalog record for this book is available from the Library of Congress

British Library Cataloguing in Publication Data
A CIP catalogue record for this book is available from the British Library

ISBN 978 1 84310 526 8

Printed and bound in Great Britain by
Athenaeum Press, Gateshead, Tyne and Wear

Contents

Part Three Conflict and Response

Part Four   Context and Culture

CHAPTER 1

Introduction

Residential Child Care

Andrew Kendrick

In many of the debates about residential child care, the voices of children and young people have not figured prominently. Or rather, in contrast to those who have detailed experiences of abuse and poor practice, the voices of children and young people who have reflected positively on their experiences of residential child care have not been heard. While not denying or down-playing negative experiences of residential child care – indeed the chapters in this book give more than enough detail of such experiences – it is very important to make sure that the balancing, positive views of children and young people are also highlighted (Social Work Inspection Agency 2006).

It is worth recalling, then, that research studies have shown that children and young people prefer residential care over foster care. Sinclair and Gibbs (1998), for example, interviewed 223 children and young people in children's homes and concluded that young people are more likely to choose residential care than any other form of care: 'even those with experience of foster care chose residential care in preference to it by a ratio of three to one' (Sinclair and Gibbs 1998, p. 46; see also Save the Children 2001). As part of the review of looked-after children in Scotland, *Celebrating Success* focused on what helps looked-after children succeed.

> We met a number of participants who had experienced feeling accepted, secure and a sense of belonging in residential care. In the best experiences, partici-pants thought of their residential carers as a kind of family... What often char-acterised the positive relationships in residential care was the continuing sense

of security and safety, which could be relied upon. (Happer, MacCreadie and Aldgate 2006, p. 17)

Policy and ambivalence

Over the years, perhaps one of the reasons that the positive messages about residential child care have not come to the fore has been a continuing ambivalence in the policy debates about the role of residential child care. Alongside exhortations to promote the positive use of residential child care and not to use it as a last resort, there have been clear messages about the primacy of the family, the preference for foster care over residential child care and the excessive cost of residential care, and arguments to reduce the use of residential care placements. Research which has stressed the positive outcomes of residential placements and the complementary nature of residential care vis-à-vis other services (Berridge 1994; Kendrick 1995a, 1995b; Rowe, Hundleby and Garnett 1989) has been overshadowed by the scandals of abuse and government enquiries which have focused attention on negative aspects of residential care (Kent 1997; Levy and Kahan 1991; Skinner 1992; Utting 1991, 1997; Waterhouse 2000).

In this context, the residential sector in the UK has changed considerably over recent years. It has reduced significantly in size, the balance between the use of residential and foster care has shifted markedly, it caters primarily for adolescents (although a significant proportion of younger children experience residential care) and for young people who have experienced significant and multiple difficulties in their lives. Residential care, however, remains a diverse sector: it includes residential child care homes, residential schools, therapeutic communities, secure accommodation services, and services for disabled children and young people. The most recent figures show that on 31 March 2005, of the 60,900 children looked after in England, 8100 were in residential care – secure units, homes, hostels and schools (DfES 2006a). A similar proportion of looked-after children and young people in Scotland are in residential care. The latest figures for Scotland relate to 31 March 2006 and there were 12,966 looked-after children on this date; 1638 children and young people were in residential care (Scottish Executive 2006).

There has been an increasing move for residential services to become more integrated with community and family support services, foster services and educational support services. There have also been major changes in the regulatory framework for services across the UK – requirements for registration of services and staff members, implementation of national standards, and qualifications and training criteria for staff members – all having significant implications for residential child care (Crimmens and Milligan 2005; Kendrick 2004; Mainey *et al.* 2006). Centres of excellence have been established to promote positive practice in residential care: in Scotland, the Scottish Institute for Residential Child Care and, in England, the National Centre for Excellence in Residential Child Care. Such developments have highlighted the continuing need for residential care in a continuum of services for vulnerable children and young people, and the complex and demanding task which is required of residential managers and practitioners (Clough, Bullock and Ward 2006; Kendrick 2005).

Two recent government publications provide further confirmation of the recognition of the positive role of residential child care: in England, the Green Paper *Care Matters: Transforming the Lives of Children and Young People* (DfES 2006b) and, in Scotland, *Extraordinary Lives: Creating a Positive Future for Looked After Children and Young People in Scotland* (Social Work Inspection Agency 2006). Both publications stress the importance of residential care, but also the need to ensure that residential care is of the highest quality. The Green Paper states that:

> Residential care will always be the placement of first choice for some children and we know that some children say that they do not want to be in foster care. We need these children to be able to enjoy a genuinely excellent care experience, drawing on the best of what homes in this country and elsewhere do now. (DfES 2006b, p. 52)

It is important, then, that all those who are involved with children and young people in residential child care draw on the latest research evidence to support their work if they are to improve quality and achieve 'excellence'. The following 15 chapters in this book address major issues relevant to residential child care today. The aim is to pull together the relevant research, to identify ongoing concerns and recent developments, and to highlight implications for policy and practice. The book is divided into four parts:

- promoting well-being and development
- addressing issues of discrimination
- conflict and response
- context and culture.

Promoting well-being and development

In Part One, five chapters address the education, health and mental health of children and young people in residential care, as well as the concept of resilience and the transition from care. Joe Francis highlights the importance of schooling in maximising children's life chances, and the long-standing evidence of the poor educational attainment of children in residential care. He describes the factors which lead to poor educational outcomes – children's social backgrounds, pre-care school experiences, placement instability, the expectations and views of professionals, poor educational support in residential establishments, and problems linked to corporate parenting and ineffective communication – and the recent policy and practice initiatives which address educational attainment.

Children and young people admitted to residential care also suffer from poor health and mental health outcomes. These have not been given the same attention as the education of looked-after children although they are moving up the agenda. Jane Scott, Harriet Ward and Malcolm Hill identify the link between poverty and poor health outcomes and that the factors associated with poorer outcomes in the general population are over-represented in the backgrounds of children in residential care. They identify four sets of factors which affect children's health: organisational processes, change and placement instability, health-related behaviour and lifestyle choices of young people, and the preparation of carers. Recent initiatives adopt more flexible approaches to service delivery to ensure appropriate access to health care. There are close parallels between the issues affecting the general health and the mental health of children and young people in residential child care. Michael van Beinum identifies high rates of mental health problems among young people in residential care and discusses linked risk and resilience factors. He describes similar issues to those examined by Scott, Ward and Hill in the provision of services, and discusses the development of 'whole systems approaches' which offer training and consultancy to carers and residential staff, as well as direct work with individual children and young people.

In Chapter 5, Brigid Daniel develops further the concept of resilience and its relevance to residential care. She outlines a conceptual framework which in-corporates risk and adversity and internal and external protective factors, and identifies five strategies for residential practice: reducing vulnerability and risk, reducing stressors and 'pile-up', increasing available resources, mobilising protective processes and fostering resilience strings. Focusing on the strengths of children and the role of positive relationships, resilience offers an alternative framework for intervention in residential child care.

Finally, in this part, Jo Dixon addresses the transition of young people from residential care. Drawing on empirical research in Scotland, she stresses that transition from residential care at an early age is concerning. The study confirmed poor outcomes in relation to education, work, accommodation and health. The importance of a supportive social network was emphasised, particularly from family; as was continuing contact with professionals, including residential workers.

Addressing issues of discrimination

In Part Two of the book, three chapters address issues of social exclusion and discrimination in residential care. Teresa O'Neill argues forcefully why gender matters in residential child care. She identifies the lack of gender analysis and the importance of gender equality for both children and staff members. She explores the gender differences in the experience of living in residential care and the evidence of worse outcomes for girls. O'Neill stresses that more recognition must be given to the impact of gender on workers' relationships and attitudes, management practices, the abuse of children and ultimately on the quality of the residential experience and outcomes for girls and boys.

In Chapter 8, Kirsten Stalker addresses the experience of disabled children in residential settings, although she emphasises that this is a largely hidden group of children because of a lack of research and information. She highlights disabled children's vulnerability to abuse, the fact that children's views are rarely sought, and difficulties in maintaining contact with families, friends and communities at home. The benefits and positive aspects of residential placements for disabled children are also identified.

Andrew Kendrick's chapter identifies the long-standing concern about the over-representation of black and minority ethnic children in care and the failure of services to address their specific needs. Racism is central to their experience in residential care and it is crucial that this is challenged at all levels. This involves the development of cultural awareness in residential care, involving fostering links with families and communities, the composition of the residential staff group, black role models, promoting positive identity and self-worth, and cultural and religious practices.

Conflict and response

Part Three of this book consists of three chapters which address peer violence in residential care, physical restraint and the use of secure accommodation. In Chapter 10, Christine Barter shows how addressing peer violence has been neglected, despite the fact that young people in residential care have consistently identified it as an overriding concern. Her study focuses on children's experiences of the nature and contexts of peer violence. The chapter identifies children and young people's protective responses and stresses that reducing violence requires a planned, proactive approach and suggests a range of possible approaches: friendship support, mentoring, peer group initiatives, confidential support and reporting systems, and positive reward systems.

Physical restraint is frequently raised as a matter of concern by both children and young people and residential staff members. In Chapter 11, Laura Steckley and Andrew Kendrick link the findings of a recent qualitative study of the experiences of children and staff members to the research literature. They identify the complexities and ambiguities which surround the use of physical restraint, and locate these in terms of guidance, training and research.

In the final chapter in Part Three, Aileen Barclay and Lynne Hunter draw on recent research in Scotland to provide a clearer understanding of the purpose and effectiveness of secure accommodation. Outcomes of young people experiencing secure accommodation are presented. The chapter highlights two key findings: the complementary nature of secure accommodation and 'alternative' services, and the variation across local authorities in relation to the point at which young people would be introduced to 'alternative' services or considered for secure accommodation.

Context and culture

The final part of the book comprises four chapters. Ruth Emond, in Chapter 13, addresses children's rights and participation. She outlines the development of children's rights in the context of the changing construction of childhood, and addresses how this has impacted on the experiences of children and young people in care. She looks critically at how the concept of participation can be used to examine the extent to which the rights of children in care are exercised and their voices are heard.

In Chapter 14, Irene Stevens and Judy Furnivall explore therapeutic approaches in residential child care. They describe holistic therapeutic approaches in the development of therapeutic communities, as well as more specific therapeutic approaches such as lifespace or opportunity-led work, and cognitive-behavioural approaches. While raising interesting questions about children's rights and therapeutic care, they call for the development of therapeutic interventions in order for residential care to achieve its full potential.

Much has been made of the need for training in residential child care, and in Chapter 15, Claire Cameron and Janet Boddy describe recent comparative research to highlight the positive benefits of training for residential staff. Contrasting social pedagogic models in Denmark and Germany with training in England, they provide convincing evidence that staff education and practice relates directly to young people's well-being, such that a pedagogic approach was associated with substantially improved life chances for young people looked after in residential care. They argue for the professionalisation of the residential care workforce through pedagogic education, in order to address current policy objectives.

Finally, in Chapter 16, Roger Bullock identifies from research the clear links between leadership, structure and culture and positive outcomes for children and young people. He stresses the need for a strategic role for residential care in meeting the individual needs of children and young people. Effective management and leadership require that the manager feels supported and in control, with a clear strategy to make the home child-oriented, and a staff team to implement evidence-based interventions.

Conclusion

The contributions to this book address many of the most significant issues affecting residential child care. A number of themes recur over and over again in these chapters. The importance of relationships between young people and residential staff members is highlighted as crucial in the development of positive residential practice. This includes the importance of staff members in undertaking a range of sporting, cultural and leisure activities with children and young people in order to promote their well-being and development.

Unplanned change and placement instability is clearly shown to have a negative impact on a range of outcomes: education, health, mental health, work and accommodation. Efforts to promote stability and continuity must be addressed in terms of continuity of support for children and young people both within placements and through placement change and leaving care. The organisational and structural relationships between professions and agencies are crucial in developing integration and collaboration that will lead to better outcomes for children and young people. The relationship of children and young people with their families and communities, and the role of residential workers and managers in promoting and developing these relationships, is critical. Finally, the authors have underlined just how essential it is to listen to children and young people in residential care, to respect their views and feelings and to promote their rights to provision and participation.

Over the years, there have been a number of moves to reduce residential child care based on a range of factors: cost, the primacy of the family, scandals and abuse, and poor outcomes. It is important, however, to acknowledge that there is a crucial role for residential child care in the range of services for children and young people looked after away from home. The recent policy initiatives which have called for the highest quality in residential child care must address the range of challenges which continue to face children and young people. The positive experiences enjoyed by some children and young people of residential care must be made the norm to ensure the best possible prospects for all children and young people.

References

Berridge, D. (1994) 'Foster and residential care reassessed: A research perspective.' *Children & Society 8*, 2, 132–50.

Clough, R., Bullock, R. and Ward, A. (2006) *What Works in Residential Child Care: A Review of Research Evidence and the Practical Considerations.* London: National Children's Bureau.

Crimmens, D. and Milligan, I. (2005) 'Residential Child Care: Becoming a Positive Choice.' In D. Crimmens and I. Milligan (eds) *Facing Forward: Residential Child Care in the 21st Century.* Lyme Regis: Russell House Publishing.

DfES (Department for Education and Skills) (2006a) *Statistics of Education: Children: Looked After by Local Authorities Year Ending 31 March 2005 – Volume 1: National Tables.* London: National Statistics.

DfES (Department for Education and Skills) (2006b) *Care Matters: Transforming the Lives of Children and Young People in Care.* London: The Stationery Office.

Happer, H., McCreadie, J. and Aldgate, J. (2006) *Celebrating Success: What Helps Looked After Children Succeed.* Edinburgh: Social Work Inspection Agency.

Kendrick, A. (1995a) *Residential Care in the Integration of Child Care Services,* Central Research Unit Papers. Edinburgh: Scottish Office.

Kendrick, A. (1995b) 'The integration of child care services in Scotland.' *Children and Youth Services Review 17*, 5/6, 619–35.

Kendrick, A. (2004) 'Beyond the new horizon: Trends and issues in residential child care.' *Journal of Child and Youth Care Work 18*, 71–80.

Kendrick, A. (2005) 'Social Exclusion and Social Inclusion: Themes and Issues in Residential Child Care.' In D. Crimmens and I. Milligan (eds) *Facing Forward: Residential Child Care in the 21st Century.* Lyme Regis: Russell House Publishing.

Kent, R. (1997) *Children's Safeguards Review.* Edinburgh: Scottish Office.

Levy, A. and Kahan, B. (1991) *The Pindown Experience and the Protection of Children: The Report of the Staffordshire Child Care Inquiry.* Stafford: Staffordshire County Council.

Mainey, A., Milligan, I., Campbell, A., Colton, M., Roberts, S. and Crimmens, D. (2006) 'Context of Residential Child Care in the United Kingdom.' In A. Mainey and D. Crimmens (eds) *Fit for the Future? Residential Child Care in the United Kingdom.* London: National Children's Bureau.

Rowe, J., Hundleby, M. and Garnett, L. (1989) *Child Care Now. A Survey of Placement Patterns.* London: BAAF.

Save the Children (2001) *A Sense of Purpose: Care Leavers' Views and Experiences of Growing Up.* Edinburgh: Save the Children.

Scottish Executive (2006) *Looked After Children 2005–2006.* Edinburgh: Scottish Executive.

Sinclair, I. and Gibbs, I. (1998) *Children's Homes: A Study in Diversity.* London: Wiley.

Skinner, A. (1992) *Another Kind of Home: A Review of Residential Child Care.* Edinburgh: Scottish Office.

Social Work Inspection Agency (2006) *Extraordinary Lives: Creating a Positive Future for Looked After Children and Young People in Scotland.* Edinburgh: Social Work Inspection Agency.

Utting, W. (1991) *Children in the Public Care: A Review of Residential Child Care.* London: HMSO.

Utting, W. (1997) *People Like Us: The Report on the Review of Safeguards for Children Living Away from Home.* London: The Stationery Office.

Waterhouse, R. (2000) *Lost in Care: Report of the Tribunal of Inquiry into the Abuse of Children in Care in the Former County Council Areas of Gwynedd and Clwyd Since 1974.* London: Stationery Office.

PART ONE

Promoting Well-being and Development

CHAPTER 2

Could Do Better!

Supporting the Education
of Looked-after Children

Joe Francis

Introduction

Doing well at school is unquestionably a key factor in maximising children's life chances. The current Labour government placed education at the centre of its election manifesto and when the new Scottish parliament was established in 1999 it brought with it a commitment to place education at the heart of the government's policies in Scotland (Francis 2000). A number of targets, aimed at raising the educational performance and outcomes of all children, were set for the first term of the Scottish parliament which envisioned a world-class school system in which all young people, 'regardless of their background', are confident, motivated and well rounded; literate and numerate to a level at or above that of their peers in the rest of the world; able to play their part as citizens of a modern democratic society; and able to seize the opportunities open to them (Scottish Office 1999).

Giving such priority to education is, of course, welcome but the latest reports suggest that achieving these targets will be difficult, with half of all 14-year-olds in Scotland performing below the expected levels in literacy and numeracy (Scottish Executive 2006). It will be especially difficult to achieve such outcomes for looked-after children and young people as research findings across the UK demonstrate that children in public care (particularly those in residential care) experience extraordinary educational disadvantage (Dixon and Stein 2005; HMI/SWSI 2001).

Whether children do well at school is generally recognised as a major predictive factor in relation to their future life chances. This has led to an increased drive for improved performance on the part of both individuals and schools. Children are exhorted to gain more qualifications at a higher standard and schools are under constant pressure to improve their qualifications results. The effects of this 'education inflation' are significant. Without educational attainment at an early stage in a child's development, successful outcomes in training and employment will be more difficult to achieve in later life (Adams, Dominelli and Payne 2002). Young people who drop out of school without finishing a course of study, or who leave without relevant qualifications, run a higher risk of being unemployed or trapped in low-income work. These difficulties can have a major adverse effect in many other areas of their transition to adult life including poor accommodation, strained relationships with friends and family, involvement in offending behaviour, and financial difficulties.

Such effects are nowhere more apparent than among the experiences of young people who leave public care (see Dixon and Stein 2005; Chapter 6 of the present volume). This highlights a major reason for addressing the problems associated with underachievement in school and ensuring that wider educational opportunities are provided for young people in public care to enable them to gain the best possible access to future life opportunities.

The scale and persistence of the problem

It is only in the last 20 years that the unsatisfactory educational arrangements and poor educational progress of looked-after children have become more widely recognised. Prior to that the low attainment level of looked-after children was simply overlooked or taken for granted (Jackson, Ajayi and Quigley 2003). That is not to say, however, that the poor educational performance of children in the care system is a new phenomenon. Indeed, evidence from as early as the 1960s has indicated that being in care carries a high risk of educational failure (e.g. Essen, Lambert and Head 1976; Ferguson 1966; Pringle 1965; Stein and Carey 1986; Triseliotis and Russell 1984).

The endemic nature of the educational difficulties encountered by young people in public care appears to have remained largely obscure because most studies treated education as an incidental matter rather than as a central focus of enquiry. It was not until an extensive review of the literature was completed in the late 1980s that it became apparent this issue required urgent attention (Jackson 1987).

As many as 50–75 per cent of looked-after children leave school with no qualifications and the majority fail to establish themselves in education, work or training upon leaving school (e.g. Biehal *et al.* 1995; Boyce and Stevens 2005; Dixon and Stein 2005; Francis, Thomson and Mills 1996). Official inspections and reports have consistently indicated that the educational standards achieved by looked-after children are too low and that more than a quarter have a poor history of attendance or are excluded from schools and do not have regular contact with education (HMI/SWSI 2001; Social Exclusion Unit 2003; SSI/Ofsted 1995).

The latest official figures for the educational performance of care leavers in Scotland show that only 55 per cent of those cared for away from home achieved at least one qualification at SCQF level three or above and that only 39 per cent achieved qualifications in both mathematics and English at SCQF level three or above (Scottish Executive 2005a). It can be seen from these figures that the general scale and persistence of the problem has not abated, despite more than a decade of heightened awareness of the problem.

Factors influencing poor outcomes

The causes of poor educational performance among looked-after children involve a complex interplay of factors including children's social backgrounds, pre-care school experiences, placement instability, the expectations and views of professionals, poor educational support in residential establishments, and problems linked to corporate parenting and ineffective communication.

Children's social backgrounds

Many young people come into public care with a history of educational difficulties and these difficulties usually stem from their experience of social exclusion and multiple disadvantage (Brodie 2001; Francis *et al.* 1996; Packman and Hall 1998). There is a strong connection between socio-economic deprivation and poor educational attainment and even where a school's performance improves and achievement levels are raised, the *relative* achievements of children from poor and more affluent families are not likely to change (Mortimore and Whitty 1997). Social deprivation continues to have a major negative impact on the educational performance of children and this is a particular problem for those who come to the attention of social services. The underlying effects of poverty on children's educational performance therefore have to be assessed and addressed at an early stage in their care careers.

Pre-care school experiences

The families of children who come into care are characterised by poverty and unemployment, marital discord and breakdown, inadequate housing and over-crowding, health problems and social isolation (Bebbington and Miles 1989; Berridge and Brodie 1998; Brodie 2001). Such adverse circumstances inevitably have a damaging effect on the educational progress of these children and they experience high levels of exclusion, truancy and social, emotional and behavioural problems, and high referral rates to educational psychologists, *before* they become looked after (Brodie 2001; Francis *et al.* 1996; HMI/SWSI 2001).

Even when these problems are recognised at a relatively early stage in the children's primary school careers, policies of minimal intervention in situations where education is an issue often result in referrals to social work being delayed until a point of crisis (Fletcher-Campbell 1997). There are indications that this situation is changing with the move towards children's trusts in England, the establishment of children's services departments (or their equivalent) in many authorities in Scotland, and the development of integrated planning and assessment mechanisms.

Placement instability

The pre-care experiences and characteristics of looked-after children are not sufficient in themselves to explain the poor educational progress of this group. A critical association has been found between disrupted care arrangements and unsatisfactory educational performance *after* the care placement is made (Bailey, Thoburn and Wakeham 2002; Biehal *et al.* 1992; Francis *et al.* 1996). Although professionals are now more alert to the potentially harmful consequences of disrupted care placements, care episodes tend to be shorter than previously and young people often experience multiple placements (Berridge and Brodie 1998; Department of Health 1999; Sinclair and Gibbs 1998). This trend will continue to represent a barrier to improving their educational performance.

It is important that disruptions and changes in care placements should be minimised (Jackson and Thomas 2001). However, changes in care placements are often unavoidable and in these situations maintaining *continuity* in other aspects of the young person's life, including school arrangements and links with family and community, is key to supporting the young person. The importance of maintaining continuity in the educational arrangements of looked-after children was highlighted in a recent project in Bristol (Bristol City Council 2002) which provided additional educational support to looked-after children in mainstream primary schools. Even though some children moved foster placement during the course of the intervention (and experienced an initial phase of regression), sustaining their school arrangements helped them to improve their spelling and reading significantly.

Professionals' expectations

Another factor that adversely affects the educational progress of looked-after children is the low expectations that social workers and carers often hold concerning their educational achievement (Aldgate *et al.* 1993; Borland *et al.* 1998; Francis *et al.* 1996; Harker *et al.* 2003). Accounts from children who have been placed in public care indicate that they commonly experience indifference from social workers and carers in relation to their education (Jackson 1994; Triseliotis and Russell 1984). One study found that few children felt that social workers had supported their education (Harker *et al.* 2003) and where young people have been successful in their education they report that this is not due to support and encouragement from social workers (Jackson 1994).

Some social workers continue to be reluctant to set what they regard as unrealistic goals for children for fear that this might compound their feelings of failure. Where children are not attending school, workers tend to leave the education section of the 'Looking After Children' materials blank and not to identify measures that might lead to improvements in, or resolution of, the problem (Ward 1995).

Another major criticism is that social workers and carers still tend to regard 16 as the age that education ceases for young people in public care (Jackson and Sachdev 2001) and, together with teachers, frequently do not give children's educational progress and standards of achievement sufficient priority compared with the attention given to such matters as care, relationships and contact with parents (Ofsted 1995). Concern has also been expressed that social workers appear to have lost sight of the fact that, next to their families, schools have the strongest influence on children's development and the benefits of a good educational experience can be greatest for children who have experienced adverse circumstances in their home lives (Gilligan 1999).

Poor educational support

The poor educational progress of looked-after children is, in large part, a product of the system, often reflecting inadequate support and planning (Fletcher-Campbell 1997). A high proportion of residential care establishments do not provide an educationally rich environment. While much good work is being done to redress this situation, many still suffer from poor educational resources, have inadequate facilities for homework and limited privacy for study. Moreover, staff do not always make full use of a range of opportunities to enhance children's education (Berridge and Brodie 1998; HMI/SWSI 2001). There are encouraging signs that government action is beginning to have an impact on the quality of educational support in children's homes, with a recent study finding that supports are more widely available in residential settings than in foster care (Harker *et al.* 2003). Work still needs to be done, however, on getting staff to actively assist young people with their schoolwork as most of these supports are material or physical, whereas children in foster care have more personal support and interest from their carers (Harker *et al.* 2003).

Concern has also been expressed about the low level of priority given to education in care planning meetings and statutory reviews, and the failure to fully utilise school's contributions in these arenas (Francis *et al.* 1996; Ofsted 1995; Scottish Executive 2001). This is an important matter that requires further attention within the process of integrating children's service planning and delivery.

Communication, coordination and corporate parenting

Communication and coordination difficulties contribute greatly to the problem. These difficulties arise within a number of levels of the care system, including the actions and responsibilities of front-line service providers and, more generally, within organisational policies and procedures which are often fragmented and poorly coordinated (Borland *et al.* 1998; Scottish Executive 2001). A major issue is the extent to which public authorities can replicate the role and function of concerned parents. A number of features of corporate parenting hinder looked-after children's educational progress, including:

- failure of the whole local authority to act as 'good parents' (Jackson and Sachdev 2001)

- lack of effective structures and procedures to ensure that all professionals and agencies are working effectively together (Harker *et al.* 2004)

- failure to be proactive in promoting children's educational progress (Parker *et al.* 1991).

Factors such as the lack of clarity about roles and responsibilities between carers, social workers and teachers, or about maintaining effective contact with schools, are frequently cited. Although local authorities tend not to issue clear guidance on what the role of carers should be in relation to children's education, nonetheless, there is a heavy reliance on carers to promote the children's educational interests (SSI/Ofsted 1995). A number of studies have found that social workers are not actively involved with schools, nor do they have a keen interest in the children's education (e.g. Aldgate *et al.* 1993; Francis *et al.* 1996; HMI/SWSI 2001). By and large, carers, rather than field social workers, take on the key role of liaising with schools, even though there is usually no officially agreed policy or procedure in relation to this.

At the wider organisational level, there are communications failures within the education and social work recording systems and these problems have not yet been overcome through the introduction of information-sharing technology (Jackson and Sachdev 2001). As well as inadequate information within their own systems (Francis 2004; Francis *et al.* 1996), education and social work frequently have no means of recording important information that crosses over the two domains (Evans 2000).

Where local authorities adopt a more structured approach to corporate parenting responsibilities, including effective liaison between education and social work, there is some evidence of higher commitment to children's educational success and children are more likely to be maintained in school (Fletcher-Campbell 1997; Vernon and Sinclair 1998). The establishment of joint procedures and protocols (Department for Education and Employment/ Department of Health 2000) and the ongoing process of integration (both in terms of assessment and planning and in terms of organisational structures) should bring improvements in this area.

School exclusion

Exclusion from school is a highly significant issue for children in public care (Brodie 2001; Francis 2004; SSI/Ofsted 1995). The Social Exclusion Unit (1998) found that young people in care are ten times more likely to be excluded from school than their peers and the most recent investigations continue to show that up to 60 per cent of children and young people in public care have a history of school exclusion (Brodie 2001; Harker *et al.* 2003). It appears that children in residential care are particularly likely to experience permanent exclusion than children in the general school population (Francis 2004) and exclusion is often viewed as an inevitable part of life in children's homes with little action taken to counteract the problem (Berridge and Brodie 1998).

Clearly, when children are excluded from school they are not likely to make good progress with their studies and, in the longer term, permanent exclusion from school is associated with wider social exclusion from society (Hayton 1999). Conversely, it has been found that care leavers who have had *successful* educational outcomes are significantly more likely *not* to have experienced absence from school through exclusion or truancy (Jackson and Martin 1998). Measures to improve the educational progress of looked-after children must therefore address the unacceptably high levels of school exclusion in the care population.

Improving policy

The poor educational outcomes of looked-after children can be attributed to broader social factors and to failures within the corporate system of education and care, rather than simply to the young people themselves. These are matters that must be addressed within strategic policy as well as through improved practice.

Current legislation places a duty on local authorities to safeguard and promote the welfare of a child looked after by them, including a duty to promote the child's educational achievement (Children Act 1989, as amended by the Children Act 2004; Children (Scotland) Act 1995). Under the provisions of the 2004 Act (which came into force in England on 1 July 2005), local authorities must give *particular attention* to the educational implications of any decision about the welfare of those children.

The most recent statutory guidance in England (Department for Education and Skills 2005) builds on earlier developments through the Department of Health Quality Protects programme, the publication of guidance on the education of young people in public care (Department for Education and Employment/Department of Health 2000), and the findings set out in the Social Exclusion Unit's report (2003). Much emphasis is given in the present guidance to strategic planning and children's services authorities now have a duty to prepare and publish a Children and Young People's Plan which should address the specific need to make steady and significant improvements in the educational achievements of children looked after by the local authority. In addition, directors of children's services and local politicians are required to:

- focus on narrowing the gap in educational achievement between looked-after children and their peers by improving the stability of their lives

- ensure that systems and structures enable looked-after children to be supported so that they achieve their full potential

- ensure that looked-after children have access to a suitable range of care and education placement options which maximise the educational opportunities and experiences available to them

- ensure that there are agreed procedures and protocols in place to support a shared understanding of the local authority's role as corporate parent in meeting the best educational interests of looked-after children, wherever they are placed.

Another major plank in the current guidance concerns the implementation of 'personal education plans' (PEPs). These individualised plans are intended to effectively promote the educational achievement of looked-after children so that, at every age, they achieve educational outcomes comparable to their peers. The range of education and development needs that should be covered in a PEP includes:

- ongoing catch-up support for those who have fallen behind with schoolwork

- suitable education where a child is not in school, for example because of temporary or permanent exclusion

- transition support needs and integration when children begin to attend a new school or return to school (e.g. following illness or exclusion)

- out-of-school-hours learning activities/study support and leisure interests

- behaviour support

- the necessary level of support to help the child to achieve an appropriate range of approved qualifications

- support needed to achieve long-term aspirations for further and higher education, training and employment.

In Scotland, there has also been a raft of policy initiatives in recent years to develop an integrated approach to delivering children's services and to improve a range of outcomes. A key objective is to raise the educational outcomes and achievement levels of all children, with particular emphasis on raising the performance of looked-after children.

For Scotland's Children (Scottish Executive 2001) drew attention to the need to provide better integration of services at points of delivery through the development of Integrated Children's Services Plans. The Education (Additional Support for Learning) Act 2004 places new duties on local authorities and other agencies to work together to provide integrated support for individual children and young people who, for whatever reason, require additional support to benefit from education. The most recent proposals for changes to children's services, including the Children's Hearings System, *Getting it Right for Every Child*, recommend development of a single assessment framework and greater focus on outcomes for individual children (Scottish Executive 2005b). As in England, the Scottish Executive are keen to implement a system of Personal Education Plans for every child. If these proposals are implemented, key agencies will be under a duty to cooperate to develop individual plans to meet identified needs and to appoint a lead professional to plan and coordinate activity where a child requires multi-agency input. The lead professional will be required to monitor and ensure that progress is being achieved.

While it is too early to assess the impact of these policy initiatives, they undoubtedly represent a serious intention to address this issue. To be effective, however, they have to be accompanied by significant improvements in everyday practice.

Adopting a practice strategy

Professionals working with looked-after children must recognise that they play a crucial role in bringing about positive educational outcomes for this group. In order to realise the broader policy objectives outlined above, carers, social workers and teachers need to adopt a structured and coherent practice strategy, focusing on the needs and abilities of individual children. Gallagher *et al.* (2004) identified a number of essential features of such a strategy. These measures should be applied with all looked-after children, whatever the placement setting, and include the following:

- Set the scene:
  o   raise the child's awareness of the value of education (i.e. in terms of future development, opportunities etc.) and prioritise the place of education within the home
  o   establish clear expectations about the child's engagement with education – going to school is not optional!
  o   where a child is out of school, use an incremental approach to re-integrate the child in education (e.g. home tuition, educational support unit, part-time school, full-time school)
  o   prepare the child emotionally as well as practically (address fears and anxieties etc.).
- Support the child in school:
  o   take an interest!
  o   give praise!
  o   help with problems
  o   help with homework
  o   read with children
  o   give the child a place to work
  o   engage them in a wide range of interests/activities
  o   attend school events, parents' evenings etc.
- Support the school placement:
  o   ensure good home/school communication
  o   provide a support worker in class
  o   work collaboratively.

- Develop a learning culture:
  - o   identify and support the child's interests and talents
  - o   look beyond the school for learning opportunities
  - o   develop links in the community.

Clearly, there is no quick-fix solution to the educational difficulties that many looked-after children face. Equally, though, there is no reason to give up on these children and adhering to the practice strategy outlined here should greatly enhance the chance of achieving much improved outcomes.

Conclusion

The primary contextual conditions of children in public care are social adversity, poverty and fractured families. This leads to some discomfiting conclusions about the likely outcomes for these children. The difficulties they experience at home inevitably intersect and overlap with their school experiences, usually to their disadvantage. Given their antecedents, it is likely that a proportion of looked-after children will always fare badly in educational terms. Our knowledge about factors which help or hinder the educational performance of young people in public care is much improved and there is a burgeoning policy context in which to bring about improvements. There is clearly a need to intervene earlier in the school lives of those disadvantaged children who come to the attention of welfare agencies and we need to promote more effective, integrated provision to support the education of these children. Policies and practice need to address inherent structural and procedural difficulties that compound the problem. Finally, the effects of being excluded from school often compound the degree of social exclusion experienced by many children in public care. This is a matter of considerable regret and local authorities must ensure that they place those children for whom they have corporate responsibilities at the top of their agenda. If children and young people in public care continue to fail in terms of their educational performance, this will have implications which extend far beyond their schooling to their capacity to participate fully in society in later stages of their lives.

References

Adams, R., Dominelli, L. and Payne, M. (2002) *Social Work: Themes, Issues and Critical Debates*, 2nd edition. Basingstoke: Palgrave.
Aldgate, J., Heath, A., Colton, M. and Simm, M. (1993) 'Social work and the education of children in foster care.' *Adoption and Fostering 17*, 3, 25–34.

Bailey, S., Thoburn, J. and Wakeham, H. (2002) 'Using the "Looking After Children" dimensions to collect aggregate data on well-being.' *Child and Family Social Work 7*, 3, 189–203.

Bebbington, A. and Miles, J. (1989) 'The background of children who enter local authority care.' *British Journal of Social Work 19*, 5, 349–68.

Berridge, D. and Brodie, I. (1998) *Children's Homes Revisited.* London: Jessica Kingsley Publishers.

Biehal, N., Clayden, J., Stein, M. and Wade, J. (1992) *Prepared for Living? A Survey of Young People Leaving the Care of Three Local Authorities.* London: National Children's Bureau.

Biehal, N., Clayden, J., Stein, M. and Wade, J. (1995) *Moving On: Young People and Leaving Care Schemes.* London: HMSO.

Borland, M., Pearson, C., Hill, M., Tisdall, K. and Bloomfield, I. (1998) *Education and Care Away from Home: A Review of Research, Policy and Practice.* Edinburgh: Scottish Council for Research in Education.

Boyce, P. and Stevens, I. (2005) *Raising the Standards: Capturing the Views of Young People who Use Residential Care Home Services.* Glasgow: Who Cares? Scotland and Scottish Institute for Residential Child Care.

Bristol City Council (2002) *The Education of Children Looked After Service: Annual Report 2001/2002.* Bristol: Bristol City Council.

Brodie, I. (2001) *Children's Homes and School Exclusion: Redefining the Problem.* London: Jessica Kingsley Publishers.

Department for Education and Employment/Department of Health (2000) *Guidance on the Education of Children and Young People in Public Care.* London: DfEE/Department of Health.

Department for Education and Skills (2005) *Statutory Guidance on the Duty on Local Authorities to Promote the Educational Achievement of Looked After Children Under Section 52 of the Children Act 2004.* London: DfES.

Department of Health (1999) *The Children Act Report.* London: The Stationery Office.

Dixon, J. and Stein, M. (2005) *Leaving Care: Throughcare and Aftercare Services in Scotland.* London: Jessica Kingsley Publishers.

Essen, J., Lambert, L. and Head, J. (1976) 'School attainment of children who have been in care.' *Child Care Health and Development 2*, 6, 339–51.

Evans, R. (2000) 'The Education and Progress of Children in Public Care.' PhD thesis. Warwick: University of Warwick.

Ferguson, T. (1966) *Children in Care and After.* London: Oxford University Press.

Fletcher-Campbell, F. (1997) *The Education of Children who are Looked After.* Slough: National Foundation for Educational Research.

Francis, J. (2000) 'Investing in children's futures: Enhancing the educational arrangements of "looked after" children and young people.' *Child and Family Social Work 5*, 1, 23–33.

Francis, J. (2004) 'Failing Children? A Study of the Educational Experiences of Young People in Residential Care.' PhD thesis. Edinburgh: University of Edinburgh.

Francis, J., Thomson, G.O.B. and Mills, S. (1996) *The Quality of the Educational Experience of Children in Care.* Edinburgh: University of Edinburgh.

Gallagher, B., Brannan, C., Jones, R. and Westwood, S. (2004) 'Good practice in the education of children in residential care.' *British Journal of Social Work 34*, 8, 1133–60.

Gilligan, R. (1999) 'Enhancing the resilience of children and young people in public care by mentoring their talents and interests.' *Child and Family Social Work 4*, 3, 187–96.

Harker, R., Dobel-Ober, D., Berridge, D. and Sinclair, R. (2004) 'More than the sum of its parts? Inter-professional working in the education of looked after children.' *Children and Society 18*, 3, 179–93.

Harker, R., Dobel-Ober, D., Lawrence, J., Berridge, D. and Sinclair, R. (2003) 'Who takes care of education? Looked after children's perceptions of support for educational progress.' *Child and Family Social Work 8*, 2, 89–100.

Hayton, A. (1999) *Tackling Disaffection and Social Exclusion: Education Perspectives and Policies.* London: Kogan Page.

HMI/SWSI (2001) *Learning with Care: The Education of Children Looked After Away from Home by Local Authorities.* Edinburgh: Stationery Office.

Jackson, S. (1987) *The Education of Children in Care*, Bristol Papers No.1. Bristol: University of Bristol School of Applied Social Studies.

Jackson, S. (1994) 'Education in residential child care.' *Oxford Review of Education 20*, 3, 267–79.

Jackson, S., Ajayi, S. and Quigley, M. (2003) *By Degrees: The First Year, From Care to University.* London: The Frank Buttle Trust.

Jacson, S. and Martin, P.Y. (1998) 'Surviving the care system: Education and resilience.' *Journal of Adolescence 21*, 569–83.

Jackson, S. and Sachdev, D. (2001) *Better Education, Better Futures: Research, Practice and the Views of Young People in Public Care.* Barkingside: Barnardos.

Jackson, S. and Thomas, N. (2001) *What Works in Creating Stability for Looked After Children?* Barkingside: Barnardos.

Mortimore, P. and Whitty, G. (1997) *Can School Improvement Overcome the Effects of Disadvantage?* London: University of London Institute of Education.

Ofsted (1995) *Pupil Referral Units: The First Twelve Inspections.* London: Office for Standards in Education.

Packman, J. and Hall, C. (1998) *From Care to Accommodation: Support, Protection, and Control in Child Care Services.* London: Stationery Office.

Parker, R., Ward, H., Jackson, S., Aldgate, J. and Wedge, P. (eds) (1991) *Looking After Children: Assessing Outcomes in Child Care.* London: HMSO.

Pringle, M.K. (1965) *Deprivation and Education.* London: Longmans.

Scottish Executive (2001) *For Scotland's Children: Better Integrated Children's Services.* Edinburgh: Scottish Executive.

Scottish Executive (2005a) *Children's Social Work Statistics 2004–2005.* Edinburgh: National Statistics Publication.

Scottish Executive (2005b) *Getting it Right for Every Child: Proposals for Action.* Edinburgh: Scottish Executive.

Scottish Executive (2006) *Pupil Attainment Survey.* News release. Edinburgh: Scottish Executive, 26 June.

Scottish Office (1999) *Targeting Excellence – Modernising Scotland's Schools.* Cm. 4247. Edinburgh: The Scottish Office.

Sinclair, I. and Gibbs, I. (1998) *Children's Homes: A Study in Diversity.* Chichester: Wiley.

Social Exclusion Unit (1998) *Truancy and School Exclusion.* London: The Stationery Office.

Social Exclusion Unit (2003) *A Better Education for Children in Care: Social Exclusion Unit Report.* London: Social Exclusion Unit.

SSI/Ofsted (1995) *The Education of Children who are Looked After by Local Authorities.* London: Department of Health and Ofsted.

Stein, M. and Carey, K. (1986) *Leaving Care.* Oxford: Blackwell.

Triseliotis, J. and Russell, J. (1984) *Hard to Place: The Outcome of Adoption and Residential Care.* London: Heinemann.

Vernon, J. and Sinclair, R. (1998) *Maintaining Children in School: The Contribution of Social Services Departments.* London: NCB and Joseph Rowntree Foundation.

Ward, H. (ed.) (1995) *Looking After Children: Research into Practice.* London: HMSO.

CHAPTER 3

The Health of Looked-after Children in Residential Care

Jane Scott, Harriet Ward and Malcolm Hill

Introduction

The agenda for improving the health of the nation and, in particular, the health of children and young people is shared by professionals, politicians and policy-makers across the UK. In 1998, Sir Donald Acheson identified socio-economic determinants for health: insufficient household income, unemployment, poorer quality of housing or homelessness and lack of access to private means of transport were all associated with poorer health outcomes (Acheson 1998). Low income, deprivation and social exclusion were associated with poorer mental, physical and emotional health and diet, as well as a low incidence of breastfeeding (Acheson 1998; van Beinum, Martin and Bonnett 2005; Hill and Tisdall 1997).

In England and Wales, *Reducing Health Inequalities: An Action Report* (Department of Health 1999a) and *Saving Lives: Our Healthier Nation* (Department of Health 1999b) set out the government's strategy for health for the next decade. Promoting health was seen as part of an initiative to tackle the underlying causes of ill health and set within the context of a wider public health agenda to reduce smoking and teenage pregnancies, and to combat communicable diseases. This was in line with the World Health Organisation's well-known definition of health as 'a state of complete, physical, social and mental well being and not merely the absence of disease or infirmity' (World Health Organisation 1948, p. 1).

The report of the House of Commons Select Committee concluded that 'the failure of local authorities to secure good health outcomes for the children and young people they look after is a failure of corporate parenting' (House of Commons Select Committee on Health 1998, para. 265). *Quality Protects* (Department of Health 2000) in England and *Children First* (National Assembly of Wales 1999) in Wales focused on improving the life chances of children in care. *Promoting the Health Care of Looked After Children* charged chief executives of primary care trusts with improving the health care of the most disadvantaged children (Department of Health 2002). More recently, *Every Child Matters: Change for Children* (HM Government 2004) has identified 'being healthy' as one of the key outcomes which all children's services must work towards in an integrated way.

A similar drive to improve the health of the Scottish nation has been taken forward by the Scottish Executive. *For Scotland's Children* set out a vision for all children and young people in Scotland by emphasising that all should have access from birth to the services and environments necessary to ensure they fulfil their potential (Scottish Executive 2001). This vision depends on an ability to take account of and respond to the whole child including his or her health. Health policy documents such as the White Paper *Towards a Healthier Scotland* (Scottish Office 1999) and *Our National Health: A Plan for Action, a Plan for Change* (Scottish Executive 2000) were aimed at improving the health of children and young people, and tackling the inequalities in health provision, often through interventions early in life. The Cabinet Delivery Group on Children and Young People set out a vision for all Scottish children, which identified that 'children and young people need to attain the highest attainable standards of physical and mental health with access to suitable healthcare and support for safe and healthy lifestyle choices' (Scottish Executive 2005, p. 4).

Children and young people looked after

The factors which wider research has shown to be associated with poorer health outcomes in the general population are over-represented in the original family and environment of a significant number of children who enter local authority care. Many are born into families from lower socio-economic groups (Bebbington and Miles 1989), exposed to discord likely to heighten their stress (Triseliotis *et al.* 1995), and a significant proportion have become looked after as a result of physical injury, neglect or sexual abuse (Minnis and Del Priore 2001). Children who are looked after and accommodated tend to have a background and previous experiences which heighten the risk of poorer than average current and future health and well-being.

This chapter considers the health experiences of all children looked after, but focuses, where evidence is available, on the experience of those in residential care. It is important to point out that children and young people living in foster care span the age range from babies and infants to those preparing to leave care, whilst those living in residential care are predominantly in their teenage years. General health issues, such as diet and health promotion, will be relevant to all caring environments, but issues linked with health-related behaviours and lifestyle choices, such as smoking, drinking and drug use, are more likely to be present in residential settings. Moreover, residential placements are very expensive; they tend to be reserved for the more challenging and vulnerable children, with the result that potentially damaging health-related behaviours are often prevalent in such settings (Ward *et al.* forthcoming).

Despite the adverse factors in the backgrounds of children who are looked after and accommodated, the literature suggests that the general health of the majority is good. Carers of just under three-quarters of looked-after young people have described their health as good or very good (Meltzer *et al.* 2003, 2004; Triseliotis *et al.* 1995). This assertion is subject to two important qualifications. First, it applies largely to physical health; there is a high incidence of mental health problems (including conduct disorders) amongst the population of young people looked after by local authorities (see Chapter 4 of the present volume). Second, many of these young people, while remaining healthy, nevertheless have lifestyles that present major threats to their present or future well-being.

Entering the care of the local authority can offer opportunities to young people to access services that begin to address or rectify many of their health needs. Meltzer and colleagues (2003, 2004) found that the general health of children seems to improve as placements become more secure; over two-thirds of children who had been in a placement for two years or more were assessed as having very good health. This figure reduced to just under half for those who had been in a placement for less than two years. Children living with foster carers were more likely to be rated as having very good health compared with children living in other placement types, particularly residential care (Meltzer *et al.* 2003, 2004). Again this finding reflects both the age profile and the characteristics of children and young people who are placed in residential units.

Factors affecting the health of young people in residential care

Despite the efforts of policy-makers and professionals, meeting the health needs of children and young people in care continues to be a challenge and it is likely that a series of factors are acting in combination as unwitting barriers to meeting their needs.

First, different organisational structures and processes may inhibit young people from accessing services, may seem at odds with young people's wishes or may obstruct inter-agency working. Second, the constant change and placement moves experienced by many looked-after young people often impacts on the continuity of their development across all areas of their lives including health (Chambers *et al.* 2002; Ward *et al.* 2002). A third factor may be the health-related behaviour and lifestyle choices of young people themselves. Their choices may impact on their immediate health and also their future health and well-being. Finally, a fourth possible barrier may be the lack of preparation of carers reported by some practitioners and carers working with troubled young people who are exhibiting challenging behavioural or mental health difficulties.

Organisational processes

The key agencies within a young person's life have responsibility for ensuring that all their needs are met and continue to be met. The factors within a child's family circumstances may mean that they are at considerable risk of missing out on routine health surveillance such as immunisations or regular health care (Ward *et al.* 2002). Immunisation programmes can offer prevention from diseases which are likely to have long-term consequences for children whose health may be already jeopardised by a poor diet or adverse living conditions. Some young children entering the looked-after system require compensatory health care, but as Polnay and Ward (2000) comment, the 'potential for the care service to compensate for previous deficits rather than simply to provide accommodation until children reach adulthood is not always explicitly understood' (Polnay and Ward 2000, p. 661). A study of nine health districts across England, Scotland and Wales showed that 33 per cent of children in public care did not receive the meningococcal C vaccine compared with 15 per cent of children living at home and not known to social work departments (Hill, Mather and Goddard 2003).

Once a child is in the care of a local authority, the process of conducting health checks and assessments through routine or annual medical examinations has not always been satisfactory. In England, medical reports are often completed inconsistently; many young people do not wish to be removed from school to attend medical assessments undertaken by a practitioner little known to them (Butler and Payne 1997). In Scotland, a different approach has been taken in the light of such evidence. The Arrangements to Look After Children (Scotland) Regulations 1996 did require local authorities to arrange medical examinations and written health assessments for all before a young person was placed, or as soon as possible thereafter, but there was no expectation to arrange an annual health assessment. Although this may help avoid an experience that some young people find embarrassing or pointless, it means that both routine checks and the need for compensatory health care could be overlooked.

Accessing services can be seen as stigmatising by young people who often report that they do not feel listened to (van Beinum *et al.* 2005; Bundle 2002) and that professionals and the organisations can be difficult to approach (Buston 2002) leading to gaps in the young person's knowledge on how to access sensitive information on sexual health and safer sex, and also mental health issues. Sexual health programmes are often delivered through schools, but the most vulnerable children and young people may miss out if, as often happens, they are absent or excluded from school. Other studies have also shown gaps in a young person's knowledge around the risks of unsafe sex in terms of sexually transmitted disease and pregnancies (Triseliotis *et al.* 1995).

Generally, all young people identify physical fitness, healthy eating and physical attractiveness as factors which contribute to good health. Praise and encouragement are thought to promote health providing a link between how young people feel, their level of self-esteem and their ability to function in life (Daniel and Wassell 2002). However, some young people have seen living in residential care as a barrier to a healthy lifestyle because such settings do not provide enough opportunities – or enough money – to meet the cost of sports or exercise activities (Ridley and McCluskey 2003).

Changes in placement

When young people move between different homes or units there is a risk that important issues are overlooked. When a move involves changing health authority, this can result in appointments being changed, missed or delayed.

Not only is information about current health issues lost, but just as important is the potential loss of the family health history (Butler and Payne 1997).

Hill (2001) identified a number of reasons why an accurate record of the child's family health history is important. These include knowledge of inherited conditions, which may remain unnoticed or are less important during childhood, but influence important decisions in adult life. Knowledge of parental history is also important; information that the birth father of a child in foster care has suffered from coeliac disease should raise questions about introducing gluten to the infant's diet; an understanding of family history may shed some light on the cause of established or emerging emotional and behavioural difficulties. Moreover insufficient information about a child's family history and circumstances may increase the risk of the transmission of blood-borne diseases such as HIV and hepatitis.

Gathering an accurate family history is not necessarily an easy task. Some parents may be deceased or untraceable or may refuse consent, but it is essential that professionals working with children understand the importance of this information in a child's current and later life.

Furthermore, a number of studies have also identified the absence of accurate up-to-date recording of children's health needs (Butler and Payne 1997; Cleaver and Walker 2004; Ward and Skuse 1999). It seems that some social workers do not view this as part of their daily routine; 'completing the paperwork' is understandably considered a lower priority when faced with pressing matters of resolving serious family conflict or finding a bed for a young person. In authorities with a workforce struggling with vacancies and high turnover of staff, it is often difficult to gather and record systematically a chronology of an individual's life when all else around may be changing. However, it is precisely for these reasons that accurate records are crucial. Recent policy and practice developments of electronic record-keeping within the fields of health and social care, such as the Integrated Children's System, and the eHealth and Social Care Record in England and Wales, and Integrated Assessment Framework and eCare in Scotland, may go some way to addressing this.

Changes in placement can also result in changes in schools and this together with higher truancy rates can mean young people in care can miss out on routine medical checks and health promotion initiatives within school. This can include informed discussion on healthy lifestyles, contraception, sexually transmitted diseases, sexual choices and risk-taking behaviours such as misuse of drugs, tobacco and alcohol (Ward *et al.* 2002).

Health-related behaviours and lifestyles

As with the majority of the general teenage population, smoking, drinking and the use of illegal drugs are present in the behaviours and lifestyle choices of many looked-after young people. However, of greater concern is that these very vulnerable young people tend to start these activities at an earlier age than the general population (Meltzer *et al.* 2003, 2004), and that general levels of uptake within this population are often higher (Meltzer *et al.* 2003, 2004; Saunders and Broad 1997; Triseliotis *et al.* 1995).

Skuse and Ward (2003) found that many of the young people they interviewed had an established history of drug or alcohol abuse *before* they entered care. However, such behaviour patterns could also be reinforced by the culture of some residential settings. Griesbach and Currie (2001) found a significant uptake of drugs by young people with experience of care compared with other teenagers. Among the many reasons given by those in public care was that it helped them to forget 'bad things' or to relax, or gave them more confidence. Furthermore, around a third of the sample who had tried drugs had done so whilst in care, but just over two-thirds had taken drugs before coming into care. Meltzer and colleagues (2004) found that looked-after and accommodated children in Scotland aged 11–17 were twice as likely to smoke, drink or take drugs as their English counterparts.

Early pregnancy brings health risks for the mothers and an increased likelihood of poor outcomes for the children. Sexual intercourse before the age of 16 has been associated with deprivation, single-parent families, low educational levels, having a mother who also gave birth in her teens and a poor relationship with parents (Corlyon and McGuire 1999; Henderson *et al.* 2002). Ely and colleagues (2000) also found that less time spent at home at the age of 15 was associated with early pregnancy. However, it is important to stress that it is not early sexual activity *per se*, but unprotected sexual behaviour that poses a threat to the young person's health in terms of sexually transmitted diseases and unplanned pregnancies.

From research in England, it is estimated that a quarter of young women leaving care are pregnant or have a child and that the numbers of young women who give birth increase within 18–24 months of leaving care (Biehal *et al.* 1995). This is of particular concern because a significant number of looked-after young people of this age have the added pressure of moving to independent living and many experience heightened feelings of anxiety and isolation. This also echoes the feedback from young people in the care system preparing for independence (Scottish Health Feedback 2003).

Preparation of carers

Studies have found that carers' perceptions of feeling burdened were related to caring for a young person displaying high levels of behavioural problems. Foster carers have reported that where problems had been identified, indications had been present for over a year (McCarthy, Janeway and Geddes 2003). However, if behavioural difficulties are not addressed, there are increased risks of placements breaking down because of a young person's failure to form secure attachments; this has implications for his or her future health, well-being and ability to form relationships in adulthood.

Carers need to be informed of a young person's emotional and behavioural problems and supported to help him or her, otherwise, carers may feel the young person has been misrepresented to them by social workers contributing to the breakdown of a placement (Gibbs, Wilson and Sinclair 2000; Richardson and Joughin 2000). Kurtz and James (2002) found that support to carers enhanced their understanding of a young person's emotional and psychological needs and of the strategies to manage such needs more effectively.

Ways forward

Young people in residential care tend to express exactly the same concerns about their health as young people living with their families. The difference, however, is the context in which these challenges are faced and the extent of unmet need. Discord within their own families, changes of address, bereavement, changes in school or interrupted school careers, and a lack of access to the support and advice of trusted adults can load additional pressures on young and vulnerable shoulders. Some young people become accommodated in part as a result of health issues, while in some cases other reasons prompting removal from home (such as child abuse or family tensions) have health components and consequences. Also the usual arrangements for health monitoring and care may not function so well, especially when there are frequent changes of home and school.

The health issues or concerns for looked-after and accommodated young people are usually multifaceted. A concern in one area of a person's life should not be addressed in isolation to its impact on other parts of his or her development. The presence of a conduct disorder may have implications for the stability of the young person's home life and participation within school. Self-esteem and self-confidence are crucial factors in shaping how young people perceive their own health and in building their confidence in order to seek out and access advice from the more sensitive or 'stigmatising' services such as sexual or mental health. It would seem logical that the solutions to health concerns should not be seen as the sole responsibility of one agency, but as a partnership across agencies, and with young people and carers.

Certain groups have higher health risks than others; in nearly all areas of health-related behaviour, males are reportedly more at risk than females. Young males are particularly vulnerable with regard to attempting or completing suicides (Scottish Executive 2000), more have complex mental health needs (Meltzer *et al.* 2003, 2004), and levels of smoking, drinking and drug use are greater (Griesbach and Currie 2001; Meltzer *et al.* 2003, 2004; Triseliotis *et al.* 1995). A particularly vulnerable group comprises those young adults preparing to leave care and move to (semi-) independent living while still in their teens. The transition from care to independent living is considered to be detrimental in terms of health and well-being with high levels of depressive moods, low self-esteem and deliberate self-harm (Ridley and McCluskey 2003; Scottish Health Feedback 2003).

Access to appropriate health care

There is evidence that many young people in residential care do not receive the health assessments and treatments they need from conventional health services. The reasons for this have already been discussed.

Recent initiatives have begun to consider other approaches to delivering health services, especially through the developing use of specialist Looked-after Children Nurses in schools. The Looked-after Children Nurse can overcome many of the criticisms of medical assessment made by young people; however, it would be a concern if the LAC Nurse was the only route for an annual health assessment when the evidence has shown that children and young people in care often miss school and perhaps those with greater health needs are more frequently absent.

Initiatives in Scotland, such as Open Door (van Beinum, Martin and Bonnett 2002) in the west and LACES or the Residential Health Care Project

(Grant, Ennis and Stuart 2002) in the east, and the Children and Adolescent Mental Health Services (CAHMS) innovation projects in England (Kurtz and James 2002) put the needs and wishes of the young person at the centre, consider more flexible approaches to service delivery and work in partnership with those caring for looked-after children. These approaches operate on an outreach basis, taking the services to the young people who were not expected to attend clinics or surgeries they considered stigmatising or daunting. A key feature is the support and training provided for those working directly with young people to help them deal with difficult behaviours with greater under-standing and more confidence. Those involved also acknowledge the need for professionals to work together in a context of mutual respect.

It is clearly important to consider when services should be provided. Research has indicated that habits such as smoking, drinking and drug use as well as emotional and behavioural problems were often present or established before entering the care system. In order to change or modify behaviours and habits successfully, these issues need to be considered before, during and after an episode in care. Too often effective programmes are curtailed when a young person moves to a new placement or returns to his or her parents (see, for instance, van Beinum *et al.* 2005). Attention should be given to the health needs of an individual still living with the family and receiving a relatively low level of support to ensure the right supports are in place earlier in life.

Conclusion

For young people living in residential care, a number of factors may come together and impact on how their health needs are met. Residential care can offer many opportunities and be the most appropriate placements for many young people looked after, but the factors within their family history and cir-cumstances, the organisational processes in place and the choices they make relating to lifestyle and health behaviours can work in opposition rather than together and make it more difficult to ensure that all the necessary agencies collaborate to meet their needs.

The choices made by young people in residential care may impose the same risks to long-term health and well-being as those made by many young people in all communities across the nation, but these activities tend to start younger and general levels of uptake are often greater. We ignore the health needs of our looked-after population at our peril and efforts are required at individual, local and national levels to instigate organisational and attitudinal change to ensure that these needs are met; perhaps similar to the efforts in Scotland to ensure that suitable learning support has been made available to meet the educational needs of children and young people (Borland *et al.* 1998; McLean and Gunion 2003). Today, the drive and opportunities are there for all to work together to improve the health of children in our society.

Acknowledgements

Parts of this chapter have been published in a report produced by the Scottish Executive (Scott and Hill 2006).

References

Acheson, D. (1998) *Independent Inquiry into the Inequalities in Health.* London: The Stationery Office.

Bebbington, A. and Miles, J. (1989) 'The background of children who enter local authority care.' *British Journal of Social Work 19*, 5, 349–68.

van Beinum, M., Martin, A. and Bonnett, C. (2002) 'Catching children as they fall: Mental health promotion in residential child care in East Dunbartonshire.' *Scottish Journal of Residential Child Care 1*, 1, 14–22.

van Beinum, M., Martin, A. and Bonnett, C. (2005) 'Catching Children as they Fall: The East Dunbartonshire Looked After Children Mental Health Project.' In J. Scott and H. Ward (eds) *Promoting the Well-being of Children, Families and Communities.* London: Jessica Kingsley Publishers.

Biehal, N., Clayden, J., Stein, M. and Wade, J. (1995) 'Leaving care in England: A research perspective.' *Children and Youth Services Review 16*, 3/4, 231–54.

Borland, M., Pearson, C., Hill, M., Tisdall, K. and Bloomfield, I. (1998) *Education and Care Away from Home: A Review of Research, Policy and Practice.* Edinburgh: SCRE.

Bundle, A. (2002) 'Health information and teenagers in residential care: A qualitative study to identify young people's views.' *Adoption and Fostering 26*, 4, 19–25.

Buston, K. (2002) 'Adolescents with mental health problems: What do they say about health services?' *Journal of Adolescence 25*, 2, 231–42.

Butler, I. and Payne, H. (1997) 'The health of children looked after by the local authority.' *Adoption and Fostering 21*, 2, 28–35.

Chambers, H. with Howell, S., Madge, N. and Olle, H. (2002) *Healthy Care: Building an Evidence Base for Promoting the Health and Well Being of Looked After Children and Young People.* London: National Children's Bureau.

Cleaver, H. and Walker, S. with Meadows, P. (2004) *Assessing Children's Needs and Circumstances.* London: Jessica Kingsley Publishers.

Corlyon, J. and McGuire, C. (1999) *Pregnancy and Parenthood: The Views and Experiences of Young People in Care.* London: National Children's Bureau.

Daniel, B. and Wassell, S. (2002) *The School Years: Assessing and Promoting Resilience in Vulnerable Children II.* London: Jessica Kingsley Publishers.

Department of Health (1999a) *Reducing Health Inequalities: An Action Report.* London: Department of Health.

Department of Health (1999b) *Saving Lives: Our Healthier Nation.* London: Department of Health.

Department of Health (2000) *The Quality Protects Programme: Transforming Children's Services 2000/01.* LAC 2000(15). London: Department of Health.

Department of Health (2002) *Children Act (Miscellaneous Amendments) (England) Regulations 2002: New Guidance on Promoting the Health of Looked After Children.* LAC 2002(16). London: Department of Health.

Ely, M., West, P., Sweeting, H. and Richards, M. (2000) 'Teenage family life, life chances, lifestyles and health: A comparison of two contemporary cohorts.' *International Journal of Law, Policy and the Family 14*, 1, 1–30.

Gibbs, I., Wilson, K. and Sinclair, I. (2000) 'The trouble with foster care: The impact of stressful "events" on foster carers.' *British Journal of Social Work 30*, 2, 193–210.

Grant, A., Ennis, J. and Stuart, F. (2002) 'Looking after health: A joint working approach to improving the health outcomes of looked after and accommodated children and young people.' *Scottish Journal of Residential Child Care 1*, 1, 23–30.

Greishbach, D. and Currie, C. (2001) *Health Behaviours of Scottish Schoolchildren. Report 7: Control of Adolescent Smoking in Scotland.* Edinburgh: University of Edinburgh.

Henderson, M., Wright, D., Raab, G., Abraham, C., Buston, K., Hart, G. and Scott, S. (2002) 'Heterosexual Risk Behaviour among Young Teenagers in Scotland.' *Journal of Adolescence 25*, 5, 483–94.

Hill, C. (2001) 'Health inheritance: The importance of family history for children in public care.' *Adoption and Fostering 25*, 1, 75–7.

Hill, C., Mather, M. and Goddard, J. (2003) 'Cross sectional survey of meningococcal C immunisation in children looked after by local authorities and those living at home.' *British Medical Journal 326*, 364–5.

Hill, M. and Tisdall, K. (1997) *Children and Society.* Harlow: Longman.

HM Government (2004) *Every Child Matters: Change for Children.* www.everychildmatters.gov.uk/_files/F9E3F941DC8D4580539EE4C743E9371D.pdf, accessed on 30 April 2007.

House of Commons Select Committee on Health (1998) *Select Committee on Health Second Report: Children Looked After by Local Authorities.* www.publications.parliament.uk/pa/cm199798/cmselect/cmhealth/319/31902.htm, accessed on 30 April 2007.

Kurtz, Z. and James, C. (2002) *What's New? Learning from the CAMHS Innovation Projects.* London: Department of Health.

McCarthy, G., Janeway, J. and Geddes, A. (2003) 'The impact of emotional and behavioural problems on the lives of children growing up in the care system.' *Adoption and Fostering 27*, 3, 14–19.

McLean, K. and Gunion, M. (2003) 'Learning with care: The education of children looked after away from home by local authorities in Scotland.' *Adoption and Fostering 27*, 2, 20–31.

Meltzer, H., Corbin, T., Gatward, R., Goodman, R. and Ford, T. (2003) *The Mental Health of Young People Looked After by Local Authorities in England.* London: The Stationery Office.

Meltzer, H., Lader, R., Corbin, T., Goodman, R. and Ford, T. (2004) *The Mental Health of Young People Looked After by Local Authorities in Scotland.* London: The Stationery Office.

Minnis, H. and Del Priore, C. (2001) 'Mental health services for looked after children: Implications from two studies.' *Adoption and Fostering 25*, 4, 27–38.

National Assembly of Wales (1999) *Children First.* Cardiff: National Assembly for Wales.

Polnay, L. and Ward, H. (2000) 'Promoting the health of looked after children.' *British Medical Journal 320*, 661–2.

Richardson, J. and Joughlin, C. (2000) *The Mental Health Needs of Looked After Children.* London: Gaskell.

Ridley, J. and McCluskey, S. (2003) 'Exploring the perceptions of young people in care and care leavers of their health needs.' *Scottish Journal of Residential Child Care 2*, 1, 55–65.

Saunders, L. and Broad, B. (1997) *The Health Needs of Young People Leaving Care.* Leicester: De Montfort University.

Scott, J. and Hill, M. (2006) *The Health of Looked After and Accommodated Children and Young People in Scotland: Messages from Research.* Edinburgh: Social Work Inspection Agency.

Scottish Executive (2000) *Our National Health: A Plan for Action, A Plan for Change.* Edinburgh: Scottish Executive.

Scottish Executive (2001) *For Scotland's Children.* Edinburgh: Scottish Executive.

Scottish Executive (2005) *Getting it Right for Every Child: Proposals for Action.* Edinburgh: Scottish Executive.

Scottish Health Feedback (2003) *The Health Needs and Issues of Young People from Glasgow Living in Foster Care Settings.* Edinburgh: Scottish Health Feedback.

Scottish Office (1999) *Towards a Healthier Scotland.* London: The Stationery Office.

Skuse, T. and Ward, H. (2003) *Children's Views of Care and Accommodation.* Report to the Department of Health. Loughborough: CCfR, Loughborough University.

Triseliotis, J., Borland, M., Hill, M. and Lambert, L. (1995) *Teenagers and the Social Work Services.* London: The Stationery Office.

Ward, H., Holmes, L., Soper, J. and Olsen, R. (forthcoming) *The Costs and Consequences of Child Care Placements.* London: Jessica Kingsley Publishers.

Ward, H., Jones, H., Lynch, M. and Skuse, T. (2002) 'Issues concerning the health of looked after children.' *Adoption and Fostering 26*, 4, 8–18.

Ward, H. and Skuse, T. (1999) *Looking After Children: Transforming Data into Management Information: Report on the First Year of Data Collection.* Totnes: Dartington Social Research Unit.

World Health Organisation (1948) *Constitution of the World Health Organization.* Geneva: World Health Organisation.

CHAPTER 4

Mental Health and Children and Young People in Residential Care

Michael van Beinum

Introduction

This chapter will explore the mental health of children and young people placed in local authority care, with an emphasis on children in residential care. It will focus on children and young people in local authority children's homes, but will be relevant to other forms of residential provision (residential schools or young offenders institutions) and to children looked after at home or in foster care. The chapter will define what is meant by mental health and mental disorder, explore the epidemiology of mental health problems in looked-after children, outline potential risk and resilience factors, and look at recent examples of providing better specialist mental health provision for children in residential care.

Children who are looked after are subject to the same factors that predict mental health difficulties as other children, but are more likely to have experienced risk factors for developing a mental disorder, such as severe adverse life events prior to coming into care or having a parent suffering from a severe and enduring mental disorder. In addition, the experience of care itself may pose a further risk factor for developing mental disorder. For instance, while a great deal of work has been undertaken recently to address some of the negative aspects of residential care, there are also numerous accounts of how some of these children have experienced physical and sexual abuse at the hands of other children and residential care staff in the past (e.g. Hobbs, Hobbs and Wynne 1999; Kendrick 1998; Waterhouse 2000). A critical question, therefore, is to what extent the experience of local authority residential care can help these children make an adequate recovery from the many adversities they have encountered, or whether the experience of residential care further damages these already vulnerable children (Rutter 2000).

Given the high levels of adversity experienced by children who end up being looked after by their local authorities, it is not surprising that such children have greatly elevated rates of mental health disorders. Furthermore, the long-term outcome for looked-after children in adulthood is poor. For instance, care leavers experience higher levels of unemployment, homelessness, disability, teenage parenthood and exclusion from education (Mental Health Foundation 2002). Care leavers are also over-represented in adult psychiatric admissions and are more likely to become addicted, to be depressed, to harm themselves and to commit suicide (Rushton and Minnis 2002). The mental health status of a child who is looked after is likely, therefore, to be a significant predictor of how well he or she does as an adult later in life, since having a mental disorder will impair a child's ability to deal with adversity in an adaptive way. To date, however, no large prospective studies have been done on the impact of mental health status on the long-term outcome for children in residential care, making it difficult to predict which children will do well and which will do badly.

What is meant by mental health?

In children and young people, mental health can be understood in terms of a number of abilities:

- the ability to develop psychologically, emotionally, intellectually and spiritually
- the ability to initiate, develop and sustain mutually satisfying personal relationships
- the ability to become aware of others and to empathise with them
- the ability to use psychological distress as a developmental process, so that it does not hinder or impair further development.

(Health Advisory Service 1995)

When thinking about mental disorder some or all of the above abilities will have been impaired. An important consideration is that having a mental disorder is always accompanied by significant distress or impairment of functioning in the affected individual. Mental health problems in children and young people can therefore be defined as 'abnormalities of emotions, behaviour or social relationships sufficiently marked or prolonged to cause suffering or risk to optimal development in the child or distress or disturbance in the family or community' (Kurtz 1992, p. 6). Such abnormalities of emotions and behaviour frequently cluster into relatively stable and predictable patterns, allowing one to classify them into a number of different conditions, using internationally validated systems such as the International Classification of Diseases, version 10 (ICD-10) (World Health Organisation 1993) or the Diagnostic and Statistical Manual, fourth edition (DSM-IV) (American Psychiatric Association 1994). This, in turn, allows one to make predictions both about the long-term outcome of a particular condition and to predict, on the basis of clinical trials, which therapeutic interventions are most likely to be of help.

In addition, mental health problems in children are best understood in a developmental context. This is important for a number of reasons. First, since children change and grow up and thereby gain new abilities to deal with the world, behaviour that is considered normal at one age may be abnormal at another. For instance, temper tantrums at simple frustrations in a two-year-old are to be expected, but are not normal in a ten-year-old. Second, it is often more useful to think of a child as being on a normal or abnormal developmental trajectory, rather than as just having, or not having, a static mental disorder. Being on an abnormal developmental trajectory may expose a child to further risk factors that might otherwise be avoided. This can happen on a number of levels, including biological (the expression of genetic vulnerabilities), psychological (such as self-image) and social (such as how one is perceived by others). For example, a ten-year-old boy with attention deficit disorder and hyperactivity (ADHD) may, as a result of not sitting still and impulsively interrupting teachers in class, be suspended repeatedly from school, and this, in turn, may affect his ability to do well academically, lower his self-esteem and make it more difficult for him to make friends. As a result he may become more likely to form friendships with other children not at school, often because they have been behaving badly, and this, in turn, may encourage him to engage in more dangerous behaviour himself, such as early experimentation with drugs, and so on. Intervention in a case like this is therefore not just a matter of addressing his underlying ADHD, but also, among other matters, of good inter-agency work to ensure he remains in school and achieves to his ability. Such developmental pathways, where exposure to one event may go on to increase the likelihood of exposure to further harmful experiences, may be of particular importance in children who are being looked after, as they have often experienced more negative life events than children who have not been looked after. It also makes research into causal pathways particularly difficult, requiring large and prospective longitudinal studies. Such studies have not yet been done with children who become looked after, and therefore much of the discussion on risk and resilience factors later in this chapter is based on data from general population studies.

Third, many problems that first appear in childhood persist into adulthood and cause continuing impairment. There is now increasing evidence that the experience of having an impairing mental disorder can itself be toxic for affected individuals and make it more likely that they continue to suffer (Birchwood 2000). Vigorous treatment of mental disorders when they first appear, on the other hand, can in some conditions substantially improve the long-term outcome for affected individuals (see, for instance, Carbone *et al.* 1999).

Epidemiology

Over the last decade a number of studies have examined the prevalence of mental health disorders in looked-after children (Chetwynd and Robb 1999; McCann *et al.* 1996; Meltzer *et al.* 2003, 2004; Robinson *et al.* 1999). A highly influential study in Oxford (McCann *et al.* 1996) found a point prevalence rate of 67 per cent for psychiatric disorders in teenagers living in residential units and foster care, compared with 15 per cent of adolescents who lived with their own families. A significant number of looked-after children in this study were found to be suffering from severe psychiatric disorders that had gone undetected and untreated, including major psychosis. The definitive studies of the epidemiology of mental health problems in looked-after children, however, were conducted by the Office for National Statistics (ONS), first in England and Wales (Meltzer *et al.* 2003), and shortly afterwards in Scotland (Meltzer *et al.* 2004). The first study compared 1039 looked-after children in England and Wales with 10,500 children living in private households, and confirmed the findings of the earlier Oxford study. It found that 49 per cent of 11–15-year-old looked-after children had a psychiatric disorder sufficiently severe to impair their social functioning, compared to 11 per cent of children living in private households. The most common mental health problems in children who were looked after were conduct disorders (around 40% compared to 5% in children in private households), followed by emotional disorders (12% compared with 6%). Furthermore, the prevalence of mental disorder varied by placement type, with the highest rates (68%) found in those who were looked after and accommodated in residential homes, compared with 39 per cent in foster care and 42 per cent in those looked after and living with birth parents. Looked-after children living with their birth parents or in residential care were at least twice as likely as those in foster care to have anxiety disorders (20% and 16% compared with 8%), and about four times as likely to have depression (9% and 8% compared with 2%). There were no differences in prevalence rates for hyperkinetic disorders between placement type (all at around 8%). Notably, unusual psychiatric diagnoses, such as autistic spectrum disorders, were much more common in those looked after and accommodated (11% of children in residential care compared with 2% in other local authority placements (Meltzer *et al.* 2003)).

A repeat of this study in Scotland confirmed the overall findings of the English study, in that, for 11–15-year-old children, those looked after by their local authorities were about four times more likely to have a mental disorder than those in private households; 41 per cent compared with 9 per cent (Meltzer *et al.* 2004). Unlike the earlier English study, however, the Scottish study failed to find any difference in the overall rates of mental disorder according to placement type, with very similar rates in those looked after at home, those placed with foster parents and those in residential placements. The reasons for this difference are not clear, but may have to do with residential units being used in different ways between jurisdictions.

Risk and resilience factors

Children who are looked after are subject to the same resilience and risk factors that predict mental health difficulties as other children, but in addition one needs to consider events occurring to a child after he or she has been received into care. This is by no means straightforward, as most looked-after children have already, almost by definition, experienced significant adversity and entered upon a deviant developmental pathway that places them both at increased risk of further adversity and of developing a mental disorder. Furthermore, some adverse experience may be damaging for the majority of children, but for some may have a 'steeling' effect, protecting them from further adversity. It needs to be stressed that many children who come into care and who have been exposed to a range of risk factors demonstrate considerable resilience and go on to become healthy and confident adults. Children who, despite considerable earlier adverse experiences, demonstrate resilience often have a number of protective factors, including an absence of genetic predisposition to mental illness, a good supportive social network, good schooling and something that they are good at around which they can build up a positive sense of self (Rutter 1999).

In addition, general population studies indicate that resilience is promoted if one grows up in a stable and low-risk early environment, as this facilitates the development of normal internal representations and emotional coping responses (Friedman and Chase-Lansdale 2002; Rutter 1985). Attachment theory predicts that such children will show secure attachment behaviours and, despite intermittent stressful events, continue to elicit good quality care from their caregivers and continue to grow and adapt. Many children who end up in care, however, have experienced less than good enough parenting in early life, notably an absence of a consistent caregiver, neglect or severe abuse, and have experienced little in the way of a stable life that would allow them to develop long-term relationships (Kendrick 1995). A number of such children will develop long-term insecure attachment behaviours (Fonagy, Steele and Steele 1991; Rutter 2005), including indiscriminate, but superficial and shallow, friendly behaviour towards unfamiliar persons, or display unusual levels of anxiety and fear towards others. Such children have great difficulties in establishing sustaining relationships with others, and adults caring for them frequently report considerable distress about the difficulty of forming a psychological connection with the child (O'Connor 2002). In addition, there is increasing evidence that sustained abusive and depriving experiences in the first two years of a child's life can result in permanent biological changes in the infant's brain, particularly in those cerebral regions involved in the making of affective bonds (Perry 2001; Schore 2001). Consequently, what evidence is available would suggest that subsequently providing such children with high-quality and sensitive parenting may not always improve the behaviour of attachment disordered children, much to the distress of their new carers (O'Connor 2002).

Not surprisingly, therefore, risk factors for developing a mental disorder include severe disruptions in the security of intensive social relationships such as instability whilst in care, multiple placements and educational disruption, as well as negative experiences prior to entering care, such as neglect and abuse (Rutter 2005).

In addition, many children in care will have been born with a range of biologically driven risk factors for developing a mental health problem later in life, such as genetic vulnerability and intra-uterine damage secondary to poor maternal health, notably maternal smoking and substance abuse (Caspi *et al.* 2002). Furthermore, they are often raised in high-risk environments that increase the likelihood of developing emotional and behavioural problems, including living in poverty (Leventhal and Brooks-Gunn 2000), exposure to parental discord and separation (Davies and Cummings 1998), having a parent suffering from a mental illness (Beardslee, Versage and Gladstone 1998) and chronic exposure to violence (Friedman and Chase-Lansdale 2002).

Education can help foster resilience and protect the mental health of high-risk children (Rutter 1985) but many looked-after children struggle with school, both because of compromised scholastic abilities and repeated exclusions or moves of school (Fletcher-Campbell 1997). Recent studies have found greatly elevated rates of scholastic difficulties in children who are looked after, with up to 60 per cent of looked-after children assessed by their teachers as having difficulties with reading, spelling or mathematics (Meltzer *et al.* 2003). Scholastic problems were particularly prevalent in looked-after children who also had a mental disorder. For instance, the ONS study (Meltzer *et al.* 2003) found that such children were nearly twice as likely as looked-after children with no disorder to have marked difficulties with reading (37% versus 19%), mathematics (35% versus 20%) and spelling (41% versus 24%). Thirty-five per cent of those with a mental disorder were three or more years behind in their intellectual development, more than twice the rate among the no disorder group (17%).

About two-thirds of children were deemed to have special educational needs (SEN), and half of these (30%) had a statement issued by the local education authority. Among the children with a mental disorder, 42 per cent had a statement of special educational needs (SEN), twice the proportion found among looked-after children with no mental disorder.

Alcohol and substance abuse is a major risk factor for developing mental health difficulties. Unfortunately young people who are looked after are more likely to be using and abusing alcohol and drugs, particularly those who also have a mental disorder. For instance, the ONS study found that 5 per cent of children with a mental disorder reported that they drank alcohol almost every day compared with 0 per cent of looked-after children with no disorder (Meltzer *et al.* 2003). There is a number of possible reasons for this. Their parents are more likely to have abused alcohol and drugs (Kantor and Strauss 1990) and there is both a genetic influence on their overall liability to substance use (Kendler *et al.* 2000) and social transmission. Furthermore, parental alcohol and drug abuse is associated with a number of other risk factors, such as poor antenatal care, bereavement and parental abuse and neglect (Kantor and Strauss 1990).

Interventions

Providing appropriate treatment for looked-after children who have mental health problems has, until recently, been neglected (Kendrick, Milligan and Furnivall 2004). Despite the high prevalence of mental health disorders in these children, a number of studies have shown that children who become looked after are less likely to be provided with therapeutic help than those living in private households (Chetwynd and Robb 1999; Mental Health Foundation 2002). This may be for a number of reasons. Looked-after children are not a homogeneous group with respect to their mental health needs and have wide differences with respect to underlying mental health needs and coping responses (Arcelus, Bellerby and Vostanis 1999). A further problem has been to provide continuity for children who have multiple placements, something that is particularly likely if the child has a mental health problem. In addition, multiple placements may themselves further exacerbate underlying problems (Stanley, Riordan and Alaszewski 2005). Carers, particularly those working in residential establishments, may have had little or no training in mental health and may not recognise the need for specialist input (Stanley *et al.* 2005). If they do, they may not be able to access this for children in their care (Rushton and Minnis 2002). Young people in care themselves may also have a strong antipathy to using established mental health services which they frequently regard as highly stigmatising (van Beinum, Martin and Bonnett 2002; Blower *et al.* 2004), although children in care also want better service provision (Friday 1998). The main reason why looked-after children have found it difficult to access mental health services, however, has been a lack of specialist service provision for this client group (Blower *et al.* 2004; Mental Health Foundation 2002).

Fortunately, over the past ten years there has been an increased policy awareness of the mental health needs of looked-after children and the lack of appropriate services for them (Department of Health 2004; Kendrick *et al.* 2004; Polnay and Ward 2000; Ward 1995). This, in turn, has led to a number of new and specialised services designed to address some of the difficulties that looked-after children have traditionally experienced in trying to access specialist services. In all of these new initiatives there has been a recognition that existing child and adolescent mental health services, by and large, do not serve these children well and more flexible and innovative ways of delivering expert input is required. A number of descriptive reports have been published, all indicating a broadly similar approach to delivering mental health expertise for these children (van Beinum *et al.* 2002, 2005; Jones 2003; McCollam *et al.* 2006; Richardson and Joughin 2000).

Different levels of expert input have been provided. Looked-after children's nurses have been introduced to undertake health surveillance for each child who is looked after. They provide health promotion, including drug and alcohol advice and sexual health counselling. Such services are normally based on an outreach model and are not clinic-based in order to improve accessibility, identify any health needs, including mental health needs, and provide basic health interventions. In addition, they link with other statutory services in order to promote easier access for a child to specialist services. Most health boards in the UK are now also developing dedicated mental health services for looked-after children provided by multi-professional teams which may include child psychiatrists, psychologists, child psychotherapists, mental health nurses and other specialist child and adolescent mental health staff. Such dedicated looked-after children mental health teams have been characterised by taking a 'whole systems approach' and do not just work with an individual child, but attempt to address the capacity of all aspects of the wider professional network to provide mental health input to these children. This has been done by adopting a tripartite model, where these specialised services have predominantly offered both training and consultation to front-line care staff and social workers, with only a limited amount of direct clinical work with young people themselves. The basic philosophy of such interventions has been to improve the capacity of staff to tolerate, understand and deal with mental health problems in young people in their care, as well as improve their ability to recognise what sorts of problems require more specialist input. These services have been based on an outreach model in order to make mental health expertise more readily available to where young people in care can best access it, namely where they live. In addition, through closer working relationships between care staff, specialist mental health staff and looked-after children, better and more speedy referrals to specialist centres can be provided for those children most in need of such services.

Few of these specialised services have been formally evaluated using an appropriate and rigorous methodology. An early randomised single blind study in the USA demonstrated the benefits of intensive input to high-risk children in foster care, measured in terms of their emotional and behavioural functioning (Clark *et al.* 1994), but foster care in the USA is very different from foster care in the UK. A further controlled study on training foster carers in Scotland (Minnis 1999) demonstrated that intensive education and support for foster carers resulted in improved outcomes for children in foster care, but that lesser degrees of input resulted in no improvement. The majority of published studies of specialised mental health services for looked-after children in the UK, however, have used a mixture of qualitative and descriptive data, but all have demonstrated considerable success in terms of the views of users and service personnel (van Beinum *et al.* 2002, 2005; Callaghan *et al.* 2004; McCollam *et al.* 2006).

Conclusion

Using a broad definition of mental health and adopting a developmental perspective underlines that helping children to grow up in a healthy and adaptive way requires the input of all agencies working with children, and should not be seen as the province of a single specialist agency such as child and adolescent mental health services. It involves not just the provision of specialist mental health services for young people with recognised mental health problems, but also mental health promotion and early intervention. Much more work, however, needs to be done to identify at as early a stage as possible those children and young people who are likely to develop mental health problems, as well as identifying how the care experience for children who become looked after can be developed so as to maximise the best long-term health and social outcomes for each child.

References

American Psychiatric Association (1994) *Diagnostic and Statistical Manual of Mental Disorders: DSM-IV,* 4th edition. Washington, DC: American Psychiatric Association.

Arcelus, J., Bellerby, T. and Vostanis, P. (1999) 'A mental health service for young people in the care of the local authority.' *Clinical Child Psychology and Psychiatry 4,* 2, 233–46.

Beardslee, W.R., Versage, E.M. and Gladstone, T.R.G. (1998) 'Children of affectively ill parents: A review of the past 10 years.' *Journal of the American Academy of Child and Adolescent Psychiatry 37,* 1134–41.

van Beinum, M., Martin, A. and Bonnett, C. (2002) 'Catching children as they fall: Mental health promotion in residential care in East Dunbartonshire.' *Scottish Journal of Residential Child Care 1,* 1, 14–22.

van Beinum, M., Martin, A. and Bonnett, C. (2005) 'Catching Children as they Fall: Providing a Dedicated Mental Health Service to Looked After and Accommodated Children.' In J. Scott and H. Ward (eds) *Safeguarding and Promoting the Well-being of Children, Families and Communities.* London: Jessica Kingsley Publishers.

Birchwood, M. (2000) 'The Critical Period for Early Intervention.' In M. Birchwood, D. Fowler and A. Jackson (eds) *Early Intervention in Psychosis: A Guide to Concepts, Evidence and Interventions.* Chichester: John Wiley & Sons, Ltd.

Blower, A., Addo, A., Hodgson, J., Lamington, L. and Towlson, K. (2004) 'Mental health of "looked after" children: A needs assessment.' *Clinical Child Psychology and Psychiatry 9,* 1, 117–29.

Callaghan, J., Young, B., Pace, F. and Vostanis, P. (2004) 'Evaluation of a new mental health service for looked after children.' *Clinical Child Psychology and Psychiatry 9,* 1, 130–48.

Carbone, S., Harrigan, S., McGorry, P.D., Curry, C. and Elkins, K. (1999) 'Duration of untreated psychosis and 12-month outcome in first episode psychosis: The impact of treatment approach.' *Acta Psychiatrica Scandinavia 100,* 2, 96–104.

Caspi, A., McClay, J., Moffitt, T., Mill, J., Martin, J., Craig, I.W., Taylor, A. and Poulton, R. (2002) 'Role of genotype in the cycle of violence in maltreated children.' *Science 297,* 8, 851–4.

Chetwynd, P. and Robb, W. (1999) *Psychological Difficulties in Young People in Residential Care in Glasgow.* Glasgow: Greater Glasgow Health Board.

Clark, H.B., Prange, M.E., Lee, B., Boyd, L.A., McDonald, B.A. and Stewart, E.S. (1994) 'Improving adjustment outcomes for foster children with emotional and behavioural disorders: Early findings from a controlled study on individualized services.' *Journal of Emotional and Behavioral Disorders 2,* 4, 207–18.

Davies, P.T. and Cummings, E.M. (1998) 'Exploring children's emotional security as a mediator of the link between marital relations and child adjustment.' *Child Development 69,* 124–39.

Department of Health (2004) *National Service Framework for Children, Young People and Maternity Services: The Mental Health and Psychological Well-being of Children and Young People: Standard 9.* London: Department of Health.

Fletcher-Campbell, F. (1997) *The Education of Children Who are Looked After.* Slough: National Foundation for Educational Research.

Fonagy, P., Steele, H. and Steele, M. (1991) 'Maternal representations of attachment during pregnancy predict the organisation of infant–mother attachment at one year of age.' *Child Development 62*, 5, 891–905.

Friday, E. (1998) *Listen Up: Young People Talk about Mental Health Issues in Residential Care.* Glasgow: Who Cares? Scotland.

Friedman, R.J. and Chase-Lansdale, P. (2002) 'Chronic Adversities.' In M. Rutter and E. Taylor (eds) *Child and Adolescent Psychiatry*, 4th edition. Oxford: Blackwell Science.

Health Advisory Service (1995) *Together We Stand: The Commissioning, Role and Management of Child and Adolescent Mental Health Services.* London: HMSO.

Hobbs, G., Hobbs, C. and Wynne, J. (1999) 'Abuse of children in foster and residential care.' *Child Abuse and Neglect 23*, 12, 1239–52.

Jones, L. (2003) *An Evaluation of a Dedicated Service for Looked After and Accommodated Young People for Greater Glasgow Health Board and East Dunbartonshire Council by Scottish Health Feedback. Report on the Second Year.* Edinburgh: Scottish Health Feedback.

Kantor, G.K. and Strauss, M.A. (1990) 'The "Drunken Bum" Theory of Wife Beating.' In M.A. Strauss and R.J. Gelles (eds) *Physical Violence in American Families.* New Brunswick, NJ: Transaction.

Kendler, K.S., Karkowski, L.M., Neale, M.C. and Prescott, C.A. (2000) 'Illicit psychoactive substance use, heavy use, abuse, and dependence in a US-population-based sample of male twins.' *Archives of General Psychiatry 57*, 3, 261–9.

Kendrick, A. (1995) *Residential Care in the Integration of Child Care Services.* Central Research Unit Papers. Edinburgh: Scottish Office.

Kendrick, A. (1998) 'In their best interest? Protecting children from abuse in residential and foster care.' *International Journal of Child and Family Welfare 3*, 2, 169–85.

Kendrick, A., Milligan, I. and Furnivall, J. (2004) 'Care in mind: Addressing the mental health of children and young people in state care in Scotland.' *International Journal of Child and Family Welfare 9*, 4, 184–96.

Kurtz, Z. (1992) *With Health in Mind. Mental Health Care for Children and Young People.* London: Action for Sick Children.

Leventhal, T. and Brooks-Gunn, J. (2000) 'The neighbourhoods they live in: The effects of neighbourhood residence upon child and adolescent outcomes.' *Psychological Bulletin 126*, 309–37.

McCann, J.B., James, A., Wilson, S. and Dunn, G. (1996) 'Prevalence of psychiatric disorders in young people in the care system.' *British Medical Journal 313*, 1529–30.

McCollam, A., Woodhouse, A. with White, J., Halliday, E. and Myers, F. (2006) *Edinburgh Connect Evaluation: Final Report.* Edinburgh: Scottish Development Centre for Mental Health.

Meltzer, H., Corbin, T., Gatward, R., Goodman, R. and Ford, T. (2003) *The Mental Health of Young People Looked After by Local Authorities in England.* London: TSO.

Meltzer, H., Lader, D., Corbin, T., Goodman, R. and Ford, T. (2004) *The Mental Health of Young People Looked After by Local Authorities in Scotland.* London: TSO.

Mental Health Foundation (2002) *The Mental Health of Looked-After Children. Bright Futures: Working with Vulnerable Young People.* London: Mental Health Foundation.

Minnis, H. (1999) 'Evaluation of a Training Programme for Foster Carers.' Unpublished PhD thesis, University of London.

O'Connor, T.G. (2002) 'Attachment Disorders in Infancy and Childhood.' In M. Rutter and E. Taylor (eds) *Child and Adolescent Psychiatry,* 4th edition. Oxford: Blackwell Science.

Perry, B.D. (2001) 'The Neurodevelopmental Impact of Violence in Childhood.' In D. Schetky and E. Benedek (eds) *Textbook of Child and Adolescent Forensic Psychiatry.* Washington, DC: American Psychiatric Press, Inc.

Polnay, L. and Ward. H. (2000) 'Promoting the health of looked after children.' *British Medical Journal 320,* 661–2.

Richardson, J. and Joughin, C. (2000) *The Mental Health Needs of Looked After Children.* London: Gaskell.

Robinson, P., Auckland, K., Crawford, H. and Nevison, C. (1999) *Care Sick? The Physical and Mental Health Needs of a Sample of Young People in Local Authority Residential Care.* Edinburgh: Young People's Unit, Royal Edinburgh Hospital.

Rushton, A. and Minnis, H. (2002) 'Residential and Foster Family Care.' In M. Rutter and E. Taylor (eds) *Child and Adolescent Psychiatry,* 4th edition. Oxford: Blackwell Science.

Rutter, M. (1985) 'Resilience in the face of adversity: Protective factors and resistance to psychiatric disorder.' *British Journal of Psychiatry 147,* 598–611.

Rutter, M. (1999) 'Resilience concepts and findings: Implications for family therapy.' *Journal of Family Therapy 21,* 119–44.

Rutter, M. (2000) 'Children in substitute care: Some conceptual considerations and research implications.' *Children and Youth Services Review 22,* 9, 685–703.

Rutter, M. (2005) 'How the environment affects mental health.' *British Journal of Psychiatry 186,* 1, 4–6.

Schore, A.N. (2001) 'The effects of early relational trauma on right brain development, affect regulation, and infant mental health.' *Infant Mental Health Journal 22,* 201–69.

Stanley, N., Riordan, D. and Alaszewski, H. (2005) 'The mental health of looked after children: Matching response to need.' *Health and Social Care in the Community 13,* 3, 239–48.

Ward, H. (ed.) (1995) *Looking After Children: Research into Practice.* London: HMSO.

Waterhouse, R. (2000) *Lost in Care: Report of the Tribunal of Inquiry into the Abuse of Children in Care in the Former County Council Areas of Gwynedd and Clwyd since 1994.* HC 201. London: Stationery Office.

World Health Organisation (1993) *The ICD-10 Classification of Mental and Behavioural Disorders: Diagnostic Criteria for Research.* Geneva: World Health Organisation.

CHAPTER 5

The Concept of Resilience

Messages for Residential Child Care

Brigid Daniel

Introduction

Resilience is a concept that is increasingly gaining currency as a basis for practice with children and young people. This chapter will give an overview of the concept, describe some of the pitfalls of its uncritical use and set out a framework for practice. Much of what is indicated for practice is what residential staff and other practitioners already do; however, the concept of resilience helps to set a conceptual framework around that work and provides a theoretical basis for what, in many cases, seems like common sense (Daniel, Wassell and Gilligan 1999).

Resilience

Resilience is sometimes defined as an *outcome*, as in Fonagy *et al.*'s frequently quoted definition: 'normal development under difficult conditions' (1994, p. 233). Residential care staff will recognise this as the description of some young people they encounter who appear to have come through very difficult experiences relatively unscathed.

   Resilience is also defined in terms of the underlying *processes* as in Gilligan's (1997) definition:

> qualities which cushion a vulnerable child from the worst effects of adversity in whatever form it takes and which may help a child or young person to cope, survive and even thrive in the face of great hurt and disadvantage. (Gilligan 1997, p. 12)

Masten, Best and Garmezy bring both aspects together with their definition of resilience as 'the process of, capacity for, or outcome of successful adaptation despite challenging or threatening circumstances' (Masten *et al.* 1990, p. 426). Here it is an adaptive quality that is highlighted; as Schofield (2001) suggests, resilient people have both an internal and an external adaptive quality. For example, if a young person has a failure at school he or she can reflect upon that internally and see it as a temporary setback and can also seek external support, for example by asking a teacher for help with the next essay. It is this adaptive quality that appears to be an essential aspect of resilience.

Resilience is not simply an absence of psychological symptoms despite having experienced adversity, it is the possession of a positive adaptive ability that enables a person to feel competent despite risky living conditions (Sagy and Dotan 2001). Resilience is the ability to know where, how and when to put your energies to improve things for yourself and how to recruit help in that endeavour.

Pitfalls of an uncritical approach

It is important to consider some of the potential problems with an uncritical approach to resilience. First, the concept can be criticised as being a rather complex way of expressing 'good parenting'. Effective parenting should enable children to develop the qualities that equip them to cope with difficulties, but such parenting is not usually described as a process of 'promoting resilience'. Nonetheless, the concept of resilience does resonate with professionals who work with children who have been abused or neglected. Practitioners can identify differences in vulnerability amongst the young people they encounter and are often struck by the specific quality of resilience that some young people appear to possess that seems to have developed despite the absence of 'good parenting'.

Second, expressions such as 'children are resilient' and 'children bounce back' are often used in general conversation. But this rather loose application of the concept can mean that some young people's upset and hurt are not recognised. As Rutter indicates, resilience is a relative concept. It is important to avoid assuming that it is a fixed attribute, and young people who appear to cope in some circumstances may not cope with others. For example, a young person may adapt to a change in school, but not with moving away from a close friend. It is also dangerous to make the assumption that just because a young person appears to be coping well, he or she is not in fact suffering internal distress and developing unhelpful coping strategies and defences. Luthar (1991) showed that some adolescents who appeared to be coping well showed, when carefully assessed, some signs of depression and anxiety. This so called 'apparent resilience' can lead to some young people's needs for help being overlooked.

Conceptual framework

Many factors have been shown to be associated with resilience and coping, some internal and some external (Werner and Smith 1992). Resilience is a dynamic concept that refers to an interaction between stresses and adversity and the buffering features within the child (Rutter 1985) and it can be helpful when assessing a young person's circumstances to separate these.

The external protective factors that help to promote resilience can be located on a dimension of adversity and protective factors. Young people who enter residential settings will, by definition, have experienced adversity such as abuse, neglect, disruption, bullying, racism, poverty and so on. At the same time, for any young person there will be some protective factors that can be capitalised upon. Three protective factors have been shown to be particularly associated with better outcomes for all young people:

• at least one secure attachment relationship

• access to wider supports such as extended family and friends

• positive school and/or community experiences.

From a longitudinal study of resilience Werner (2000) identified additional factors that are particularly protective during school age years:

• nurturance and trust

• lack of separations

• lack of parental mental health or addiction problems

• required helpfulness

• encouragement of autonomy (girls)

• encouragement of expression of feelings (boys)

• close grandparents

• family harmony

- sibling attachment
- four or fewer children
- sufficient financial and material resources
- peer contact
- positive adult role models.

Internal factors fall on a dimension of vulnerability and resilience. Three key factors are known to be associated with levels of vulnerability or resilience at all ages:

- sense of security
- self-esteem
- self-efficacy.

(Gilligan 1997)

During school years the further specific characteristics identified by Werner (2000) as being associated with resilience are:

- female
- internal locus of control
- empathy with others
- problem-solving skills
- communication skills
- sociable
- independent
- reflective, not impulsive
- ability to concentrate on schoolwork
- autonomy (girls)/emotional expressiveness (boys)
- sense of humour
- hobbies
- willingness and capacity to plan.

Young people who enter residential care have been shown to demonstrate a range of internal and external characteristics on the range of adversity and vulnerability, including:

- chaotic behaviour, poor impulse control, proneness to harm others and property

- fearfulness of going to school or of prospect of leaving care

- sense of being lost, of having no one and having no future

- persistent and continuing offending

- inappropriate sexual behaviour, including prostitution

- difficult relations with parents, including outright rejection.

(Department of Health 1998)

The concept of resilience provides a starting point for a broader-based positive assessment and planning process that aims to:

- *capitalise* on those protective factors that promote resilience and

- *nurture* the adaptive coping process (or resilience) that enables the young person to make use of the protective factors.

Assessment

To date the research on resilience has focused upon identifying the characteristics associated with resilience. There has been far less research into deliberate attempts to boost resilience in young people, and especially those who have experienced abuse and neglect (Heller *et al.* 1999). However, there is now sufficient evidence about the factors associated with resilience to support the benefits of intervention aimed at nurturing those factors in young people in residential settings. Several publications set out ways in which the concept can be used in a range of practice settings (Daniel and Wassell 2002a, 2002b; Gilligan 2001; Newman 2004; Unger 2005).

The concept of resilience is entirely compatible with the Looking After Children materials and provides a framework for developing a carefully targeted plan for intervention that aims to improve the likelihood of better outcomes for the young person in the short and longer term (Daniel and Wassell 2002a). The materials provide less guidance on how to assess protective and resilience factors but the messages from the research on resilience can offer pointers.

External characteristics

SECURE ATTACHMENT

When assessing attachment there is still a tendency for social workers to focus on the relationship with the mother, but there is evidence that children can have different attachment relationships with each parent (Fox, Kimmerly and Schafer 1991). It is, therefore, equally important to find out who is important to the young person without making assumptions. For some young people the father may be an important attachment figure, even if he is not resident in the family (Daniel and Taylor 2001).

ACCESS TO WIDER SUPPORTS

There may also be other people who are important to the young person such as members of the extended family, neighbours, friends and their parents. It is known to be protective for young people to have a network of people around them, but too often their importance is not recognised by professionals who often focus on immediate family relationships.

SCHOOL AND COMMUNITY RESOURCES

Similarly, it is essential to assess the quality of the school experience. Even if a young person does not achieve at a high academic level he or she can still derive considerable support from positive nursery or school experiences. School is, often, also a bridge into other community resources such as clubs and activities.

Internal characteristics

SENSE OF SECURITY

There is considerable evidence that having a secure attachment base is protective. It is not necessarily the same as having an attachment figure: some attachment relationships are not secure and do not engender an internal feeling of comfort and safety. It is important, therefore, to assess the young person's experience of the attachment relationship because even when a parent says that he or she loves the child and describes the relationship as close it may not feel that way to the young person. For example, when a parent's behaviour is erratic because of alcohol abuse he or she may be inconsistent in availability to the young person; this will not promote feelings of security, rather it can lead to anxiety.

SELF-ESTEEM

If a young person has high self-esteem he or she has an internal sense of worth and competence. However, self-esteem is a more complex characteristic because it is also an interpersonal feature; therefore, good self-esteem should entail the young person also having an appreciation of the worth of others. Good self-esteem is best fostered by achievement in things that matter to the young person rather than simple assertions of worth.

SELF-EFFICACY

Self-efficacy is concerned with the extent to which a person has an accurate knowledge of his or her own limits and strengths, an accurate understanding of what things he or she can or cannot influence and an understanding of how to have some control over events. For example, two young people may fail a maths test: the one with a good sense of self-efficacy may think, 'Well, the test was hard, but perhaps I didn't revise enough; next time I'll try harder.' The one with poor self-efficacy is likely to think, 'Everyone else did all right, I am useless at maths, there is nothing I can do about it.'

In summary, these three internal qualities have been summed up by researchers of the International Resilience Project as enabling resilient young people to say:

'I HAVE'…for example, 'people I trust and love.'

'I AM'…for example 'a loveable person.'

'I CAN'…for example 'find ways to solve problems.'

(Grotberg 1997, pp. 22–3)

Intervention

For some young people the assessment will indicate that they already demonstrate high levels of resilience. For these young people the aim of intervention is to build on the capacities that have enabled them to cope, and to assist them to avoid some of the potentially negative outcomes of particular coping strategies. In their study of adult offspring of parents who abused alcohol, Velleman and Orford (1999) found that strategies that were effective in childhood could become unhelpful under some circumstances. For example they found that some children were able to remove themselves from the emotional disruption in the household, for example by staying with a friend. This strategy was very effective. But if young people removed themselves from the household, by entering into marriage at an early age or moving into some other unsatisfactory situation, the outcomes were poorer. The message from this is that it is important to honour the strategies that young people have developed, but to assist them to limit the potential negative consequences.

If the aim is to nurture resilience five strategies have been identified:

1. reduce vulnerability and risk

2. reduce the number of stressors and 'pile-up'

3. increase the available resources

4. mobilise protective processes

5. foster resilience strings (where an improvement in one domain has a positive knock-on effect in other domains).

(Masten 1994)

Reduce vulnerability and risk

Many looked-after and accommodated adolescents have already experienced many of the situations that they were 'at risk' of when younger. The residential setting may protect them from some of the risks associated with living at home, but may also open them to different risks. Indeed, as these young people enter young adulthood the risks are likely to emanate more and more from their own behaviour. As the recent Child Protection Review in Scotland indicated, young people who are looked after and accommodated have a higher mortality rate than children in the general population with suicides, substance misuse and road accidents (often as a result of stealing cars) being the main causes of death (Scottish Executive 2002).

When young people engage in such risky behaviour it can indicate that they lack a sense of future and purpose. As a result of his research with young men who had committed serious violent crime, including murder, in the USA, Garbarino (1999) highlighted the extent to which such young men lived in the 'here and now'. They were unable to engage in discussions about the future and certainly did not see the point in changing their lifestyles because they could not visualise themselves having a future. Bombarding a young person with messages about the riskiness of their behaviour if they have no regard for their own safety and no sense of future can be counterproductive. Instead the focus of work must be in helping them to develop a narrative of their lives that foresees some future. In other words, such young people need to develop a sense of hope. Part of the key to young people being able to develop a narrative for the future is to support them in having a narrative about their past by giving them the opportunity to reflect upon their experiences and to develop a 'coherent story' of their lives (Main and Goldwyn 1984). The aim is to encourage young people towards a position where they want to protect themselves from risky situations and where they see themselves as having some choices of direction.

Reduce the number of stressors and 'pile-up'

Adolescents cope best when they can deal with issues one by one (Coleman and Hendry 1990). Looked-after young people, though, are often bombarded with a number of life stresses at once. For example, a move in placement will also entail losses of previous attachments and connections. Even the most resilient of people can be overwhelmed when the number of stressors multiplies. When assessing and planning, therefore, it is important to look at ways that potential stresses can be staggered. For example, it will not be helpful for a young person to negotiate a return to school at the same time as re-establishing contact with an estranged family member.

Paradoxically, however, it is also important that young people are not overly protected from risk. The development of resilience is helped if young people are allowed to experience risk and be supported to cope with it (Newman and Blackburn 2002). Currently society is risk averse, and there is a strong emphasis on protecting children. The disadvantage of this is that young people are often deprived of opportunities to learn from experience. Within residential settings, therefore, the challenge is to enable positive risk-taking that provides young people with opportunities to learn coping strategies. Outdoor activities with an element of challenge are particularly effective for this.

Increase the available resources

Residential staff, in conjunction with field social workers, can play a major role in increasing the available human resources for a young person. As key workers staff will be a resource in themselves and the potential for these relationships cannot be underestimated. There is evidence that young people can learn new patterns of attachment on the basis of positive relationships (Feeney and Noller 1996). Through the opportunity to experience different types of relationships with adults young people can experience:

- trust
- having their views listened to
- being given choices
- being appreciated for their individuality
- the chance to talk over their options
- support.

Staff can also work with young people to identify other people in the formal and informal network who can offer support. Many of the young people will have experienced a number of moves and placements. They may well also have a large extended family. Their ability to maintain contacts is likely to be impaired and key workers can act as a bridge to re-establishing contacts. Kendrick suggests that the potentially supportive role of the group setting is often underestimated (Kendrick 2005). He cites Emond's (2002) study of group processes that showed a range of ways in which young people draw upon the support and knowledge of different members of the group.

Mobilise protective processes

When mobilising protective processes the aim is to build the young person's sense of self-efficacy so that he or she can say 'I can...'. Many young people who have experienced abuse and/or neglect do not make accurate appraisals of situations and are not clear about the kind of strategies they can adopt. They may have difficulty in recognising the situations that they can have some influence over and the ones that they can't. However, focused intervention can help young people to improve their ability to appraise situations and choose appropriate strategies. For example, a young woman who frequently finds herself in conflict with others might believe that 'Everyone is out to get me.' A skilful helper can help her to identify her own part in such conflict and help her to devise strategies to defuse it. A young man whose mother drinks to excess and blames him for her drinking can be assisted to recognise the limits of his own power in the situation, to stop blaming himself and to cease attempting to stop his mother from drinking.

Foster resilience strings

There are a number of domains of a young person's life where intervention can be targeted including:

- secure base
- education
- friendships
- talents and interests
- positive values
- social competencies.

(Daniel and Wassell 2002a, 2002b)

In fostering resilience strings, the aim is for improvements in one domain to have a positive spin-off in another. A study that examined the value of assessing these domains in children living in foster care suggested that they helped enhance knowledge of the child, and self-knowledge by the child: 'I think that she's maybe got a better understanding of where she is...it's reinforced positives that she has [*social worker*]' (Daniel with Wassell 2005, p. 18). There was one cautionary note to this in that it was identified in the case of one child that positive factors could be 'kind of masking the gaps that are there' (p. 18). This again is a reminder to distinguish between resilience and 'apparent resilience' (Luthar 1991).

Current practice often concentrates on the establishment of a secure base. However, although crucial, this work should not eclipse the other aspects of a young person's life (Gilligan 1997). The comments in Daniel and Wassell's study (2005) suggest both that the secure base underpins a lot of the other areas, and that a careful assessment of the other domains can help to highlight difficulties with the secure base. It is as if practitioners sometimes need to look away from the secure base in order to see it in greater relief. Indeed, improvements in other aspects of the young person's life may enhance his or her ability to make attachments. For example, if a young person develops a better sense of self-esteem because of achievements in a pursuit or hobby that interests him or her, he or she is likely to feel more worthy of attention and love. Fifteen young people who were interviewed as part of a review of services in a local authority (Dearden 2004) identified many of these factors as making a difference to them. They valued stability and continuity and could identify the importance of a significant adult who believed in them but they also valued access to educational and leisure facilities.

Aspects of one domain can, therefore, be used to boost another, for example, there may a relative who would be interested in supporting a young person with his or her schooling, thus improving relationships and education together. There is a growing body of evidence about the strong association between better long-term outcomes and educational attainment and there is tremendous scope for a two-way positive flow between aspects that support education. Young people identified as having done well educationally, including a number who had gone on to further and higher education, were interviewed about the factors that they would identify as having helped (Jackson and Martin 1998; Martin and Jackson 2002). Again, the issue of stability emerged, as well as having a parent or significant adult who valued education. The interplay of a number of domains is clear from the young people's accounts. For example, Jackson found that having a belief in one's own effectiveness was a significant factor, and that this was not dependent upon self-esteem. Belief in personal effectiveness may lead to educational achievements, but at the same time emerging achievements can boost self-belief thus creating a positive feedback loop. Dent and Cameron (2003) review the role that the educational psychologist can play in assisting schools to create an ethos that aims to nurture resilience in young people, including making classrooms more supportive and recognising the potential of school for positive change.

Friendships can be encouraged if young people are involved in structured activities with other young people. There is evidence that the most successful activities for young people are those that naturally occur in their environment (Newman and Blackburn 2002). The message from this is that it may be more useful to use resources to support existing community and youth organisations to include looked-after young people rather than to set up special projects for looked-after children.

It is particularly important to encourage pro-social behaviour and positive values towards others. Just as self-esteem entails an appreciation of the worth of others, so resilience is boosted when young people have the opportunity to contribute to others and society. Social workers in Daniel and Wassell's study picked this out as an area worth paying much more attention to (Daniel with

Wassell 2005). It is important, therefore, to explore ways in which young people can help others, for example through peer support, buddying, volunteering and so on. The main influences on the development of positive values are adult role models; therefore, staff have a major role to play in creating an ethos of mutual respect and caring. Within such an ethos it is also possible to encourage social competence and the group situation can be used to good advantage as a locus for learning how to interact with others. As Hicks *et al.* (2003) have found, residents in homes where the manager was assessed as having clear strategies for promoting education and good behaviour were more likely to do well on a wide range of outcomes.

A resilience-based approach

The concept of resilience increasingly offers an alternative framework for intervention, the focus being on the assessment of potential areas of strength within the young person's whole system. As suggested, much of the practice that is indicated by taking a resilience-led approach may not be markedly different from the kind of activities that residential staff are carrying out already. However, it is often the kind of work that is 'squeezed in' or seen as a luxury. If staff are armed with the evidence base that the concept of resilience presents they are in a stronger position to make the case for the time and resources to incorporate such approaches into the heart of their work with young people.

Finally, the research on resilience emphasises the role of positive relationships in the promotion of self-belief and well-being. For many young people in residential settings, therefore, quality of the relationships with staff are going to be key to the efficacy of strategies of intervention. In order to provide young people with consistent and supportive relationships, staff themselves have to be robust and resilient. It is possible to apply the concept of resilience to the understanding of what promotes the well-being of staff. For example, staff need to feel secure in their jobs, to have a sense of self-esteem about their work and to feel effective. There is evidence that residential staff would like to be more involved in therapeutic work (Department of Health 1998) and if the conditions of the unit support staff in this way they will be resilient enough to stick with the most demanding young people. The research on resilience shows how powerfully protective it can be for young people to have the experience of someone taking an interest in them, to have someone who appreciates their worth as individuals and who believes in them. Often it can be the very small things that make a difference. Young people look back and say things like 'I remember that time you took me to get that pair of jeans I wanted.' Brooks describes the importance to young people of a 'charismatic' adult (Brooks 1994). On the same theme Benard identifies three qualities that characterise individuals who help young people resist stress, what she calls 'turnaround people':

- a caring relationship
- high expectations
- opportunities for contribution and participation.

A residential setting has huge potential to enable staff to be 'turnaround' people for the young residents.

Acknowledgements

This chapter is based upon a paper that was published in *The Scottish Journal of Residential Child Care* and material has been reproduced by kind permission of the publishers, The Scottish Institute for Residential Child Care.

References

Benard, B. (2002) 'Turnaround people and places: Moving from risk to resilience.' *The Strengths Perspective in Social Work Practice.* London: Ally.

Brooks, R.B. (1994) 'Children at risk: Fostering resilience and hope.' *American Journal of Orthopsychiatry 64*, 4, 545–53.

Coleman, J.C. and Hendry, L. (1990) *The Nature of Adolescence*, 2nd edition. London: Routledge.

Daniel, B. and Taylor, J. (2001) *Engaging with Fathers: Practice Issues for Health and Social Care.* London: Jessica Kingsley Publishers.

Daniel, B. and Wassell, S. (2002a) *Adolescence: Assessing and Promoting Resilience in Vulnerable Children III.* London: Jessica Kingsley Publishers.

Daniel, B. and Wassell, S. (2002b) *The School Years: Assessing and Promoting Resilience in Vulnerable Children II.* London: Jessica Kingsley Publishers.

Daniel, B. with Wassell, S. (2005) *Resilience: A Framework for Positive Practice.* Edinburgh: Scottish Executive. www.scotland.gov.uk/Resource/Doc/920/0011997.pdf, accessed on 30 April 2007.

Daniel, B., Wassell, S. and Gilligan, R. (1999) '"It's just common sense isn't it?": Exploring ways of putting the theory of resilience into action.' *Adoption and Fostering 23*, 3, 6–15.

Dearden, J. (2004) 'Resilience: A study of risk and protective factors from the perspective of young people with experience of local authority care.' *Support for Learning 19*, 4, 187–93.

Dent, R.J. and Cameron, R.J.S. (2003) 'Developing resilience in children who are in public care: The educational psychology perspective.' *Educational Pyschology in Practice 19*, 1, 3–18.

Department of Health (1998) *Caring For Children Away From Home: Messages From Research.* Chichester: Wiley.

Emond, R. (2002) 'Understanding the resident group.' *Scottish Journal of Residential Child Care 1*, 1, 30–40.

Feeney, J. and Noller, P. (1996) *Adult Attachment.* Thousand Oaks, CA: SAGE Publications.

Fonagy, P., Steele, M., Steele, H., Higgitt, A. and Target, M. (1994) 'The Emanuel Miller Memorial Lecture 1992: The theory and practice of resilience.' *Journal of Child Psychology and Psychiatry 35*, 2, 231–57.

Fox, N.A., Kimmerly, N.L. and Schafer, W.D. (1991) 'Attachment to mother/attachment to father: A meta-analysis.' *Child Development 62*, 1, 210–25.

Garbarino, J. (1999) *Lost Boys: Why Our Sons Turn Violent And How We Can Save Them.* New York: The Free Press.

Gilligan, R. (1997) 'Beyond permanence? The importance of resilience in child placement practice and planning.' *Adoption and Fostering 21*, 1, 12–20.

Gilligan, R. (2001) *Promoting Resilience: A Resource Guide on Working with Children in the Care System.* London: BAAF.

Grotberg, E. (1997) 'The International Resilience Project.' In M. John (ed.) *A Charge Against Society: The Child's Right to Protection.* London: Jessica Kingsley Publishers.

Heller, S.S., Larrieu, J.A., D'Imperio, R. and Boris, N.W. (1999) 'Research on resilience to child maltreatment.' *Child Abuse and Neglect 23*, 4, 321–38.

Hicks, L., Gibbs, I., Byford, S. and Weatherley, H. (2003) *Leadership and Resources in Children's Homes.* York: The University of York, Social Work Research and Development Unit.

Jackson, S. and Martin, P.Y. (1998) 'Surviving the care system: Education and resilience.' *Journal of Adolescence 21*, 5, 569–83.

Kendrick, A. (2005) 'Social Exclusion and Social Inclusion: Themes and Issues in Residential Child Care.' In D. Crimmens and I. Milligan (eds) *Facing Forward: Residential Child Care in the 21st Century.* Lyme Regis: Russell House Publishing.

Luthar, S.S. (1991) 'Vulnerability and resilience: A study of high-risk adolescents.' *Child Development 62*, 600–12.

Main, M. and Goldwyn, R. (1984) 'Predicting rejection of her infant from mother's representations of her own experience: Implications for the abused–abusing intergenerational cycle.' *Child Abuse and Neglect 8*, 203–17.

Martin, P.Y. and Jackson, S. (2002) 'Educational success for children in public care: Advice from a group of high achievers.' *Child and Family Social Work 7*, 2, 121–30.

Masten, A. (1994) 'Resilience in Individual Development.' In M.C. Wang and E.W. Gordon (eds.) *Educational Resilience in Inner-City America.* Hillsdale, NJ: Erlbaum.

Masten, A.S., Best, K.M. and Garmezy, N. (1990) 'Resilience and development: Contributions from the study of children who overcome adversity.' *Development and Psychopathology 2*, 425–44.

Newman, T. (2004) *What Works in Building Resilience*. London: Barnardo's.

Newman, T. and Blackburn, S. (2002) *Transitions in the Lives of Children and Young People: Resilience Factors*. Edinburgh: Scottish Executive Education Department.

Rutter, M. (1985) 'Resilience in the face of adversity: Protective factors and resistance to psychiatric disorder.' *British Journal of Psychiatry 147*, 598–611.

Sagy, S. and Dotan, N. (2001) 'Coping resources of maltreated children in the family: A salutogenic approach.' *Child Abuse and Neglect 25*, 1463–80.

Schofield, G. (2001) 'Resilience and family placement: A lifespan perspective.' *Adoption and Fostering 25*, 3, 6–19.

Unger, M. (ed.) (2005) *Handbook for Working with Children and Youth: Pathways to Resilience Across Cultures and Contexts*. Thousand Oaks, CA: Sage.

Velleman, R. and Orford, J. (1999) *Risk and Resilience: Adults Who Were the Children of Problem Drinkers*. Amsterdam: Harwood Academic Publishers.

Werner, E.E. (2000) 'Protective Factors and Individual Resilience.' In J. Schonkoff and S. Meisels (eds) *The Handbook of Childhood Intervention*, 2nd edition. Cambridge, MA: Cambridge University Press.

Werner, E.E. and Smith, R.S. (1992) *Overcoming the Odds: High Risk Children from Birth to Adulthood*. Ithaca and London: Cornell University Press.

CHAPTER 6

Young People Leaving Residential Care

Experiences and Outcomes

Jo Dixon

Introduction

Each year, across England and Scotland, around 8000 young people aged 16 and over leave care. Despite a general decline in the use of residential care, a significant proportion will leave from a residential placement.

For some young people, the transition from care will run smoothly; however, for others it will bring disadvantage and difficulties. The difficulties associated with leaving care have been widely acknowledged by professionals working with care leavers and are evidenced by national statistics and an increasing body of research carried out over the past three decades (see Stein 2004). The over-representation of care leavers in statistics on homelessness and unemployment, together with reports of the high incidence of mental and physical health problems and early parenthood, give some indication of the vulnerability of this group and of the problems they face.

Research suggests that young people leaving residential care are amongst the most vulnerable in the care system. As a group, they are more likely to have experienced greater difficulties prior to and during their care careers. Many will already have experienced one or more foster placement breakdowns and a high proportion will exhibit challenging or complex difficulties (Biehal *et al.* 1995; Rowe, Hundleby and Garnett 1989). The fact that young people leaving residential care may be more disadvantaged is likely to be a reflection on the type of young person accommodated in residential placements rather than the residential system *per se*. There is indeed evidence to suggest that residential units are better able to cope with difficult behaviour and may prove more appropriate for older children entering care, for whom foster placements are less likely to succeed (Farmer, Moyers and Lipscombe 2004; Sinclair and Gibbs 1998).

The collective voice of young people leaving residential care has long been central to our understanding of the issues facing all care experienced by young people. The Who Cares? project of the 1970s, which brought together young people living in children's homes to explore their care experience, was at the forefront of raising awareness of the difficulties associated with living in and leaving care. This was followed by a number of small exploratory studies, mainly focusing on residential care, which highlighted negative in-care experiences coupled with poor post-care outcomes and a lack of sustained support (Morgan-Klein 1985; Triseliotis 1980; Stein and Carey 1986).

Increased awareness of the difficulties facing care leavers served to raise the profile of leaving care on the political agenda and drive forward developments in policy and practice aimed at improving outcomes. Key developments included the Children Act 1989 and the Children (Scotland) Act 1995, which brought about specific duties and powers for local authorities in respect of supporting care leavers. There has also been a steady increase since the 1980s in specialist leaving-care projects, which provide direct support to care leavers.

Leaving care continues to feature prominently on the political and social care landscape but what does leaving care mean for young people, and what challenges do they face in the early stages of post-care living? What helps them to prepare for leaving care and how best can they be supported to achieve positive post-care outcomes? This chapter addresses these questions using a recent study of Scottish care leavers to highlight key issues and outcomes, and draws mainly on the experiences of young people leaving residential care.

The residential group

The Scottish study, carried out between 2000 and 2001 and prior to changes in legislation affecting care leavers, involved a survey of 107 young people leaving care in three Scottish local authorities. It included information from young people and their social worker or leaving-care worker (support worker). Young people were surveyed approximately six months after leaving care, and a subset of 61 were followed up with an interview 12 to 18 months after leaving care. Analysis looked at starting points (e.g. outcomes across accommodation, career, health and well-being six months on from leaving care) and outcomes at the follow-up point to chart progress.

Young people came from a range of care backgrounds. As with most looked-after young people, many had experience of a combination of placement types, including being looked after on a home supervision requirement. The diverse care backgrounds of these young people make it difficult to completely isolate the residential experience, however, by focusing on those who left care from a residential placement, it is possible to trace the pattern of the residential experience and situate it within the general experience of leaving care.

Research suggests that around three-fifths of children looked after away from home for two or more years will have experience of residential care (Bullock 1999). Around a third of young people in the Scottish study had been looked after in a residential placement at some point during their last care episode. Almost a quarter had left care from residential placements (children's home – 10%; residential schools – 11%; secure units – 1%), and it is this group whose views and experiences are used in this chapter.

Living in residential care

Residential care has undergone considerable changes in organisation and use in recent years. Having moved through a period of crisis and criticism, recent research suggests greater optimism for the future of residential care, in offering a positive placement choice for some looked-after children. As Bullock (1999) notes, good residential care can provide young people with a stable and stimulating environment.

For young people in the Scottish study who had left residential care, the care experience was mixed both within and across individual accounts and generally mirrored the overall experience of the wider group. When asked about the good aspects of being in care, young people talked about social and material advantages, such as going on holidays or trips out and having money to buy clothes or pursue hobbies. More commonly, they described the importance of finding company and comfort, feeling safe and having someone to talk to who had similar experiences. Susan told us, 'good things were a bit of security with staff there all the time and I could relate to the other young persons in the unit' and Gill valued the support she had received from her children's home where there were 'people who look after you and make you feel loved and wanted'.

Less positive aspects included a lack of privacy, feeling restricted by 'rules and regulations', and being punished. Brian talked of being 'restrained by staff'. He added, 'even if it was the best place I would still have hated it because it was not home'. Missing home and feeling cut off from family and friends was particularly apparent. Rona told us, 'the most bad thing about being in care was being so far away from home and not being able to see your friends and family when you wanted'. Sharon's experience highlighted some of the key aspects of being looked after:

> You know you will be looked after if your own parents can't look after you properly. [but] children's homes can get overcrowded...[and] there's not a lot of choice about where you go and a lot of moving around.

'Moving around' was a common experience for young people in the study with a third having moved on four or more occasions. Those leaving residential care appeared to have more moves, experiencing on average three placement moves. Only six per cent had remained in the same placement throughout their last care episode.

Existing research highlights the tendency for looked-after young people to experience movement and disruption in their lives. A recent English study found that 17 per cent had experienced ten or more care placements (Dixon *et al.* 2004). Such disruption carries implications for educational stability, identifying and meeting needs and for forming positive and lasting relationships. Research and practice evidence has emphasised the importance of continuity and stability in care for providing a basis for positive life chances. Indeed, placement stability has been associated with improved outcomes in educational attainment, career and social relationship skills, and accommodation (Biehal *et al.* 1995; Department of Health 1998).

Leaving residential care

Most looked-after young people leave care earlier than other young people leave home. Research suggests that on average, young people leave care at 16 years old whilst their non-care peers are more likely to leave home in their early twenties (Heath 1999). Explanations for this pattern of early transitions are many and vary from personal choice: 'I had been in care too long, it was time to move on,' and individual circumstances: 'I was out of place, one of the oldest in the residential school,' to wider strategic pressures: 'Staff thought it was time for me to move on.' In recent years, the prevailing culture has been to reverse this trend by introducing measures aimed at preventing unplanned and early moves from care to independent living.

Almost all young people in the Scottish study (93%) had moved on from care before 18 years of age and two-thirds had done so at 16. There was some evidence that young people leaving residential care did so earlier than those moving on from foster care (at an average age of 16 compared to 17 for the foster group). Furthermore, all those who left care at 18 or over had left from a foster placement.

Making the transition from care at an early age is a concern and is likely to impact upon post-care outcomes. However, for some young people it can represent a positive step on the pathway to independence. For example, a move to supported carers can provide a breathing space where young people can develop their skills and confidence before embarking upon fully independent living. Of equal importance to age, therefore, is that young people are well prepared, are able to leave care in a planned and supported manner, and, given that a third of the residential group said they had no choice when they left care, are able to have a say in when they leave.

The process of preparing young people for leaving care, known in Scotland as 'throughcare', should be holistic and well planned, taking on a natural and gradual progression in accordance with age and development (Stein and Wade 2000). However, support workers reported that only half of those leaving residential care had received a programme of preparation. Young people from foster care and those looked after at home were less likely to have done so (47% and 16% respectively). In addition, six out of ten young people in the survey had not had a formal leaving-care review to help them plan their transition from care. Most of those who had, however, were from residential care.

After residential care

Care leavers take on the responsibilities of independent adult living, such as setting up and managing a home, finding a career and starting a family, much sooner and often in a shorter space of time than their non-care peers. The post-care outcomes of young people in the Scottish study highlighted some of the difficulties associated with leaving care and the factors that influenced positive outcomes after care.

Education and career

Although some young people succeed in their education whilst looked after, research and government statistics suggest that the educational outcomes for looked-after young people are generally poor. In a survey of English care leavers, half of the sample had no qualifications (Biehal *et al.* 1995) whilst *Learning with Care* reported that up to 75 per cent of looked-after adolescents across five Scottish authorities had left school without qualifications (HM Inspectors of Schools and the Social Work Services Inspectorate 2001).

Attending school is also an essential part of a child's development and can provide a source of structure and stability in an otherwise uncertain or troubled life. However, high levels of educational disruption as well as poor attainment were evident within the Scottish group. Most (83%) had truanted and fewer than half (39%) had standard grades. The extent to which these young people are educationally disadvantaged is highlighted by national data which shows that 95 per cent of all Scottish school leavers achieved at least one qualification (Scottish Executive 2003).

There was some evidence that those leaving residential care fared worse educationally. Ninety-five per cent had experienced truancy and exclusion and less than 30 per cent had qualifications. For those who had, the average was three standard grades, fewer than the national average of seven for all Scottish school leavers. Young people in the study highlighted unmet educational needs and regrets at missing out on schooling. Colin, who had attended residential school, commented:

> My experience in classrooms wasn't good, people walking in and out, not taking it seriously. As a result I can't read and write very well and I feel bad about it. I didn't get the help I needed from teachers and care workers.

The trend for care leavers to have poor educational attainment and participation rates may result from the complex inter-relationship of pre-care disadvantage and family experiences and the difficulties that led them into care (Bynner and Parsons 2002; Stein 1994). However, that looked-after children are persistently failing to reach their full potential has raised the possibility that the care experience itself can exacerbate pre-care educational difficulties rather than compensate for them. Indeed, past research suggests a tendency for carers and social workers to afford limited attention to the education of looked-after children.

Young people can be supported to reach their full potential through the provision of a stable, supportive and educationally encouraging care environment, backed up by strategies to address the causes of truancy and exclusion (Jackson 2002). In the current survey, those young people who had achieved good educational outcomes tended to have been in long-term placements, most often in foster care, had experienced fewer placement moves, had not truanted or been excluded and had continued to receive a consistent package of support.

Educational disadvantage can impact upon progress after care. Indeed, most young people in the study were unemployed in the early months after leaving care, with only a quarter in education or training and one-tenth in work. Although young people leaving residential care were three times more likely to be in training than those leaving other care placements (27% and 9% respectively), more than seven in ten were unemployed and none were in education or work.

High levels of non-participation cannot be disconnected from wider social trends, which have seen an increasingly competitive youth labour market and a general delay in entry to employment. However, care leavers in the survey fared considerably worse than the general youth population with 61 per cent not participating in employment, education or training compared to ten per cent of 16–18-year-olds in general (Department for Education and Skills 2003).

Most young people participating in work, education or training had been assisted by professionals or family and social networks to identify or finance opportunities. Brian, for example, had left residential care without any qualifications but had been helped into education by the social work department. He told us, 'They got me straight into college, I hope I stick in and get a decent job.' Abby had received support from family: 'I have no standard grades and it's much harder to get a job...my mum and sisters helped me to get in to training.' Several common factors were associated with good career outcomes. For example, those with good outcomes tended to have been in long-term, stable care placements and had received an integrated package of support before and after leaving care. They were also more likely to have stable post-care accommodation.

Accommodation

An important issue for care leavers, and indeed leaving-care policy and practice, is accommodation. In Scotland, the Social Justice Milestones for tackling social exclusion state that all young people leaving care 'should have access to appropriate housing options' (Scottish Executive 1999, p. 11).

A third of young people who had left residential placements were living in hostels and a quarter had returned to live with parents in the early months after leaving care. In comparison to those leaving foster care, the residential group appeared less likely to be living in supported lodgings (26% and 11% respectively) and their own tenancy (25% and 6% respectively). This may reflect the earlier age at which the residential group left care and the age at which they are able to take on their own tenancy.

The housing experience of the group showed that most had received assistance in finding accommodation and most (87%) felt generally positive about their housing situation. However, many commented on the difficulties of managing and maintaining their own home. Coping with finances: 'the bills I still find difficult', shopping and caring for themselves: 'I don't eat meals just snacks and crisps', together with isolation and adjustment issues were common. Deb, who had moved to her own tenancy, commented, 'It's really difficult when you leave a [residential] school that's full of lassies and go and live by yourself' and Gill, who had returned home, found that '[Mum] still treated me like I was a wee lassie.'

Problems of transitory and insecure housing were also evident. Staying with friends and family temporarily was common and 60 per cent of young people had moved accommodation between one and four times during the year since leaving care. There was evidence that those leaving residential care had difficulty settling after care. The average number of moves for the residential group was five, with three-quarters having at least one subsequent move since leaving care. Although some young people moved for positive reasons, such as better accommodation, many moved through crisis or necessity. Rachel told us, 'I couldn't stay at my own flat because it isn't safe,' whilst Carol explained, 'I got chucked out of my first house and then got chucked out of my mum's then I was in a homeless unit.'

Homelessness had been an issue for almost four in ten young people. Over a third of the residential group had been homeless since leaving care. Most often this included staying with friends or family temporarily or staying in a homeless hostel. The fact that young people were helped out of homelessness and re-housed despite accommodation breakdown reflects the high priority given to the accommodation needs of care leavers. Most local authorities reported access to a range of housing options and had formal agreements with housing departments and providers (Dixon and Stein 2005). However, leaving-care staff highlighted the dilemma of matching young people's expectations with their abilities and the housing options available, particularly when dealing with an unplanned move or crisis situation.

Lifestyle, health and well-being

In terms of outcomes across other life areas, the Scottish study showed that pro-portionally, those leaving residential care were more likely to be young parents when compared to those from other care placement (13% and 8% respectively). Early parenthood amongst care leavers has been well documented (Corlyon and McGuire 1997; Garnett 1992). In the Scottish survey, nine per cent of all young men were parents and 16 per cent of young women had a child or were pregnant by the age of 17. This compares to seven per cent of all Scottish young women in the 16–19 age group who experience pregnancy (NHS Scotland 2000).

Health issues were also more prevalent within the residential group with almost twice as many reporting a physical heath problem. A recent study of the health of Scottish care leavers reported that young people considered leaving care to have had a negative impact on their health and that many displayed health risk behaviours, such as substance misuse, smoking, poor diet and lack of physical exercise (Scottish Health Feedback 2001).

Research also suggests that looked-after children have a greater vulnerabil-ity to learning difficulties, emotional and behavioural difficulties and mental illness (McCann *et al.* 1996; Meltzer *et al.* 2003). Mental health difficulties were apparent amongst the Scottish sample with young people reporting depression, agoraphobia, eating disorders and self-harming. Those leaving residential care were more likely to be described by their support worker as having mental health and emotional and behavioural difficulties than young people leaving from other placements (60% compared to 42%). The higher incidence of such difficulties amongst young people leaving residential care may be explained by the tendency for residential care to be used to accommodate older children, who often present more challenging behaviours (Berridge 2000).

Support

Finally, like all young people making the transition to adulthood, care leavers will require support to help them negotiate the inherent challenges. Many, however, will have fractured family relationships and may lack a social support network – particularly if they have experienced movement in and after care. The Children (Scotland) Act 1995 makes provisions for the formal support of young people transitioning from care, within the principles of throughcare (support to prepare a young person for leaving care) and aftercare (support for care leavers).

Building effective formal and informal support systems is an integral part of preparing for and assisting the transition to post-care living. In terms of informal support, this study found that maintaining family links had been encouraged whilst young people had been looked after with the majority having some contact with family within 12 months of leaving care. Almost all (95%) of those leaving residential care were in contact with family and two-thirds felt that they could turn to a family member if they needed help. Friends, partners and partners' families were also identified as a source of support. However, some young people commented on the loss of friendships after leaving care. Taking up accommodation far from their local neighbour-hood or family and friends could lead to feelings of isolation.

The importance of a supportive social network was emphasised. Many of those who experienced housing crisis were able to turn to family and friends for short-term shelter, as was the case for Josh when he lost his tenancy: 'I was fortunate really not to be sleeping rough, I always had a kip on somebody's floor.' Family and friends could also provide practical support with careers, and for young parents, with child care. Furthermore, those who lacked a social network were more likely to have poorer well-being and self-esteem and cope less well after care.

Loss of contact with ex-carers was also an issue, with only half of the group having contact with ex-foster or residential carers six months on from leaving care. For some, this contact involved infrequent visits or phone contact only. Half of the residential group, however, still had monthly contact with a residential worker and many welcomed the opportunity to 'drop in and see members of staff'. Such contact offers an important source of continuity. A third of local authorities identified strategies for facilitating ongoing contact, such as subsidising visits, activities and overnight returns to ex-placements. It was, however, acknowledged that workload and new responsibilities posed a barrier for ongoing support. One throughcare manager commented that, 'staff and carers are not disinterested but do have a recognisable new focus'.

In terms of formal support, providing effective aftercare support relies on contact with support workers – whether a specialist leaving-care worker or a social worker. Young people from residential care were more likely to be in contact with a social worker (65%) or a leaving-care worker (65%) when compared to those from foster care (42%, 62%) and those looked after at home (12%, 4%), although contact decreased over time for all young people. A year on from leaving care, only half of the residential group still had contact with a leaving-care worker and 15 per cent had contact with a social worker.

Young people also identified a range of other professionals who had assisted them after care. This included teachers, health professionals, drug and alcohol support services, youth offending teams and advocacy workers, demonstrating the diversity of need amongst the group and the importance of inter-agency links and multidisciplinary working.

Young people clearly valued the support they had received: 'My careers advisor is very good and listens to me,' 'My social worker, he's been a brilliant help to me,' 'My carers are always there for me.' Furthermore, analysis across a range of life areas consistently showed that the mediating factor between poor starting points and good outcomes was the existence of support, whether formal or informal.

Conclusion

Care leavers are a diverse group and a vulnerable group. Research also indicates that young people leaving residential care may be particularly at risk of poor outcomes. They are more likely to experience in-care movement, leave care at an earlier age, have fewer qualifications and are more likely to experience unemployment and housing movement in the early months after care.

The difficulties facing all care leavers are recognised in the recent legislative changes aimed at strengthening and widening the scope of the policy framework to provide assistance to young people in and leaving care. The Children (Leaving Care) Act 2000 represents a major reshaping of the leaving-care landscape in England and Wales. It legislated for the transfer of financial support of 16- and 17-year-olds from the Department of Works and Pensions to the local authority, a duty to assess and meet the needs of young people in and leaving care, pathway planning, the appointment of personal advisors, assistance with education and training up to the age of 24, maintenance in suitable accommodation and a duty to keep in touch by the 're-sponsible authority.' Section 6 of this Act, concerning financial support, was introduced in Scotland in April 2004. Additionally, the Scottish Parliament introduced the Regulation of Care (Scotland) Act 2001 and the Supporting Young People Leaving Care in Scotland, Regulations and Guidance, implemented in April 2004, to strengthen responsibilities and broaden the support offered to young people leaving care. Also, the introduction in Scotland of Pathways, and in England and Wales, Pathway Plans, which provide a framework for needs assessment and action planning for young people leaving care, offers the potential for a more consistent and structured approach to needs assessment and aftercare planning.

The challenge now is whether these developments will improve the experience and outcomes for young people in and leaving care. Research suggests that to be most effective, they will need to operate alongside further developments across the overall care experience.

First, aftercare support needs to build upon effective and positive substitute care. Placement stability and continuity in care are the foundation stones, along with maintaining links with family, carers and community and identifying and meeting educational, health and emotional needs early and effectively.

Second, if the age of leaving care is to reflect normative transitions to adulthood, adequate resources to maintain young people in suitable supported placements are necessary. It requires a change in culture amongst policy-makers, social workers, carers and young people themselves, so that remaining in care past the age of 16 is viable and those who want to remain in their residential unit or foster home are able to do so in an age-appropriate manner.

Third, young people's access to education, training and employment should be maximised. This should be integrated with improving the education of looked-after children. Recent strategies introduced by the Scottish Executive include a series of targets aimed at driving up the educational participation and performance of looked-after children.

Fourth, strategies to address the needs of young parents, young disabled people and those vulnerable to difficulties with health, well-being and risk behaviour, require further consideration. Such issues are particularly pertinent for those young people in and leaving residential care, who may have more complex needs.

Fifth, the provision of formal and informal support in care and the continuation of support across a range of life areas after care are pivotal to facilitating good outcomes. Pathway planning and needs assessments should ensure that reliable, consistent and appropriate support is made available.

Finally, improving the life chances and choices of young people living in and leaving care is an enduring challenge. Key objectives are providing greater stability, continuity and preparation whilst young people are looked after; giving them the opportunity for a more gradual transition from care; and increasing the help in and after care. In working towards meeting these challenges, local authorities and those working with young people in and leaving care can and do make a difference.

References

Berridge, D. (2000) *The Importance of Stability.* Quality Protects Research Briefing Number 2. Dartington: Department of Health/Research in Practice/Making Research Count.

Biehal, N., Clayden, J., Stein, M. and Wade, J. (1995) *Moving On: Young People and Leaving Care Schemes.* London: HMSO.

Bullock, R. (1999) 'Work with Children in Residential Care.' In M. Hill (ed.) *Effective Ways of Working with Children and their Families.* London: Jessica Kingsley Publishers.

Bynner, J. and Parsons, S. (2002) 'Social exclusion and the transition from school to work: The case of young people not in education, employment or training.' *Journal of Vocational Behavior 60*, 289–309.

Corlyon, J. and McGuire, C. (1997) *Young Parents in Public Care.* London: National Children's Bureau.

Department for Education and Skills (2003) *Statistics of Education: Care Leavers, 2002–2003, England.* National Statistics Bulletin. London: DfES.

Department of Health (1998) *Caring for Children Away from Home: Messages from Research.* Chichester: Wiley.

Dixon, J., Lee, J., Wade, J., Byford, S. and Weatherly, H. (2004) 'Young People Leaving Care: A Study of Costs and Outcomes.' Unpublished report to the Department of Health.

Dixon, J. and Stein, M. (2005) *Leaving Care: Throughcare and Aftercare in Scotland.* London: Jessica Kingsley Publishers.

Farmer, E., Moyers, S. and Lipscombe, J. (2004) *Fostering Adolescents.* London: Jessica Kingsley Publishers.

Garnett, L. (1992) *Leaving Care and After.* London: National Children's Bureau.

Heath, S. (1999) 'Young adults and household formation in the 1990s.' *British Journal of Sociology of Education 20*, 4, 545–61.

HM Inspectors of Schools and the Social Work Services Inspectorate (2001) *Learning with Care. The Education of Children Looked after Away from Home by Local Authorities.* Edinburgh: Scottish Executive.

Jackson, S. (2002) 'Promoting Stability and Continuity of Care Away from Home.' In D. McNeish, T. Newman and H. Roberts (eds) *What Works For Children?* Buckingham: Open University Press.

McCann, J.B., James, A. Wilson, S. and Dunn, G. (1996) 'Prevalence of psychiatric disorders amongst young people in the care system.' *British Medical Journal 313*, 1529–30.

Meltzer, H., Gatward, R., Corbin, T., Goodman, R. and Ford, T. (2003) *The Mental Health of Young People Looked After by Local Authorities in England.* London: National Statistics.

Morgan-Klein, B. (1985) *Where am I Going to Stay?* Edinburgh: Scottish Council for Single Homeless.

NHS Scotland (2000) *Scottish Health Statistics 2000.* Edinburgh: NHS Information and Statistics Division.

Rowe, J., Hundleby, M. and Garnett, L. (1989) *Child Care Now. A Survey of Placement Patterns.* London: BAAF.

Scottish Executive (1999) *Social Justice…a Scotland Where Everyone Matters.* Edinburgh: Scottish Executive.

Scottish Executive (2003) *Children's Social Work Statistics 2002–2003.* Edinburgh: Scottish Executive National Statistics Publication.

Scottish Health Feedback (2001) *A Study of the Health Needs of Young People with Experience of Being in Care in Glasgow.* Edinburgh: Scottish Health Feedback.

Sinclair, I. and Gibbs, I. (1998) *Children's Homes: A Study in Diversity.* Chichester: Wiley.

Stein, M. (1994) 'Leaving care, education and career trajectories.' *Oxford Review of Education 20*, 3, 349–60.

Stein, M. (2004) *What Works for Young People Leaving Care?* Barkingside: Barnardos.

Stein, M. and Carey, K. (1986) *Leaving Care.* Oxford: Blackwell.

Stein, M. and Wade, J. (2000) *Helping Care Leavers: Problems and Strategic Responses.* London: Department of Health.

Triseliotis, J. (1980) 'Growing up in foster care.' In J. Triseliotis (ed.) *New Developments in Foster Care and Adoption.* London: Routledge and Kegan Paul.

PART TWO

Addressing Issues
of Discrimination

CHAPTER 7

Gender Matters in Residential Child Care

Teresa O'Neill

Introduction

There are almost equal numbers of boys and girls 'looked after' by local authorities (Department for Education and Skills 2005) and increasing numbers of girls in the criminal justice system (Youth Justice Board 2005), so it is surprising that so little is known about the different gender needs of girls and boys. Traditionally, boys have been in the majority and there has been little recognition that the needs of girls may be different or that alternative policies and strategies may be necessary to respond to them (Berridge and Brodie 1998; Farmer and Pollock 1998; O'Neill 2001). As more than 13 per cent of young people 'looked after' are in children's homes, this chapter will examine why gender matters in residential child care.

Background

It is rare to find gender analysis in child welfare: policies, practice guidance and most academic literature either misrepresent or completely omit gender issues. For example, *Every Child Matters*, the government Green Paper for children's services in England (Department for Education and Skills 2003), fails to address gender issues relating to children or adults; many of the inquiries into abuse in children's homes ignore gender issues (Pringle 1993) or reinforce prejudiced misconceptions in relation to gender (for example, Utting 1991, 1997; Warner 1992); and very few research studies even mention gender. In the Department of Health research programme on residential care for children, *Caring for*

Children Away from Home (Department of Health 1998), little recognition is given to the importance of gender in understanding the needs of girls and boys in residential children's homes, how these settings operate and the role of gender in defining staff attitudes (Green 2005); and only two of the studies (Berridge and Brodie 1998; Farmer and Pollock 1998) comment on gender differences. Furthermore, in a recent examination of progress in the implementation of safeguards for children living away from home since *People Like Us* (Utting 1997), gender issues were neglected altogether (Stuart and Baines 2004). 'Gender mainstreaming' (Daniel *et al.* 2005) is now needed in child welfare to make explicit the different impact of social systems, policies, initiatives and actions on and among men and women, boys and girls, and as a means to promote gender equality (Rees 1999).

In the context of residential care, gender is of tremendous importance not only in understanding differences between boys and girls and the implications of these for children's services, but also in understanding the different management styles of male and female workers; the relationships between gender, organisations and power; and the abuse and exploitation of children (Green 2005). It is evident from all the inquiries that concepts of masculinity and power are relevant to many of the contexts of institutional abuse (for example, Brannan, Jones and Murch 1993; Kirkwood 1993; Levy and Kahan 1991; Waterhouse 2000; Williams and McCreadie 1992). Many recommendations have emerged from these inquiries although it has been argued that few have successfully been implemented (Gallagher 1999); that little real effort has yet been made to analyse the causes of abuse in children's homes (Colton 2002; Wolmar 2000); and that research on residential care has contributed little in this regard, focusing on government priorities and policy rather than challenging practice (Bullock, Millham and Little 1993). An in-depth understanding of why things have gone wrong in the past is needed, and gender has a critical part to play in this analysis.

Gender equality

Gender equality is about gender, equality and power relationships. Gender has come to be understood as a socially constructed phenomenon which has varied historically and culturally, and is the product of socialisation rather than nature (Green 2005; Oakley 1972). In the past, the term 'gender' has been associated with women and gender equality seen as women's business (Hearn 2001). As gender relations have begun to change in recent years, one effect has been 'the gradually growing realisation that men and masculinities are just as gendered as are women and femininities' (Hearn *et al.* 2003, p. 8) and, furthermore, that within one society there are many types of masculinities and femininities which are affected by other dimensions such as class and race 'with white middle-class hegemonic masculinities being exalted and celebrated, and complicit and alternative masculinities as well as all types of femininities being negated and marginalized' (Green 2005, p. 461).

Power relations are structured so that one group of people benefits at the expense of another (McNay 1992) and in our patriarchal society, men have benefited disproportionately in terms of power and resources (Hearn 1987). The structural and personal power (Waldby 1989) accorded to men has also enabled them to enact socially condoned violence such as rape and domestic violence in order to maintain power. Even now this continues to be excused on the basis of their 'biological' inability to exercise sexual control with the blame transferred to the 'provocative' female: 'the male sexual incontinence theory' (Dyer 1985 cited by Green 2005, p. 460). Children, particularly girls, are also vulnerable to this type of abuse of power: in a society that reflects ambivalence about the nature of childhood and childhood sexuality, they have also been labelled 'provocative'. Children's position in the hierarchy affords them little power, status or rights, and those in residential care who lack worth in the eyes of the wider community are even more powerless and vulnerable to abuse and social exclusion (Myers, O'Neill and Jones 1999).

Residential children's homes are organisations which 'present themselves as agendered and asexual entities' (Green 2005, p. 465) although, in fact, gender is a key factor in how they function. Organisations are based in the public world of work and are associated with male characteristics and power, while women's ascribed feminine role is located in the private life of the family and associated with qualities such as emotionality and nurturing. Although residential children's homes sit between the public and private domains because they are simultaneously a 'home' for children and part of the world of organisa-tions, they operate largely under the rules in the public domain (Parkin 1989) within hierarchical structures of authority. Men still disproportionately hold the management and senior positions and women predominate in the lower-status welfare or caring roles (Adkins 1992). This has been the case in social work and in residential children's homes, although there is some evidence that this is now starting to change (Milligan, Kendrick and Avan 2004). The style of leadership and the regime and culture established in the home influence the quality of the residential experience for staff as well as children and there are many examples of abusive, institutionalised practices in settings where masculine, heterosexual hierarchies are allowed to be dominant (Jones 1993; Parkin and Green 1997; Stein 1993). In such regimes, women workers' inequality is institutionalised through the maintenance of traditional gender roles (Aymer 1992) and their relative powerlessness, compounded by their lack of knowledge, training and confidence, contributes to their inability to intervene to protect children. How the organisation, managers and staff in children's homes interpret and respond to the gendered and sexual behaviour of looked-after children is of great importance.

Looked-after children

Girls and boys have different patterns of help-seeking and respond to different services, and girls' routes into care and their needs whilst in care are also different from those of boys. Criminal behaviour is often the reason for boys' admission to care, but is rarely the reason for that of girls, which is much more likely to result from problems in family relationships (including violence and abuse), concerns about 'moral' welfare, and health issues, particularly the use of drugs and/or alcohol. Unlike boys, girls often request their own admission to care as an escape route from emotional pressures at home, and from abuse (Hudson 1989): this is despite the fear shared by boys and girls of involvement with formal agencies and the risk of breach of trust and confidentiality (MacLeod 1999). There is some evidence that adolescent girls are more likely to experience placement in care as a result of the divorce of parents, are more negatively affected by separation and divorce than are boys, experience more difficulties in adapting to stepfamilies and have more conflicts with stepfathers than their male peers (Berridge and Brodie 1998; Fombonne 1996).

There are further striking differences between boys and girls in the assessment of 'risk' and what is judged by social workers and the courts to constitute 'significant harm'. These differences are much more likely to result in heavy interventionist responses with girls than with boys. Adolescent girls face conflicting personal and political expectations: adolescence is about challenge, whilst femininity is about conformity, and some behaviours which are normalised for boys through conceptions of emerging masculinities are seen as a transgression of the female role for girls (Carlen 1987; Hudson 1984). For example, aggressive or violent behaviour that is tolerated in boys attracts deep and widespread condemnation in girls (Chesney-Lind 1997; Lagree and Lew Fai 1989). The behaviour of girls is policed in ways that the behaviour of boys is not, and they are labelled troublesome even when their behaviour may constitute no more than an extension of normal adolescent behaviour that is unacceptable to parents or other adults (O'Neill 2005).

Girls' sexuality rather than their victimisation is often perceived as the problem: it is central to the definition of risk and is the reason for professional intervention with most adolescent girls. It has been argued (Hudson 1984) that while such intervention is legitimated on the basis of girls' need for protection, hidden beneath the 'welfare as protector' discourse lies a fear of the young woman who is sexually active. The sexual behaviour of girls is frequently problematised whilst the sexual behaviour of boys is largely ignored (Brogi and Bagley 1998; O'Neill 2001; O'Neill, Goode and Hopkins 1995; Shaw and Butler 1998).

Residential care

Residential children's homes are provided for almost 6000 children in England, with a further 2000 placed in other residential settings including secure children's homes, young offender institutions, residential schools and mother and baby units (Department for Education and Skills 2005). The large majority are adolescents, most of whom have complex needs, and many have histories of abuse, including sexual abuse (Aymer 1992; Kahan 1994; Kendrick 1995; Madge 1994; Rowe, Hundleby and Garnett 1989; Sinclair and Gibbs 1998; Triseliotis *et al.* 1995).

There are gender differences in the experience of living in residential care and, whilst outcomes for both boys and girls in residential care are poor overall, there is evidence that they are worse for girls (Hobcraft 1998). Problems include low educational attainment and expectations, and high mobility and exclusion rates (Fletcher-Campbell, Archer and Tomlinson 2003) with the majority of children leaving care with no educational qualifications (Biehal *et al.* 1992) and career choices heavily determined by gender, with girls at a disadvantage as a result (Trust for the Study of Adolescence 2000). Although girls perform better than boys (reflecting the pattern in the general population), recent guidance from the Social Exclusion Unit (2003) does not make any reference to gender or acknowledge the different needs of boys and girls in care, and whilst there is concern about boys' performance and a need to address this discrepancy, there is also evidence that little attention is being given to the girls who *are* failing in school (Trust for the Study of Adolescence 2000).

The health needs of looked-after children have long been neglected with low priority given to routine medical care. These children's mental health needs are greater than those in the general population of the same age, and show stark gender differences, with higher rates of depression, eating disorders and self-harm among young women and suicide more common among young men (Berridge and Brodie 1998; Farmer and Pollock 1998; Howard League 1995; Sinclair and Gibbs 1998; Trust for the Study of Adolescence 2000). There has been a virtual absence of health education, including sexual health education (Utting 1997) and insofar as it occurs is aimed more at girls than boys. This might be thought surprising given the high risk for all young people of contracting sexually transmitted diseases including HIV/AIDS and the dispro-portionate number of young women who become pregnant whilst in care (Biehal *et al.* 1992).

One effect of the contraction of the residential sector is that there are fewer and less specialised children's homes which limits the opportunity for matching children's needs with the most appropriate provision, something that could arguably address some of the problems referred to above and improve outcomes. This is exacerbated by the absence in many homes of a clear theoretical orientation and statement of purpose (Berridge and Brodie 1998; Sinclair and Gibbs 1998) and this 'theoretical void' (Stein 1993) has allowed abusive regimes to become established (Levy and Kahan 1991). Furthermore, the 'we take all comers' approach (Rose 2002, p. 191) results in the combination in homes of girls with boys, children who abuse with the victims of abuse and different categories of offender with non-offenders, despite repeated recom-mendations that some groups should be accommodated separately (Farmer and Pollock 1998; Green and Masson 2002; Utting 1991). Concerns have been expressed that residential homes are not equipped to work with the range of problems this combination presents (Barter 1997) and that children are exposed to risks from their peers of which they are unaware, without the provision of adequate staff protection. Policy and practice in recent years has resulted in the majority of residential homes accommodating boys and girls together, although it has been shown that any benefits of this 'normalising' arrangement are predominantly benefits for the boys, with girls' needs subordinated or unrecognised, even where they are in the majority in homes (Berridge and Brodie 1998; Farmer and Pollock 1998).

Gender, sexuality and abuse

The relationship of gender to issues of sexuality and abuse in residential child care has been neglected and few commentators have appreciated its importance in understanding how residential institutions operate and the abuse and exploitation of children (Colton 2002; Green 2005; Green and Masson 2002).

The risk of children suffering some kind of abuse in residential care is up to six times higher than that for young people in the general population (Rushton and Minnis 2002) and the way in which many homes operate minimises the possibility that children will disclose peer or adult abuse to staff or other children (Green and Masson 2002). There are important gender differences in the levels of vulnerability to abuse and in the effects and outcomes for girls and boys and it has been suggested that whilst boys are most at risk in residential schools, girls are at the greatest risk in children's homes (Westcott and Clement 1992). Some residential homes have been found to have a criminal peer culture increasing the incidence of offending for boys and girls (Wade *et al.* 1998) and a recent study found that 40 per cent of young people admitted to residential care without any previous caution or conviction received one if they stayed in the home for six months or more (Sinclair and Gibbs 1998). Peer violence, bullying and exploitation have been found to be serious problems (Berridge and Brodie 1998; Cawson *et al.* 2004; Farmer and Pollock 1998; Sinclair and Gibbs 1998) and it is also now emerging that residential care presents a high risk of sexual violence, particularly for girls by male peers, and of initiation into prostitution by peers within and outside the residential home and by paedophiles, drug dealers and pimps (Cawson *et al.* 2004; Farmer and Pollock 1998; Green and Masson 2002; Oliver and Candappa 2003; O'Neill *et al.* 1995; Shaw and Butler 1998). Boys known to have been sexually abused by adult males are also vulnerable and at risk of bullying by other boys and male staff who see them as weak and 'feminised' (Bacon and Richardson 2000; Green 2005; Parkin and Green 1997).

A matter of particular concern is the normalization and acceptance of peer sexual abuse within residential settings with 'denial and invisibilization' (Green and Masson 2002, p. 156) the most common staff response to sexuality. Staff uncertainty about what constitutes 'peer sexual abuse' and what is normal sexual experimentation compounds the problem and leaves children, particularly girls, highly vulnerable and young male sexual abusers continuing to present a risk to others, without their therapeutic needs being met. This vulnerability to sexual exploitation is further increased in the 'macho' cultures of some residential homes (Berridge and Brodie 1998). Many such institutions are characterised by stereotypical gender roles and unequal power relationships between male and female staff who often collude, knowingly or inadvertently, with sexist attitudes (Goldson 2002; Green and Parkin 1999; O'Neill 2001).

Issues of sexuality in residential care have been found to be mishandled and staff responses to be reactive and punitive (Green and Parkin 1999). Male staff frequently abdicate responsibility for issues of sexuality, seeing it as women's business, and both male and female staff blame girls for any sexual activity, colluding with the myths about girls' provocativeness and boys' inability to exercise sexual control (Green 2005; Green and Masson 2002; O'Neill 2001). Both male and female workers respond negatively to girls who are seen as sexually active or involved in prostitution and there is substantial evidence that children's homes afford little protection to girls already involved in or at risk of initiation into prostitution (Farmer and Pollock 1998; Jesson 1993; O'Neill 2001; O'Neill *et al.* 1995; Shaw and Butler 1998). Boys' sexuality (as long as it is heterosexual) is invisible and boys are not seen either as potentially abusive or at risk of abuse. Boys who are assumed to be gay, either because of their sexual behaviour or identity or because they do not conform to the stereotypical notions of macho masculinity, are often marginalised and ridiculed (Green 2005). At the same time they are perceived as 'predatory', reflecting deeply entrenched but misconceived views about male homosexuality and the sexual abuse of boys: although gay men may be abusers, boys and girls are predominantly abused by heterosexual men (Finkelhor 1986; Kelly, Regan and Burton 1991).

Girls' sexuality is 'perceived as something to be punished, controlled, forbidden, made invisible and seen as taboo' (Parkin and Green 1997, p. 80). Farmer and Pollock's (1998) study of sexually abused and abusing children found that 'the sexualised behaviour of girls was a particularly neglected area, and their behaviour excited rejection by male workers and only a passive stance by many caregivers' (Farmer and Pollock 1998, p. 131). Furthermore, girls placed in male-dominated secure children's homes for protection from risks in the community were marginalised and subjected to a greater level of surveillance and restriction than the boys, even though most of the boys had been sexually active and some of them had been convicted of serious sexual offences. The girls were afforded little protection from sexual bullying and harassment by the boys: those who retaliated in an attempt to protect themselves were punished and others, who were traumatised by the abuse and self-harmed, were restrained and isolated in their cells (O'Neill 2001).

The view appears to be widespread that girls are more difficult to work with than boys (Berridge and Brodie 1998; Hudson 1989; O'Neill 2001). Many workers fail to understand the complexity of girls' needs, expressing uncertainty and a lack of confidence in how to work with them (Hudson 1989; O'Neill 2001) and demonstrating an ill-preparedness to deal with some of the behaviour presented by girls, such as deliberate self-harm. One male residential worker said:

> the boys will fight if they're upset, they'll thump someone in the face and that's a lot easier to deal with – you restrain them, sit on them until they calm down, but with the girls, I'm very nervous that someone's going to cut themselves or try to hang themselves... I find working with girls much more stressful. (O'Neill 2001, p. 161)

Many workers withdraw from working with girls who often constitute a small minority among boys, and in so doing they add weight to the view that girls are 'difficult', justify their own lack of engagement and further compound the marginalisation of girls who are already socially excluded.

In many residential settings, women workers are required to take primary responsibility for the girls, and their enforced compliance with this and with the expectation to 'police' the girls' sexuality (Aymer 1992; Parkin and Green 1997) mirrors the powerlessness of the children themselves (Morrison 1990). This practice by residential workers also reinforces rather than challenges the negative stereotype of the sexually 'predatory' or 'dangerous' young woman, particularly where men justify their defensive practice with girls on the basis that they will make false allegations of sexual misconduct against them (O'Neill 2001). It denies women and girls' 'shared vulnerability from adult males' (Aymer 1992, p. 192) and fails to provide positive, empowering role models for girls; but, perhaps most dangerous of all, it presents role models to the boys that collude with abusive male behaviour, sexist images of women and sexual stereotypes which disadvantage and objectify females (Green 2005) and does nothing to address the boys' poor relationships with women.

Conclusion

Boys and girls looked after in residential children's homes share some common concerns and experience of disadvantage, and they experience the risks, problems and poor outcomes associated with placement in residential care. However, they also face problems and have needs which are unique to their gender and there has been little recognition that the needs of girls may be different from those of boys, or that alternative approaches and policies may be needed to respond to them. This has compounded the marginalisation of already socially excluded girls in institutional care, who are expected to 'fit into' provision primarily designed for boys, resulting in even worse outcomes for girls than for their male peers (Berridge and Brodie 1998; Farmer and Pollock 1998; Hobcraft 1998; O'Neill 2001).

Residential children's homes provide an essential resource for young people but if they are to be the placement of choice providing a positive experience of being looked after and achieving good outcomes for girls as well as boys, they need to be better resourced with workers afforded higher status and more opportunities to increase their knowledge and skills. A good under-standing of what has gone wrong in the past is essential so that *appropriate* responses to problems can be implemented, and gender matters in this analysis. Gender inequalities in residential children's homes need to be illuminated and challenged, and more recognition given to the impact of gender on workers' relationships and attitudes, management practices, the abuse and exploitation of children and ultimately on the quality of the residential experience and outcomes for girls and boys.

References

Adkins, L. (1992) 'Sexual Work and the Employment of Women in the Service Industries.' In M. Savage and A. Witz (eds) *Gender and Bureaucracy.* Oxford: Blackwell.

Aymer, C. (1992) 'Women in Residential Work: Dilemmas and Ambiguities.' In M. Langan and L. Day (eds) *Women, Oppression and Social Work.* London: Routledge.

Bacon, H. and Richardson, S. (2000) 'Child Sexual Abuse and the Continuum of Victim Disclosure: Professionals Working with Children.' In C. Itzin (ed.) *Home Truths and Child Sexual Abuse: Influencing Policy and Practice.* London: Routledge.

Barter, C. (1997) 'Who's to blame: Conceptualising institutional abuse by children.' *Early Child Development and Care 133*, 101–14.

Berridge, D. and Brodie, I. (1998) *Children's Homes Revisited*. London: Jessica Kingsley Publishers.

Biehal, N., Clayden, J., Stein, M. and Wade, J. (1992) *Prepared for Living ? A Survey of Young People Leaving the Care of Three Local Authorities*. London: National Children's Bureau.

Brannan, C., Jones, J. and Murch, J. (1993) *Castle Hill Report: A Practice Guide*. Shrewsbury: Shropshire County Council.

Brogi, L and Bagley, C. (1998) 'Abusing victims: Detention of child sexual abuse victims in secure accommodation.' *Child Abuse Review 7*, 5, 315–29.

Bullock, R., Millham, S. and Little, M. (1993) *Residential Care for Children: A Review of the Research*. London: HMSO.

Carlen, P. (1987) 'Out of Care into Custody.' In P. Carlen and A. Worrell (eds) *Gender, Crime and Justice*. Milton Keynes: Open University Press.

Cawson, P., Berridge, D., Barter, C. and Renold, E. (2004) *Physical and Sexual Violence Between Children Living in Residential Settings: Exploring Perspectives and Experiences*. End of Award Report to ESRC. London: NSPCC and University of Luton.

Chesney-Lind, M. (1997) *The Female Offender: Girls, Women and Crime*. London: Sage.

Colton, M. (2002) 'Factors associated with abuse in residential child care institutions.' *Children and Society 16*, 1, 33–44.

Daniel, B., Featherstone, B., Hooper, C.-A. and Scourfield, J. (2005) 'Why gender matters for Every Child Matters.' *British Journal of Social Work 35*, 8, 1343–55.

Department for Education and Skills (2003) *Every Child Matters*. London: Department for Education and Skills.

Department for Education and Skills (2005) *Statistics of Education: Children Looked After by Local Authorities year ending 31 March 2004 – Volume 1: Commentary and National Tables*. London: National Statistics.

Department of Health (1998) *Caring for Children Away from Home: Messages from Research*. Chichester: Wiley.

Farmer, E. and Pollock, S. (1998) *Sexually Abused and Abusing Children in Substitute Care*. Chichester: Wiley.

Finkelhor, D. (1986) *A Sourcebook on Child Sexual Abuse*. London: Sage.

Fletcher-Campbell, F., Archer, T. and Tomlinson, K. (2003) *The Role of the School in Supporting the Education of Children in Public Care*. Research Brief No RB 498. www.dfes.gov.uk/research/data/uploadfiles/RB498.pdf, accessed on 19 July 2007.

Fombonne, E. (1996) 'Depressive Disorders: Time Trends and Possible Explanatory Mechanisms.' In M. Rutter and D. Smith (eds) *Psychosocial Disorders in Young People: Time Trends and their Causes*. Chichester: Wiley.

Gallagher, B. (1999) 'The abuse of children in public care.' *Child Abuse Review 8*, 357–65.

Goldson, B. (2002) *Vulnerable Inside: Children in Secure and Penal Settings*. London: The Children's Society.

Green, L. (2005) 'Theorizing sexuality, sexual abuse and residential children's homes: Adding gender to the equation.' *British Journal of Social Work 35*, 4, 453–81.

Green, L. and Masson, H. (2002) 'Adolescents who sexually abuse and residential accommodation: Issues of risk and vulnerability.' *British Journal of Social Work 32*, 2, 149–68.

Green, L. and Parkin, W. (1999) 'Sexuality, Sexual Abuse and Children's Homes – Oppression or Protection.' In The Violence Against Children Study Group (ed.) *Children, Child Abuse and Child Protection: Placing Children Centrally.* Chichester: Wiley.

Hearn, J. (1987) *The Gender of Oppression: Men, Masculinity and a Critique of Marxism.* Brighton: Wheatsheaf.

Hearn, J. (2001) 'Men and Gender Equality: Resistance, Responsibilities and Reaching Out.' Keynote paper, 'Men and Gender Equality Conference', 15–16 March 2001, Orebro, Sweden.

Hearn, J., Pringle, K., Mueller, U., Oleksy, E., Lattu, E., Chernova, J. and Ferguson, H. (2003) *Critical Studies on Men in Ten European Countries: the State of Academic Research.* Helsinki: European Research Network on Men in Europe Project.

Hobcraft, J. (1998) *Intergenerational and Life-Course Transmission of Social Exclusion: Influences and Childhood Poverty, Family Disruption and Contact with the Police.* London: LSE Centre for the Analysis of Social Exclusion.

Howard League (1995) *Banged Up, Beaten Up, Cutting Up: Report of the Howard League Commission of Inquiry into Violence in Penal Institutions for Young People.* London: Howard League.

Hudson, B. (1984) 'Adolescence and Femininity.' In A. McRobbie and M. Nava (eds) *Gender and Generation.* London: Macmillan.

Hudson, B. (1989) 'Justice or Welfare.' In M. Cain (ed.) *Growing Up Good: Policing the Behaviour of Girls in Europe.* London: Sage.

Jesson, J. (1993) 'Understanding adolescent female prostitution: A literature review.' *British Journal of Social Work 23*, 5, 517–30.

Jones, J. (1993) 'Child Abuse: Developing a Framework for Understanding Power Relations in Practice.' In H. Ferguson, R. Gilligan and R. Torode (eds) *Surviving Childhood Adversity: Issues for Policy and Practice.* Dublin: Social Studies Press.

Kahan, B. (1994) *Growing Up in Groups.* London: HMSO.

Kelly, L., Regan, L. and Burton, S. (1991) *An Exploratory Study into the Prevalence of Sexual Abuse in a Study of 16–21 Year Olds.* London: University of North London, Child Abuse Studies Unit.

Kendrick, A. (1995) *Residential Care in the Integration of Child Care Services.* Edinburgh: The Scottish Office.

Kirkwood, A. (1993) *The Leicestershire Inquiry 1992.* Leicester: Leicestershire County Council.

Lagree, J. and Lew Fai, P. (1989) 'Girls in Street Gangs in the Suburbs of Paris.' In M. Cain (ed.) *Growing Up Good: Policing the Behaviour of Girls in Europe.* London: Sage.

Levy, A. and Kahan, B. (1991) *The Pindown Experience and the Protection of Children.* Stafford: Staffordshire County Council.

MacLeod, M. (1999) 'Children's Perspectives.' In N. Stanley, J. Manthorpe and B. Penhale (eds) *Institutional Abuse: Perspectives Across the Life Course.* London: Routledge.

Madge, N. (1994) *Children and Residential Care in Europe.* London: National Children's Bureau.

McNay, M. (1992) 'Social Work and Power Relations: Towards a Framework for an Integrated Practice.' In M. Langan and L. Day (eds) *Women, Oppression and Social Work.* London: Routledge.

Milligan, I., Kendrick, A. and Avan, G. (2004) *'Nae Too Bad': A Survey of Job Satisfaction, Staff Morale and Qualifications in Residential Child Care in Scotland.* Glasgow: Scottish Institute for Residential Child Care.

Morrison, T. (1990) 'The emotional effects of child protection work on the worker.' *Practice 4*, 4, 253–71.

Myers, J., O'Neill, T. and Jones, J. (1999) 'Preventing Institutional Abuse: An Exploration of Children's Rights, Needs and Participation in Residential Care.' In The Violence Against Children Study Group (ed.) *Children, Child Abuse and Child Protection: Placing Children Centrally.* Chichester: Wiley.

Oakley, A. (1972) *Sex, Gender and Society.* London: Temple Smith.

Oliver, C. and Candappa, M. (2003) *Tackling Bullying: Listening to the Views of Children and Young People.* London: Department for Education and Skills.

O'Neill, T. (2001) *Children in Secure Accommodation: A Gendered Exploration of Locked Institutional Care for Children in Trouble.* London: Jessica Kingsley Publishers.

O'Neill, T. (2005) 'Girls in Trouble in the Child Welfare and Criminal Justice System.' In G. Lloyd (ed.) *Problem Girls: Understanding and Supporting Troubled and Troublesome Girls and Young Women.* London: Routledge.

O'Neill, M., Goode, N. and Hopkins, K. (1995) 'Juvenile prostitution – The experience of young women in residential care.' *ChildRight 113*, 14–16.

Parkin, W. (1989) 'Private Experiences in the Public Domain: Sexuality and Residential Care Establishments.' In J. Hearn, D.L. Sheppard, P. Tancred-Sheriff and G. Burrell (eds) *The Sexuality of Organisations.* London: Sage.

Parkin, W. and Green, L. (1997) 'Cultures of abuse within residential child care.' *Early Child Development and Care 133*, 73–86.

Pringle, K. (1993) 'Gender politics.' *Community Care*, 4 March, 16–17.

Rees, T. (1999) 'Mainstreaming Equality.' In S. Watson and L. Doyal (eds) *Engendering Social Policy.* Buckingham: Open University Press.

Rose, J. (2002) *Working with Young People in Secure Accommodation: From Chaos to Culture.* Hove: Brunner-Routledge.

Rowe, J., Hundleby, M. and Garnett, L. (1989) *Child Care Now: A Survey of Placement Patterns.* London: BAAF.

Rushton, A. and Minnis, H. (2002) 'Residential and Foster Family Care.' In M. Rutter and E. Taylor (eds) *Child and Adolescent Psychiatry*, 4th edition. Oxford: Blackwell Science.

Shaw, I. and Butler, I. (1998) 'Understanding Young People and Prostitution: A Foundation for Practice?' *British Journal of Social Work 28*, 2, 177–96.

Sinclair, I. and Gibbs, I. (1998) *Children's Homes: A Study in Diversity.* Chichester: Wiley.

Social Exclusion Unit (2003) *A Better Education for Children in Care.* London: Social Exclusion Unit.

Stein, M. (1993) 'The Uses and Abuses of Residential Care.' In H. Ferguson, R. Gilligan and R. Torode (eds) *Surviving Childhood Adversity: Issues for Policy and Practice.* Dublin: Social Studies Press.

Stuart, M. and Baines, C. (2004) *Progress on Safeguards for Children Living Away from Home: A Review of Action since the People Like Us Report.* York: Joseph Rowntree Foundation.

Triseliotis, J., Borland, M., Hill, M. and Lambert, L. (1995) *Teenagers and the Social Work Services.* London: HMSO.

Trust for the Study of Adolescence (2000) *Young People and Gender.* London: Cabinet Office and Home Office.

Utting, W. (1991) *Children in the Public Care: A Review of Residential Care.* London: HMSO.

Utting, W. (1997) *People Like Us: The Report of the Review of the Safeguards for Children Living Away from Home.* London: HMSO.

Wade, J., Biehal, N., Clayden, J. and Stein, M. (1998) *Going Missing: Young People Absent from Care.* Chichester: Wiley.

Waldby, V. (1989) 'Theoretical Perspectives on Father–Daughter Incest.' In E. Driver and A. Droisen (eds) *Child Sexual Abuse: Feminist Perspectives.* London: Macmillan.

Warner, N. (1992) *Choosing with Care: the Report of the Committee of Inquiry into the Selection, Development and Management of Staff in Children's Homes.* London: HMSO.

Waterhouse, R. (2000) *Lost in Care: Report of the Tribunal of Inquiry into the Abuse of Children in Care in the Former County Council Areas of Gwynedd and Clwyd since 1994.* HC 201. London: Stationery Office.

Westcott, H. and Clement, M. (1992) *NSPCC Experience of Child Abuse in Residential Care and Educational Placements: Results of a Survey.* London: NSPCC.

Williams, G. and McCreadie, J. (1992) *Ty Mawr Community Home Inquiry.* Cwmbran: Gwent County Council.

Wolmar, C. (2000) 'The Untold Story Behind Child Abuse.' *Guardian*, 16 February. www.guardian.co.uk/comment/story/0,,234042,00.html, accessed on 19 July 2007.

Youth Justice Board (2005) *Youth Justice Annual Statistics 2004/05.* London: Youth Justice Board.

CHAPTER 8

Disabled Children in Residential Settings

Kirsten Stalker

Introduction

> At my old school, I used to get told off for not listening; they never gave me a chance... I get more help with learning at my new [residential] school... I'm more into the things they do, it's more exciting. I'm going to France on a school trip. (Anne, quoted in Abbott, Morris and Ward 2001a, p. 55)

> They just said to me that there was a school in [X] that I could be going to that most people, everyone there's got at least something a bit wrong with them and first of all I thought I might not get on with people there, then I thought, I'm going to miss my friends as well. (Carl, quoted in Abbott *et al.* 2001a, p. 49)

This chapter reviews research about a largely hidden group of children – young disabled people in residential settings. The focus will be on residential schools, since that is where the majority of disabled children living away from home are placed, although some attention will be paid to health-care settings and short-term ('respite') homes. I have not been able to identify any recent research about disabled children in children's homes (although see Hawthorn (2005) for an excellent discussion of 'giving a voice' to young disabled people in residential care). It seems that most studies about children in residential settings exclude those with impairments, do not report whether or not the sample included any young people with impairments or, if they do, fail to analyse these children's experiences as a separate group. In particular, we know very little about what residential settings feel like to the disabled children living there (Cook, Swain and French 2001; Morris 1995).

Readers interested in the history of residential care for disabled children should turn to Oswin (1971) and Shearer (1980). This chapter draws on material published between 1995 and 2005, primarily in the UK. Given the paucity of research, it also includes policy documents and official reports. The focus is on children and young people with physical, sensory or cognitive impairments rather than those with emotional or behavioural difficulties (EBD), (although the latter are the biggest group of children in residential 'special' schools).

Numbers and characteristics of disabled children in residential settings

Following concerns that basic information about the numbers and circumstances of disabled children in residential settings was lacking (Davies 2002; Department of Health 2001; Paul and Cawson 2002; Utting 1997), the Department for Education and Skills/Department of Health (2003) produced a paper drawing together information from various sources. However, as Stuart and Baines (2004) point out, the status of this paper, which was published on the Quality Protects website, is unclear and any action to be taken as a result of its findings, unspecified. There has been no equivalent initiative in Scotland.

The Department for Education and Skills/Department of Health (2003) report does not contain the most recent figures but, based on further analysis of official statistics and recent research, it provides more detail than is normally available. On 31 March 2002, in England and Wales, there were 1320 disabled children with 'looked-after' status in residential settings. Of these, 595 were at residential schools, 620 in children's homes and the remainder in a hotchpotch of settings which do not appear well placed to meet children's needs, such as residential care homes for adults, unregulated accommodation, NHS establishments and secure units. The vast majority of these children were white and aged between 10 and 15. Thirty-nine per cent were placed outside their home authorities. Nevertheless, since looked-after children are subject to regular review, the report states that there is less 'professional disquiet' about this group than others.

In March 2002, about 10,500 disabled children attended residential special schools in England and Wales (Department for Education and Skills/Department of Health 2003). Of these, 3400 were boarding for up to seven nights a week in maintained special schools, with 2700 in non-maintained special schools (non-profit-making independent schools run by charitable trusts). A further 4400 youngsters attended 99 independent residential special schools. Although nearly all these pupils had statements of special educational need, it is not known how many had impairments. The vast majority of boarders at maintained and non-maintained schools were white, a majority were aged 11–15 and three-quarters were boys. The largest group in all types of school were children with EBD, followed by those with learning disabilities. Children with physical and/or sensory impairments were a relatively small proportion.

Turning to Scotland, in March 2004 there were 193 young people in homes for disabled children, which had an average of six places each (Scottish Executive 2004). In September 2004, there were 938 children with a Record of Needs (equivalent to a 'Statement' south of the border) in publicly funded and independent schools in Scotland (personal communication, Scottish Executive Education Department 2005). Excluding those with diagnoses of EBD, 391 had physical, sensory and/or cognitive impairments, the biggest single group being children with an autistic spectrum disorder, of whom there were 126. However, there may have been other children with impairments in residential settings who did not have a Record of Need.

McConkey *et al.* (2004) examined the characteristics of looked-after disabled children spending 90 days or more away from home within a 12-month period, in one part of Northern Ireland. Thirty-four were in residential provision, but fewer than half this group were in schools or children's homes falling within the requirements of the Children's Order (NI) – clearly a cause for concern. Fifty-nine per cent were boys and 41 per cent, girls. Their median age was 15; most had learning disabilities and 'challenging behaviour', followed by children with communication difficulties, autism and those who were technologically dependent.

The quality of information about disabled children in health-care settings is particularly poor. Neither impairment nor ethnicity is routinely recorded in NHS hospital admission data. Analysis of HES (hospital episode statistics) indicates that, between 1998 and 2001, 2200 children spent longer than six months in hospital in England and Wales, with 245 apparently having been there for more than five years (Department for Education and Skills/ Department of Health 2003). Among those in hospital for longer than six months, nearly 80 per cent were classified as having 'mental and behavioural disorders'. The HES data indicated that children with learning disabilities (included under 'mental disorders') are particularly likely to have long admissions. In a cross-border study of children with complex needs in health-care settings, delays in discharge were primarily attributed to insufficient support in the community (Stalker *et al.* 2003). In Northern Ireland, McConkey *et al.* (2004) report difficulty tracking disabled children admitted to hospitals on a short- or long-term basis.

The past ten years has seen increasing use of children's hospices for short-term care for children with life-limiting conditions and those with profound multiple impairments but, again, we lack a national overview of numbers and needs. Research has shown a range of benefits to families and children (Jackson and Robinson 2003; Phillips and Burt 1999) and high levels of satisfaction among parents. On the other hand, the appropriateness of offering 'respite' and terminal care in the same setting, and the impact of the hospice environment on children who are not dying, have been questioned (Morris 1998a).

Paul and Cawson (2002) identify two reasons for the poor quality of information about disabled children in residential settings. First, the numbers of disabled children are relatively small in systems geared to collecting data needed for planning services for majority populations. Second, there is evidence that 'disability leads to invisibility' caused by:

> a combination of social attitudes which are reluctant to acknowledge disability or to listen to disabled people, and administrative systems which set up barriers to learning and multi-disciplinary working… (Paul and Cawson 2002, p. 270)

However, the Department for Education and Skills/Department of Health (2003) predicted that data should improve, at least in England and Wales, following the introduction of enhanced returns on looked-after children, the Children in Need census, the Pupil Level Annual Schools Census and the work of new regional SEN partnerships.

Reasons for placement

The Department for Education and Skills/Department of Health (2003) admits that, in relation to looked-after disabled children, 'We do not have a clear view of the specific reasons for their being in care' (Department for Education and Skills/Department of Health 2003, p. 15). Reviewing research about admission to residential special schools, two main factors, which may be related, emerge – inability to meet a child's educational needs locally and pressure on families. Abbott *et al.* (2001a), who examined decision-making about residential school placements in 21 English local authorities, note that the most common reason for placement cited by education and social services was 'social' – 'the impact of the child's impairment on the family' (p. 2). Davies (2002), in a comprehensive review of research about residential schools throughout the UK, found that referrals and admissions can be socially driven rather than determined by a child's clinical or educational needs. McConkey *et al.* (2004) found that families whose disabled children are in residential placements have a mixture of complex problems which mainstream services struggle to meet, not least through failures in coordinated planning.

Most of the 34 parents interviewed by Abbott *et al.* (2001a), whose children were at residential school, had been very reluctant to let their child go. However, other evidence suggests that some parents prefer residential school placements to residential homes, adoption or fostering, which are considered more stigmatising (Green 2004; Morris 1995; Russell 1995). Where there are concerns about a child's welfare at home, residential school is sometimes seen as a good way to ensure the child has a better standard of care and educational opportunities (Abbott *et al.* 2001a).

Legal status

The legal status of disabled children in residential settings is not always clear. This has serious implications for their welfare, since those who are not 'looked after' under the Children Acts do not have the same legislative rights and protection as those who are. Placements funded by education authorities may attract little or no attention from social services (Abbott *et al.* 2001a). Most of the 21 education authorities in this study were unaware of their duty under the Children Act 1989 to notify social services of any disabled child going to residential school. Where information was shared, this was more by default than design. Most education officers took what Abbott *et al.* call a 'minimalist' approach to ensuring children's welfare, with involvement in annual reviews very variable. Reviews were organised and coordinated by the schools. Social workers were only invited where they were actively involved with the family. Sometimes social workers by accident came across children who had been attending residential schools for 48–52 weeks a year, for several years.

Most social services departments in Abbott *et al.*'s study treated children as looked after and accommodated under the Children Act 1989 but four did not. Even where disabled children in residential settings are supposed to be looked after, they may not be afforded their full rights. Most authorities in Abbott *et al.*'s study admitted they did not always manage their legal responsibilities. Only one social services department fully implemented 'looked after' procedures for disabled children at residential schools. Abbott *et al.* (2001b) come to the worrying conclusion that:

> It is not possible to be confident about the welfare of disabled children at residential schools given the wide variations in practices in following the guidance set out in the Children Act. For children in placements funded solely by education, there is unlikely to be anybody other than a parent actively checking whether or not a child is safe and happy (p. 4)

Eyre, Thompson and Gillroy (1999) report that 186 disabled children remained in hospitals in Newcastle for at least three weeks, and in some cases much longer, after completion of treatment. Stalker *et al.* (2003) found confusion among health and social care agencies in four health authorities/ boards in England and Scotland about the legal status of disabled children spending three months or more in health-care settings. Under the Children Act 1989, health authorities in England must notify local authorities when children are in hospital for three months. Local authorities should then determine whether the child's welfare is being adequately safeguarded and if they should exercise any of their functions under the Act. Utting (1997) noted that health authorities often fail to notify local authorities. The Children (Scotland) Act 1995 only requires health authorities to do so when a child has had (or is unlikely to have) no parental contact for three months.

Misunderstandings also occur about how the Children Act regulations apply to children in short-term care. When placed in a residential (or family) setting for more than 24 hours, children become 'looked after' by the local authority – and should therefore have care plans and regular reviews. However, Morris (1998b) found some disabled children having short breaks without any knowledge or involvement by social services. Problems associated with 'drift' are noted by Priestley, Rabiee and Harris (2003) who found some young people living full-time in 'respite care.' Again, mainstream children's services were not always aware of such children, many of whom did not have an allocated social worker. Small numbers of disabled children also receive 'short-term care' for social reasons in hospitals (Connors and Stalker 2003; Department for Education and Skills/Department of Health 2003; Stalker and Hunter 1999). Sometimes these placements drift into long-term care, where there is a lack of planning and/or, in practitioners' view, no suitable alternative. The 24-hour rule mentioned above does not apply to health-care settings.

Child protection

There are no large-scale data sets about abuse of disabled children in the UK comparable to information available from the USA, Canada and Australia. Analysis of computer records for over 40,000 children in one US city found that, compared to non-disabled children, disabled children were:

- 3.8 times more likely to be neglected
- 3.8 times more likely to be physically abused
- 3.1 times more likely to be sexually abused
- 3.9 times more likely to be emotionally abused.

(Sullivan and Knutson (2000) cited in Miller 2003, pp. 19–20)

A number of factors can increase disabled children's vulnerability to abuse (Miller 2003), including greater use of institutional care, physical dependency and barriers to communication. There is sometimes an assumption, captured in the title of a report by the National Working Group on Child Protection and Disability, that 'it doesn't happen to disabled children' – reflecting a long-held view that these young people are somehow intrinsically different from others.

Given the inconsistency in monitoring and review of disabled children in residential settings, it is not surprising that concerns have been expressed about their vulnerability to abuse. Yet as Paul and Cawson (2002) point out, there is little hard information or research on this topic. Utting (1997), who reviewed safeguards for children living away from home, concluded that disabled children were 'extremely vulnerable to abuse of all kinds, including peer abuse, and high priority needs to be given to protecting them and ensuring that safeguards are rigorously applied' (Utting 1997, p. 79). Kendrick and Taylor (2000) drew attention to the often unidentified abuse of children in hospital. They report evidence from the USA suggesting that abuse is more common in hospital than at home.

Williams and Morris (2003) review developments in child protection systems for young disabled people in residential care, following the Utting report. They note a number of policy initiatives in England and Wales, including the Commission for Social Care Inspection, new safeguarding duties for schools under the Education Act 2002 and the introduction of national minimum standards for children's homes and residential schools under the Care Standards Act 2002. A residential school is now treated as a children's home if it provides accommodation for more than 42 weeks per year.

Children's views and experiences

Seeking children's views when decisions are made about their lives is both good practice and a legislative requirement. As noted already, we do not know much about disabled children's views and experiences of residential care. Morris (1998b) found little evidence of social workers exploring children's wishes and feelings when making decisions about short-term care placements. In the authority she studied over a six-month period, in only 12 out of 66 cases was there any attempt to find out the child's views. In at least five cases, social workers had not even seen the child. Similarly, Abbott, Morris and Ward (2000) reported that education departments rarely sought children's views about how best to meet their needs. Although social services had a better record in consulting children, they sometimes failed to ensure children's views were acted on, while young people with communication impairments were routinely excluded.

An example of good practice in seeking the views of young people with communication impairments in residential settings, and supporting them to speak up for themselves, comes from an advocacy group at Chailey Heritage School (Virgo 1998). Issues raised by the group include relationships, practical issues (for example, about equipment), personal preferences, finding friends, public transport and boredom. The young people had strong feelings about the outside world disabling them, and about their right to make choices and be heard, and expressed mixed views about whether school or home was better. The group's experiences suggest that quality of life in residential settings is significantly improved where young people are facilitated to voice their preferences and feelings. Support from an independent advocate is crucial.

Lightfoot and Sloper (2002) highlight good practice in consulting disabled children about hospital services. They recommend approaching young people while they are in hospital but to be sensitive about timing. Having a 'starter list' of topics can be helpful, but young people need to know they can add issues that matter to them. While stressing there is no 'right' method for consulting, the authors outline the advantages and disadvantages of various approaches ranging from questionnaires to group work.

Across the studies reviewed by Davies (2002), a majority of disabled youngsters thought that residential special school placement had a positive impact, helping them socially and emotionally. They reported improved skills in various areas and had developed better relationships. Abbott *et al.* (2001a) spoke to, or observed, 32 young people in residential schools. These children recounted some unhappy experiences in local schools and, in that sense, most were positive about the opportunities afforded by residential school. Some thought they got a better education at boarding school. Nevertheless, most would still have preferred to be at home. They missed their families and they missed having their own space and routines. Most, but not all, went home for visits during term time and holidays. A few did not like anything about residential school. Other research has shown children can feel very homesick in short-term care units (Oswin 1984) and longer-term placements (Cook *et al.* 2001; Stalker *et al.* 2003).

It can be difficult for parents to maintain regular contact with, and visit, disabled children in residential settings, especially if they are placed far from home (Abbott *et al.* 2001a; Priestley *et al.* 2003). This is exacerbated where parents lack or cannot afford transport, where the child has multiple placements and where the nature of the child's impairment makes communication difficult by telephone or letter. Abbott *et al.* found that although social services usually acknowledged their duty to help parents keep in touch, support was almost entirely discretionary, decisions being made on an individual basis through negotiation with parents.

The Children Act 1989 requires local authorities to appoint independent visitors for children who are looked after and have had no parental contact for at least 12 months. Knight (1998) studied 23 independent visitor schemes in England and Wales (although not all the children were in residential placements). Knight found that only about a third of authorities were using independent visitors. Of the 235 children who had an independent visitor, only 32 were disabled. Some social work staff were unclear about the role of independent visitors, there was insufficient funding to run schemes properly and those located in social services departments were not always perceived as independent. Nevertheless, children linked to independent visitors benefited from the contact. They were offered friendship, outings, support and an opportunity to do ordinary things and experience some family life.

One of the main concerns about residential care for disabled children is that it cuts young people off not only from their families but also from friends and communities at home (Cook *et al.* 2001). They may lead fairly enclosed lives in a residential home or school, with limited opportunities to participate in mainstream leisure activities. In an age where social inclusion is a major policy and practice goal for disabled children, residential care may seem an undesirable option. Ordinary social opportunities are very important to disabled children (Murray 2002) and parents of children at residential schools consider social inclusion a priority (Morris 2004).

The limited evidence available gives a mixed picture. The children in Abbott *et al.*'s study (2001) experienced their 'free time' differently, some feeling bored, with little to do and insufficient staff available to support them going out. Others felt they had a good deal of independence and choice of activities. Often, they had better social lives at school than at home although it could be difficult having a boyfriend or girlfriend. Stalker *et al.* (2003), in a case study of a Scottish residential school, report that pupils spent most of their free time with staff and flat mates within the residential setting and had little contact with any young people outside. On the other hand, Davies (2002) notes that 'an increasing variety of appropriate and purposeful extra curricular activities is being provided in many residential schools' (Davies 2002, p. 13). Berridge and Brodie (1998) report that short-break homes for disabled children had a better record than long-stay units (not specifically for disabled children) in organising outings, despite some logistical difficulties in terms of transport and practical arrangements.

Staff in residential settings occupy a powerful position in relation to children. Abbott *et al.* (2001) report that some residential staff were very committed to the children they worked with and engaged with them thoughtfully. Others were disrespectful, sometimes passing very negative comments about the young people and not bothering to communicate with them. Davies (2002) reports evidence of therapeutic relationships with staff, noting many pupils in the studies he reviewed valued the 'caring aspect' of residential schools.

Conclusions and implications for policy and practice

While the actual numbers are relatively low, disabled children are more likely to be 'looked after', and more likely to be in residential settings, than their non-disabled peers. The legal status of some of these placements is unclear and, despite their particular vulnerabilities, young disabled people are not always afforded the same rights and protection as others. In particular, there must be concern about children living away from home without care plans and regular reviews, about those in 52-week-a-year placements at residential schools and those who spend much of their school holidays in short-term care placements. In addition, as we have seen, some children are living in health-care settings, in adult establishments or unregulated homes – would such arrangements be tolerated for non-disabled children? Given the paucity of research on residential settings for disabled children, and the poor quality of information available, there is need for further investigation. However, there is also an urgent need for better policy and practice, for example:

- Improved data collection systems, particularly about the numbers, needs and circumstances including the ethnicity of disabled children in independent residential schools and those who have long or repeat admissions to hospital.

- All disabled children at residential special schools should be treated as 'looked after' and afforded the legal rights and protection accompanying that status.

- Better community services are needed to support families looking after disabled children with complex needs at home. More family-based short-break schemes are needed, with carers trained and supported to look after children with complex needs. Townsley, Abbott and Watson (2004) give examples of good practice in multi-agency working with families bringing up children with complex health-care needs at home.

- Consideration could be given to recruiting more 'professional' foster and adoptive parents to care for children with complex needs.

- To safeguard disabled children's welfare, residential settings must be placements of choice rather than a last resort (Russell 1995). The aims and intended outcomes of placements should be agreed by all, including parents and children, and inclusion and participation in local communities promoted. Well-supported family contact plans and robust reviewing systems are required (Williams and Morris 2003).

- Efforts should always be made to explore disabled children's views, both prior to and during placement. Social workers, education officers and staff in residential settings would benefit from training in communication.

- Disabled children should have access to independent advocates, especially where their views differ from those of parents and professionals.

- Local authorities should actively support parents to keep in touch with disabled children in residential settings and support children to return home as much as possible.

Berridge and Brodie (1998) highlighted aspects of good practice in short-break homes for disabled children: a clear sense of purpose, a structured and 'expert-led' programme, a high level of one-to-one interaction, 'normalising' activity, a positive approach to the children's development, good relationships with parents actively involved in the children's care, and constructive inter-agency planning and involvement. They argue that such good practice features provide a useful template for residential care for all children.

Acknowledgements

Thanks to Colin Gallacher of the Scottish Executive Education Department for providing statistical data and David Abbott of Bristol University for comments on this chapter.

References

Abbott, D., Morris, J. and Ward, L. (2000) 'Disabled Children and Residential Schools: A Survey of Local Authority Policy and Practice.' *Findings 420*. York: Joseph Rowntree Foundation.

Abbott, D., Morris, J. and Ward, L. (2001a) *The Best Place To Be? Policy, Practice and the Experiences of Residential School Placements for Disabled Children.* York: York Publishing Services.

Abbott, D., Morris, J. and Ward, L. (2001b) 'Residential Schools and Disabled Children: Decision-Making and Experiences.' *Findings 31*. York: Joseph Rowntree Foundation.

Berridge, D. and Brodie, I. (1998) *Children's Homes Revisited.* London: Jessica Kingsley Publishers.

Connors, C. and Stalker, K. (2003) *The Views and Experiences of Disabled Children and their Siblings: A Positive Outlook.* London: Jessica Kingsley Publishers.

Cook, T., Swain, J. and French, S. (2001) 'Voices from segregated schooling: Towards an inclusive education system.' *Disability and Society 16*, 2, 293–310.

Davies, J.D. (2002) 'Review of the Impact of Special Education Residential Provision in the United Kingdom.' Unpublished report prepared for Kent County Council. Bristol: University of the West of England.

Department for Education and Skills/Department of Health (2003) *Disabled Children in Residential Placements.* www.dfes.gov.uk/qualityprotects/docs/Disabled%20children%20Revised%20Final%202April04.doc, accessed on 19 July 2007.

Department of Health (2001) *Valuing People: A New Strategy for Learning Disability for the 21st Century.* London: Stationery Office.

Eyre, J., Thompson, J. and Gillroy, V. (1999) 'Children with Disabilities Resident in Newcastle Hospitals for Longer than Three Weeks.' Unpublished report to Newcastle and North Tyneside Health Authority.

Green, S. (2004) 'The impact of stigma on maternal attitudes toward placement of children with disabilities in residential care homes.' *Social Science and Medicine 59*, 4, 799–812.

Hawthorn, M. (2005) 'Giving a Voice to Disabled Young People in Residential Care.' In D. Crimmens and I. Milligan (eds) *Facing Forward: Residential Care in the Twenty-first Century.* Lyme Regis: Russell House.

Jackson, P. and Robinson, C. (2003) 'Children's hospices: Where do they fit?' *Critical Social Policy 23*, 1, 103–12.

Kendrick, A. and Taylor, J. (2000) 'Hidden on the ward: The abuse of children in hospitals.' *Journal of Advanced Nursing 31*, 3, 565–73.

Knight, A. (1998) *Valued or Forgotten? Disabled Children and Independent Visitors.* London: National Children's Bureau.

Lightfoot, J. and Sloper, P. (2002) *Having a Say in Health: Guidelines for Involving Young Patients in Health Services Development.* University of York: Social Policy Research Unit.

McConkey, R., Nixon, T., Donaghy, E. and Mulhern, D. (2004) 'The characteristics of children with a disability looked after away from home and their future service needs.' *British Journal of Social Work 34*, 4, 561–76.

Miller, D. (2003) 'Disabled Children and Abuse.' In National Working Group on Child Protection and Disability (2003) *'It Doesn't Happen to Disabled Children': Child Protection and Disabled Children.* London: NSPCC.

Morris, J. (1995) *Gone Missing? A Research and Policy Review of Disabled Children Living Away from their Families.* London: The Who Cares? Trust.

Morris, J. (1998a) *Accessing Human Rights: Disabled Children and the Children Act.* Barkingside: Barnardos.

Morris, J. (1998b) *Still Missing? Disabled Children and the Children Act.* London: Who Cares? Trust.

Morris, J. (2004) 'They have to be special.' *Community Care*, 8–14 January, 36.

Murray, P. (2002) *'Hello! Are You Listening?' Disabled Teenagers' Experience of Access to Inclusive Leisure.* York: York Publishing Services.

Oswin, M. (1971) *The Empty Hours: A Study of the Weekend Life of Handicapped Children in Institutions.* London: Allen Lane, The Penguin Press.

Oswin, M. (1984) *They Keep Going Away: A Critical Study of Short-Term Residential Care Services for Children who are Mentally Handicapped.* London: King's Fund.

Paul, A. and Cawson, P. (2002) 'Safeguarding disabled children in residential settings.' *Child Abuse Review 11*, 5, 262–81.

Phillips, R. and Burt, M. (1999) *Rachel House: An Independent Evaluation, The Views of Children, Young People and Families.* Edinburgh: Children's Hospice Association Scotland.

Priestley, M., Rabiee, P. and Harris, J. (2003) 'Young disabled people and the "new arrangements" for leaving care in England and Wales.' *Children and Youth Services Review 25*, 11, 863–90.

Russell, P. (1995) *Positive Choices: Services for Children with Disabilities Living Away from Home.* London: The Council for Disabled Children, National Children's Bureau.

Scottish Executive (2004) *Children's Social Work Statistics 2003–04.* Edinburgh: Scottish Executive National Statistics Publication. www.scotland.gov.uk/stats/bulletins/h 00369-00.asp, accessed on 19 July 2007.

Shearer, A. (1980) *Handicapped Children in Residential Care: A Study of Policy Failure.* London: Bedford Square Press of the National Council for Voluntary Organisations.

Stalker, K., Carpenter, J., Phillips, R., Connors, C., MacDonald, C. and Eyre, J. with Noyes, J., Chaplin, S. and Place, M. (2003) *Care and Treatment? Supporting Children with Complex Needs in Healthcare Settings.* Brighton: Pavilion Publishing.

Stalker, K. and Hunter, S. (1999) 'To close or not to close: The future of learning disability hospitals in Scotland.' *Critical Social Policy 19*, 2, 177–94.

Stuart, M. and Baines, C. (2004) *Safeguards for Vulnerable Children: Three Studies on Abusers, Disabled Children and Children in Prison.* York: York Publishing Services.

Townsley, R., Abbott, D. and Watson, D. (2004) *Making a Difference? Exploring the Impact of Multi-Agency Working on Disabled Children with Complex Health Care Needs, Their Families and the Professionals who Support Them.* Bristol: Policy Press.

Utting, W. (1997) *People Like Us: The Report of the Review of the Safeguards for Children Living Away from Home.* London: HMSO.

Virgo, S. (1998) 'Group Advocacy in a Residential Setting.' In C. Robinson and K. Stalker (eds) *Growing Up with Disability.* London: Jessica Kinglsey Publishers.

Williams, A. and Morris, J. (2003) 'Child Protection and Disabled Children at Residential School.' In National Working Group on Child Protection and Disability (eds) *'It Doesn't Happen to Disabled Children': Child Protection and Disabled Children.* London: NSPCC.

CHAPTER 9

Black and Minority Ethnic Children and Young People in Residential Care

Andrew Kendrick

Introduction

A written answer of 17 May 2006 in the House of Commons highlighted that in England the number of children from black and minority ethnic groups in care rose by over 25 per cent between 2001 and 2005 – from 10,020 to 12,800. This compares to a fall over the same period for the number of white children in care (Dhanda 2006). Black and minority ethnic children make up 21 per cent of the looked-after population, compared to only 13.5 per cent of all children in the England (Thoburn, Chand and Proctor 2005). This highlights concerns over the years about the over-representation of children from black and minority ethnic groups in the care population (for example, Barn 1993; Rowe, Hundleby and Garnett 1989). There is considerable variation across the UK, however. In Scotland, although there has also been a significant rise in the proportion of looked-after children from black and minority ethnic groups, these children represent two per cent of the looked-after population; and this compares to three per cent of the 0–18 population (Scottish Executive 2004).

There has also long been a concern that services provided for black and minority ethnic children and their families often do not address their specific needs (Ahmad 1990; Ahmed, Cheetham and Small 1986; Barn 1993; Singh 2005; Thanki 1994). Barn (2001) notes that, in the 1950s, the Family Welfare Association stated that there was no difference in the problems of minority families and the indigenous population, and they were making adequate use of services. Since then, research has shifted this view. Caesar, Parchment and Berridge (1994) identify three ways in which access to social services is impeded: first, 'the prevention of *initial* access; secondly, by denying *equal* access; and, finally, through the lack of services to meet the specific cultural, physical, emotional and religious needs of Black children' (Caesar *et al.* 1994, pp. 23–4). More recently, there have been concerns about the social work response to unaccompanied asylum-seeking children and young people (Hayes and Humphries 2004; Lyons, Manion and Carlsen 2006; Mitchell 2003; Stanley 2001).

It is important that such concerns are considered in the context of broader issues of racism and power at societal, institutional and individual levels: 'ethnicity and "race" are contested and troubling categories because they have become sites in which and through which relations of oppression are constituted' (Dominelli, Lorenz and Soydan 2001, p. 1). Barn (2001) identifies the ways in which research has focused on family structures and lifestyles to understand the situations of black and minority ethnic families, rather than exploring the impact of structural racism. Racial stereotypes lead to black and minority ethnic families being pathologised and seen as 'deviant' (Barn 1993; Chakrabarti 2001; Scott 1999; Singh 1992). Jones and Waul (2005) identify how structural and institutional racism impact on the way in which residential child care must address the needs of black children and young people:

> effective care for black children must be rooted in a willingness to understand and deal with racism in all its manifestations; to meet needs that arise for black children, including those that are linked to racism, those that are 'simply' to do with them being children and those that are to do with being a specific child with specific needs, history, background and life experiences in a specific context. (Jones and Waul 2005, p. 44)

We must also be aware of the difficulties around definition and the use of terms in times of increasing international mobility and globalisation where 'ethnic identities and the idea of ethnicity are highly uncertain' (Fook 2001, p. 9). Jones and Waul (2005) use the term 'black' as a political and unifying term to refer to the 'colour' of the experience of racism rather than simply the colour of a skin (Jones and Waul 2005, p. 34; see also Mehra 1996; Singh 2005). However, they acknowledge that it is not a concept that has a universal appeal or acceptance. Prevatt Goldstein (2005) also notes that use of the term 'minority ethnic children' as a synonym for black ethnicities can render invisible the experiences of white minority ethnic children. This has particular significance with increasing number of asylum-seeking children from Eastern Europe. There are also particular issues in relation to the racial and ethnic identity of children of inter-racial parentage (Barn and Harman 2006). In this chapter, I have used the term 'black and minority ethnic' in order to reflect both the commonalities and heterogeneity across the children and young people (Chakrabarti *et al.* 1998), although in some cases I retain the terminology of the research literature.

Article 30 of the UN Convention on the Rights of the Child (UNCRC) stresses the rights of children belonging to ethnic, religious or linguistic minorities. Where children are placed away from their family, 'regard shall be paid to the desirability of continuity in a child's upbringing and to the child's ethnic, religious, cultural and linguistic background' (Article 20, UNCRC). In the UK, the Children Act 1989 and the Children (Scotland) Act 1995 make it a duty to consider race, culture, religion and language (Chakrabarti *et al.* 1998). It is also important to recall that many of the issues which affect black and minority ethnic children in residential care, will be common to all children: 'much of what is to be learned about caring for black children is neither unique to black children nor does it speak to the experiences and needs of *all* black children' (Jones and Waul 2005, p. 33).

Placement in care

Rowe *et al.* (1989) was one of the first studies to provide detailed information on patterns of foster and residential care for black and minority ethnic children. The study confirmed that 'black children were disproportionately represented in admissions to care' and 'this was mainly accounted for by the large number of young black children being admitted for temporary care during family emergencies' (Rowe *et al.* 1989, p. 160). While there were wide variations across the six authorities (3% to 51%), the study concluded that black children were over-represented in admissions to care in all six authorities. Rowe and colleagues also comment on 'the remarkably high overall admission rate for children of mixed parentage' (Rowe *et al.* 1989, p. 164) which accounted for 44 per cent of the admissions of black children in the study. In a study in one local authority, Barn (1993) found that black children (predominantly African-Caribbean and children of mixed parentage) were twice as likely as their white peers to be admitted into care within four weeks of referral. Barn considered that the rapidity at which black children entered care highlighted unsatisfactory preventive work with black families and children (Barn 1993). More recently, Lees (2002) also identified an over-representation of African-Caribbean and mixed heritage children in her study of girls and young women entering care in one local authority.

In relation to Asian children, however, Rowe *et al.* (1989) found they were under-represented. Subsequent research has consistently shown that Asian children are under-represented in the care system. Thoburn *et al.* (2005) compared the ethnicity of those in care and the census figures for the child population: black/black British (3.0% of population and 6.5% of children in care); mixed heritage (3.2% and 7.4%); South Asian (6.6% and 2.3%). They also show, however, that there are significant variations between different local authorities.

Placement in residential care

Studies in the 1970s highlighted the disproportionate placement of black and minority ethnic children and young people in residential care (Barn 1993, 2001; Thoburn *et al.* 2005). This has been attributed to the difficulty in finding suitable family placements (Cheetham 1986). More recent studies have identified different patterns. Rowe *et al.* (1989) found that 'fostering rates for white, Afro-Caribbean and mixed parentage children were almost identical… Proportionately more black teenagers went into specialist foster homes' (Rowe *et al.* 1989, p. 170). Similarly, Barn (1993) found that 'more white children than black were placed in institutional settings…black children had a much better chance of being placed in substitute family settings than white children' (Barn 1993, p. 69; see also Barn, Andrew and Mantovani 2005; Barn, Sinclair and Ferdinand 1997).

Research on residential care has identified both variation across authorities and variation across different types of placement. Sinclair and Gibbs (1998) found that the proportion of black and minority ethnic children in children's homes over the past year was 7.5 per cent, but this ranged between 2 and 15 per cent across different authorities. Generally, they made up a small proportion of the residents in the home. Roughly a third of the homes had had no black and minority ethnic resident in the previous year, a third had less than 11 per cent and a further third had had between 11 and 27 per cent (Sinclair and Gibbs

1998). Berridge *et al.* (2003) studied a sample of 257 adolescents from four local authorities. While one-quarter of the sample came from minority ethnic groups, there were wide variations across placement types. Only 2 of the 63 young people in residential special schools were from minority ethnic groups, compared to almost one-third of the children in foster care and nearly half of the residents of children's homes. A significant number of these were unaccompanied young people from abroad, and one children's home was exclusively for this group.

Thoburn *et al.* (2005) also highlight that a significant proportion of unaccompanied asylum-seeking children are spending much of their adolescence in residential care and hostels. Wade, Mitchell and Baylis (2005) found that residential care was 'mainly used for an initial period of assessment and preparation before young people moved to semi-independent settings' (Wade *et al.* 2005, p. 74). Some local authorities have developed specialist children's homes for unaccompanied asylum-seeking children, and there are conflicting views about whether specialist children's homes are an appropriate model (Mitchell 2003). On the one hand, they are more able to address the specific cultural needs of the children in their care (Stanley 2001); on the other, it must not be assumed that unaccompanied asylum-seeking children are a homogeneous group, and there can be friction between children from different minority ethnic groups (Wade *et al.* 2005). However, young people living in foster and residential care appear to receive more support from social workers and carers than those living in independent and semi-independent accommodation (Mitchell 2003; Stanley 2001). More generally, Jones and Waul (2005) highlight the positive practice developed in the Bibini Centre for Young People, which provides residential and community-based services for black children and families.

The experience of being in residential care for black and minority ethnic children and young people

Only a small number of studies have focused on black and minority ethnic children in care, and an even smaller number on residential care. There are, however, clear messages about the issues which need to be addressed in providing quality residential care for black and minority ethnic children; and central to this is the issue of addressing racism: 'It has often been said that anti-racist practice is simply good practice' (Jones and Waul 2005, p. 43).

Racism in residential child care

At the most fundamental level, racism must be confronted and addressed. There has been clear evidence over the years that individual and institutional racism has been a central feature of the experience of black and minority ethnic children in care:

> It was very weird to me, especially the officer in charge. He was racist, definitely. Residential workers need training. (Denzil) (Quoted in Ince 1998, p. 69)

In 1984, at the first national conference of black children in care, overt racism by staff was highlighted (Black and In Care 1992). Racism and racial abuse can also come from other young people and Berridge and Brodie (1998) found that residential staff expressed concern at the extent of prejudice among the resident group. Sinclair and Gibbs (1998) found that while black and minority ethnic children and young people were no more likely than others to complain about bullying or sexual harassment, they did 'find the homes an uneasy and uncomfortable place in which to be' (Sinclair and Gibbs 1998, p. 267). Wade *et al.* (2005) found that unaccompanied asylum-seeking children could feel 'unsettled and fearful as a result of turbulence generated between residents from different ethnic or national groups' (Wade *et al.* 2005, p. 81).

Barter *et al.* (2004) researched racism in residential care in the context of a wider study of peer violence. All residential homes stated that racism would not be tolerated and that any occurrence was taken very seriously (Barter *et al.* 2004, p. 93). Indeed, the researchers wrote of their surprise at 'the low level of expressed racism and the rarity with which young people in the homes seemed to deploy racist insults and attacks…' (Barter *et al.* 2004, p. 215). Young people were very conscious that racism was unacceptable and that it would be taken seriously by staff. Staff generally considered that young people viewed the use of racism negatively, 'and were as likely as staff to reprimand a young person for racist behaviour or views' (Barter *et al.* 2004, p. 94). Staff, however, confirmed that some young people held entrenched racist views and many staff had themselves been victims of racist abuse. Staff also considered that certain groups, in particular asylum seekers and South Asian males, were most at risk of racial abuse from other young people.

Barter *et al.* contrasted the conceptualisation of racist violence to the other forms of violence in residential care, and considered that racist violence was placed within wider social relations of inequality rather than in the context of blaming individual pathology.

> It was notable that racism was one area where staff were well prepared in these homes. Most homes had multi-cultural staff groups, and there were clear anti-racism polices…with which both young people and staff were familiar. There were clearly stated sanctions against racism of which young people were aware, and staff had often received in-service training on how to deal with racism. (Barter *et al.* 2004, p. 215)

This research highlights, then, that positive practice and training can make significant inroads into the issue of racism in residential child care, although not suggesting that this is a problem solved.

Cultural awareness

Maximé (1986) stressed the emotional harm caused by racist practice which denies black and minority ethnic children and young people a positive sense of their racial identity. The importance of cultural continuity, set out in the UNCRC, is reflected in research, legislation and guidance (Prevatt Goldstein and Spencer 2000). It is important, therefore, that residential child care provides the opportunities for black and minority ethnic children and young people to experience their culture, religion and history on a day-to-day basis.

LINKS WITH FAMILIES AND COMMUNITIES

Links with birth families are of crucial importance for all children and young people in residential child care (Kendrick 2005). The families of black and minority ethnic children and young people can be put off, however, if residential child care is not perceived as a welcoming place: 'Any family is likely to find it difficult to approach a children's home with its connotations of parental failure and its potentially powerful staff, but families who are wary of differences in culture and of racist responses may find such approaches particularly difficult' (Sinclair and Gibbs 1998, p. 268). Barn (1993) found that having black staff in residential homes was important in maintaining family links and 'gave black parents the confidence to make regular visits to their children' (Barn 1993, p. 95). Jones and Waul (2005) also exemplify the positive work that can be done with families in the context of residential care.

The location of residential establishments is another important factor. Black and minority ethnic children can be placed at a distance from their home, leading to alienation and deprivation of family, community and identity (Barn 1993; Caesar *et al.* 1994). This is also an issue for unaccompanied asylum-seeking children who may be 'isolated in communities where they have no contacts, friends or relevant refugee community organizations...' (Mitchell 2003, p. 187). Berridge and Brodie (1998) found that staff in homes in virtually all-white areas could be defensive about the placement of black and minority ethnic children, although the researchers 'did observe some good practice taking place in these settings' (Berridge and Brodie 1998, p. 97).

COMPOSITION OF STAFF GROUP AND BLACK ROLE MODELS

Residential services have been criticised for not providing black role models for the children in their care (Caesar *et al.* 1994; Jones and Waul 2005). O'Neale (2000) comments that the provision of role models was mainly achieved when children remained in their communities and it was more difficult if they were placed in mainly white neighbourhoods. The make-up of residential staff teams is also important. Sinclair and Gibbs (1998) found that seven per cent of the staff were black and minority ethnic, a similar figure to Mainey (2003). However, there was wide variation between authorities ranging from none to one in eight (Sinclair and Gibbs 1998) and wider variation in the homes, in one case 64 per cent. However, 'there was almost no correspondence between the proportion of black and ethnic minority young people in the home and the proportion of black and ethnic minority staff' (p. 266).

Most of the young people in Ince's (1998) study reported problems with their racial identity: 'an absence of positive black role models left them with major questions about their own identity. Were they white? Were they black?' (Ince 1998, p. 61; see also Maximé 1986; Mehra 1996).

IDENTITY AND SELF-WORTH

Issues of race and ethnicity are central to identity and self-worth. Voice for the Child in Care (2004) highlights that how:

> These aspects of a child's heritage, culture and personal reality were fully inte-grated into the care system made a critical difference to young people, how they saw themselves, how they integrated as adults into their minority

community and how they were able to cope with discrimination (Voice for the Child in Care 2004, p. 2)

Robinson (2000) compared the racial identity attitudes and self-esteem of a sample of young people in residential care and a sample living with their own families. She found that both groups had relatively high levels of self-esteem and internalisation attitudes (characterised by positive views toward oneself, acceptance of the black reference group and a decline in anti-white feelings). Robinson suggests that the positive attitudes among the young black people in residential care could be due to factors identified above: the number of black and minority ethnic staff members in the residential units, or the fact that the residential homes were located in areas where the young people were able to maintain links with their family and community. Robinson also highlighted that racial identity attitudes in the two groups were commonly expressed through immersion attitudes: 'illustrated by an investment in African Caribbean culture, as evidenced by wearing ethnic clothing and hairstyles, choosing African Caribbean entertainment forms, and associating primarily with other African Caribbeans' (Robinson 2000, p. 18). She stresses that practitioners need to be aware of the theories of racial identity in order to be able to recognise racial identity stages that children and young people have reached, and to understand how black and minority ethnic children and young people may respond to both white and black care workers (see also Maximé 1986).

Central to this is the development of relationships with children and young people and with highlighting their voice and story. Kohli (2006a), for example, outlines the role of social workers with unaccompanied asylum-seeking children in relation to cohesion (a focus on the practicalities of resettlement), connection (responding to the emotional life of young people who were at times deeply distressed and attempting to connect events, people and feelings) and coherence (regenerating the rhythm of ordinary life) (see also Kohli 2006b). Bernard (2002) similarly stresses the impact of societal racism on the way in which maltreatment and trauma is understood and conceptualised by black and minority ethnic children and young people: 'to be able to hear what black children are telling us, and perhaps more importantly, paying attention to the silences surrounding what they are not telling us, is a crucial component of risk assessments' (Bernard 2002, p. 249).

CULTURAL AND RELIGIOUS PRACTICES

It is vital for residential work to provide black and minority ethnic children both culture-specific and multicultural experiences. Caeser *et al.* (1994) identify food and diet as perhaps the most obvious example of integrating culture into the day-to-day experience of residential child care. The need to address the appropriate care and cosmetics for the skin and hair care of black and minority ethnic children is also important (Caesar *et al.* 1994; Ince 1998; Mehra 1996). The failure to address these issues, however, has been frequently highlighted (Barn 1993; Sinclair and Gibbs 1998; O'Neale, 2000). Jones and Waul (2005) describe the development of a food policy in a residential service for black children and young people:

> The policy determined that children would regularly experience the range of foods they were accustomed to or wanted to try (cooks prepared meals as diverse as fish and chips, fufu and groundnut stew). All meat prepared was Halal and a vegetarian option was always available. (Jones and Waul 2005, p. 41; see also Berridge and Brodie 1998)

They highlight that the policy was challenged less by children and young people and their families, but 'it was usually professionals who persisted in challenging the policy…through the guise of "children's rights"' (Jones and Waul 2005, p. 41). Berridge and Brodie (1998) identify good practice in residential care homes where lists had been made of food stores and places of worship for different minority ethnic groups, where children and young people were taken shopping in black areas and culturally appropriate educational materials were in evidence.

O'Neale (2000) identified concerns about how the religious needs of children were being met and highlighted that some young people felt that residential staff who were atheists did not support and encourage them to fulfil their religions duties: 'it is easy to see that a lack of religious input and back up could lead to cultural alienation for some children looked after' (O'Neale 2000, p. 16). Wade *et al.* (2005) note the importance of religion for many unaccompa-nied asylum-seeking children where membership of churches or mosques provided not only for religious needs, but also 'provided a symbolic connection with home and opened up a social space in which new social relationships could grow' (Wade *et al.* 2005, p.176). The research found that practitioners were generally supportive of this involvement, aware of the benefits for young people.

Leaving care

Issues of lack of contact with families and communities highlighted above can have significant impact on the transition from care for black and minority ethnic children and young people (Stein 2005). Barn *et al.* (2005), however, found a complex pattern of ethnicity and disadvantage for young care leavers: African and Asian young people experienced least instability in care and education; Caribbean and mixed parentage young people were at a higher risk of disadvantage; but white young people experienced worst outcomes in relation to placement disruption, educational attainment, homelessness and risky behaviour such as the use of illicit drugs.

Voice for the Child in Care (2004) found that black and minority ethnic young people wanted practical help in leaving care, but also wanted emotional support, guidance, advice and friendship. While young people may not perceive their needs to be different from any other young person leaving care, Ince (1998) stresses that dealing with racism in the wider society should be part of the preparation for young black people leaving care. Social work services, however, have tended to provide little support in addressing prejudice and discrimination, although there was some good practice, for example in guidance provided by residential staff members. Agencies lacked a policy framework and 'these departments were on the whole reliant on the competence and commitment of individual workers' (Barn *et al.* 2005, p. 61).

Conclusion

Recent studies have identified a range of positive developments in residential child care for black and minority ethnic children and young people. At the root of such positive residential practice is an explicit need to challenge racism in all its forms. We have seen that a number of interlinking issues are important: links to family and community, the composition of the staff group, role models for black and minority ethnic children, identity and self-worth, and support and promotion of religious and cultural practices. Residential workers and managers have a crucial role in providing positive culturally specific experiences for the children and young people in their care, in supporting the development of their cultural and ethnic identity and in assisting young people in their transitions to adulthood.

References

Ahmad, B. (1990) *Black Perspectives in Social Work.* London: Venture Press.

Ahmed, S., Cheetham, J. and Small, J. (eds) (1986) *Social Work with Black Children and their Families.* London: Batsford.

Barn, R. (1993) *Black Children in the Public Care System.* London: Batsford.

Barn, R. (2001) *Black Youth on the Margins: A Research Review.* York: Joseph Rowntree Foundation.

Barn, R., Andrew, L. and Mantovani, N. (2005) *Life After Care: The Experiences of Young People from Different Ethnic Groups.* York: Joseph Rowntree Foundation.

Barn, R. and Harman, V. (2006) 'A contested identity: An exploration of the competing social and political discourse concerning the identification and positioning of young people of inter-racial parentage.' *British Journal of Social Work 36,* 1309–24.

Barn, R., Sinclair, R. and Ferdinand, D. (1997) *Acting on Principle: An Examination of Race and Ethnicity in Social Services Provision for Children and Families.* London: British Agencies for Adoption and Fostering.

Barter, C., Renold, E., Berridge, D. and Cawson, P. (2004) *Peer Violence in Children's Residential Care.* Basingstoke: Palgrave.

Bernard, C. (2002) 'Giving voice to experiences: Parental maltreatment of black children in the context of societal racism.' *Child and Family Social Work 7,* 239–51.

Berridge, D., Beecham, J., Brodie, I., Coles, T., Daniels, H., Knapp, M. and MacNeill, V. (2003) 'Services for troubled adolescents: Exploring user variation.' *Child and Family Social Work 8,* 4, 269–79.

Berridge, D. and Brodie, I. (1998) *Children's Homes Revisited.* London: Jessica Kingsley Publishers.

Black and In Care (1992) *Black and In Care Annual Report 1991/1992.* London: Black and In Care.

Caesar, G., Parchment, M. and Berridge, D. (1994) *Black Perspectives on Services for Children in Need.* Barkinside: Barnardos & National Children's Bureau.

Chakrabarti, M. (2001) 'Ethnicity and Social Services.' In M. Chakrabarti (ed.) *Social Welfare: Scottish Perspective.* Aldershot: Ashgate Publishing.

Chakrabarti, C., Thorne, L., Hosie, A., Lindsay, M., Brown, J., Hill, M. and Khand, I. (1998) *Valuing Diversity: Having Regard to the Racial, Religious, Cultural and Linguistic Needs of Scotland's Children.* Edinburgh: Scottish Office.

Cheetham, J. (1986) 'Introduction.' In S. Ahmed, J. Cheetham and J. Small (eds) *Social Work with Black Children and their Families.* London: Batsford.

Dhanda, P. (2006) *House of Commons written answer (Hansard),* 17 May 2006: col 974W. www.publications.parliament.uk/pa/cm200506/cmhansrd/cm060517/text/6051 7w0006.htm, accessed on 30 April 2007.

Dominelli, L., Lorenz, W. and Soydan, H. (eds) (2001) *Beyond Racial Divides: Ethnicities in Social Work Practice.* Aldershot: Ashgate.

Fook, J. (2001) 'Emerging Ethnicities as a Theoretical Framework for Social Work.' In L. Dominelli, W. Lorenz and H. Soydan (eds) *Beyond Racial Divides: Ethnicities in Social Work Practice.* Aldershot: Ashgate.

Hayes, D. and Humphries, B. (eds) (2004) *Social Work, Immigration and Asylum: Debates, Dilemmas and Ethical Issues for Social Work and Social Care Practice.* London: Jessica Kingsley Publishers.

Ince, L. (1998) *Making It Alone: A Study of the Care Experiences of Young Black People.* London: British Agencies for Adoption and Fostering.

Jones, A. and Waul, D. (2005) 'Residential Care for Black Children.' In D. Crimmens and I. Milligan (eds) *Facing Forward: Residential Care in the 21st Century.* Lyme Regis: Russell House Publishing.

Kendrick, A. (2005) 'Social Exclusion and Social Inclusion: Themes and Issues in Residential Child Care.' In D. Crimmens and I. Milligan (eds) *Facing Forward: Residential Child Care in the 21st Century.* Lyme Regis: Russell House Publishing.

Kohli, R.K.S. (2006a) 'The comfort of strangers: Social work practice with unaccompanied asylum-seeking children and young people in the UK.' *Child and Family Social Work 11*, 1–10.

Kohli, R.K.S. (2006b) 'The sound of silence: Listening to what unaccompanied asylum-seeking children say and do not say.' *British Journal of Social Work 36*, 707–21.

Lees, S. (2002) 'Gender, ethnicity and vulnerability in young women in local authority care.' *British Journal of Social Work 32*, 907–22.

Lyons, K., Manion, K. and Carlsen, M. (2006) *International Perspectives on Social Work: Global Conditions and Local Practice.* Basingstoke: Palgrave Macmillan.

Mainey, A. (2003) *Better Than You Think: Staff Morale, Qualifications and Retention in Residential Child Care.* London: Children's Bureau.

Maximé, J.E. (1986) 'Some Psychological Models of Black Self-concept.' In S. Ahmed, J. Cheetham and J. Small (eds) *Social Work with Black Children and their Families.* London: Batsford.

Mehra, H. (1996) 'Residential Care for Ethnic Minorities Children.' In K.N. Dwivedi and V.P. Varma (eds) *Meeting the Needs of Ethnic Minority Children: A Handbook for Professionals.* London: Jessica Kingsley Publishers.

Mitchell, F. (2003) 'The social services response to unaccompanied children in England.' *Child and Family Social Work 8*, 179–89.

O'Neale, V. (2000) *Excellence Not Excuses: Inspection of Services for Ethnic Minority Children and Families.* London: Social Services Inspectorate.

Prevatt Goldstein, B. (2005) 'Introduction.' In J. Thoburn, A. Chand and J. Proctor, *Child Welfare Services for Minority Ethnic Families.* London: Jessica Kingsley Publishers.

Prevatt Goldstein, B. and Spencer, M. (2000) *'Race' and Ethnicity: A Consideration of Issues for Black, Minority Ethnic and White Children in Family Placement.* London: BAAF.

Robinson, L. (2000) 'Racial identity attitudes and self-esteem of black adolescents in residential care: An exploratory study.' *British Journal of Social Work 30*, 1, 3–24.

Rowe, J., Hundleby, M. and Garnett, L. (1989) *Child Care Now: A Survey of Placement Patterns.* London: British Agencies for Adoption and Fostering.

Scott, P. (1999) 'Black People's Health: Ethnic Status and Research Issues.' In S. Hood, B. Mayall and S. Oliver (eds) *Critical Issues in Social Research: Power and Prejudice.* Buckingham: Open University Press.

Scottish Executive (2004) *Children's Social Work Statistics 2003–04.* Edinburgh: Scottish Executive National Statistics Publication. www.scotland.gov.uk/stats/bulletins/ 00369-00.asp, accessed on 30 April 2007.

Sinclair, I. and Gibbs, S. (1998) *Children's Homes: A Study in Diversity.* Chichester: Wiley.

Singh, R. (1992) *Race and Social Work: From 'Black Pathology' to 'Black Perspectives'.* Bradford: Race Relations Research Unit.

Singh, S. (2005) 'Thinking Beyond "Diversity": Black Minority Ethnic Children in Scotland.' In D. Crimmens and I. Milligan (eds) *Facing Forward: Residential Care in the 21st Century.* Lyme Regis: Russell House Publishing.

Stanley, K. (2001) *Cold Comfort: Young Separated Refugees in England.* London: Save the Children.

Stein, M. (2005) *Resilience and Young People Leaving Care: Overcoming the Odds.* York: Joseph Rowntree Foundation.

Thanki, V. (1994) 'Ethnic diversity and child protection.' *Children and Society 8,* 3, 232–4.

Thoburn, J., Chand, A. and Proctor, J. (2005) *Child Welfare Services for Minority Ethnic Families.* London: Jessica Kingsley Publishers.

Voice for the Child in Care (2004) *The Care Experience: Through Black Eyes.* London: Voice for the Child in Care.

Wade, J., Mitchell, F. and Baylis, G. (2005) *Unaccompanied Asylum Seeking Children: The Response of Social Work Services.* London: BAAF.

PART THREE
Conflict and Response

CHAPTER 10

Prioritising Young People's Concerns in Residential Care

Responding to Peer Violence

Christine Barter

Introduction

Peer violence has been largely absent from the official, professional and academic agendas despite the fact that young people in care have consistently highlighted it as one of their overriding concerns. This chapter seeks to provide insights into the dynamics of this form of abuse as well as exploring possible responses. To begin with, official guidance and policy initiatives will be discussed and the limited research evidence and relevant wider literature relating to peer violence will be considered. Following this, research undertaken by the current author and colleagues will be presented, which for the first time focuses exclusively on the problem of peer violence in residential children's homes. Finally, possible strategies for preventing and reducing peer violence within residential children's homes will be offered.

Policy and guidance on peer violence in children's homes

Child-care policy has had little to say about violence between young people in children's homes. Good practice guidance for residential care was produced to accompany the Children Act 1989 (Department of Health 1991); however, peer relationships are not mentioned. Similarly the two detailed reviews of residential child care conducted by Sir William Utting in the 1990s contain little guidance on peer violence (Utting 1991, 1997). Reports along similar lines were also commissioned in Scotland (Kent 1997) and Wales (Waterhouse 2000). Once again although both acknowledge the problem of peer abuse, neither make particular mention of it in their list of recommendations.

Another important policy initiative in the 1990s was the work of the Warner committee on staffing in children's homes (Department of Health 1992), also set up in response to a major scandal (Kirkwood 1993). The only evidence the committee cited was a small-scale exercise by the National Association of Young People in Care based on 50 young people, mostly living in institutions, who had complained to them about abuse. Although half of the perpetrators were other young people, none of its 83 recommendations concerned abuse by children.

The most recent government initiative to raise standards in the management and delivery of children's social services is Quality Protects (Department of Health 1998), set up following the Waterhouse public inquiry (Waterhouse 2000). Once again the focus was on the competence and effectiveness of professionals with no specific indicators concerning violence between young people as measures of quality in residential services.

Last, the *National Minimum Standards for Children's Homes* included a specific requirement for countering bullying (Department of Health 2002). However, there is no more general strategic guidance available other than a single paragraph (para. 18, 1–5, pp. 26–7) relating solely to bullying. Similarly, the Scottish equivalent on standards mentions exploitation, abuse and bullying but again provides no specific guidance. (Scottish Executive 2002). Given the lack of emphasis contained in official guidance, it is unsurprising that children's homes have lagged behind other services in having clear policies to respond to peer violence (Berridge 2004). As we shall see, research has also failed to comprehensively address this issue, contributing to the lack of recognition and understanding surrounding this form of abuse.

Evidence on peer violence in residential settings

In spite of the many scandals concerning the institutional abuse of children in residential homes (Colton 2002; Committee of Inquiry into Children's Homes and Hostels 1986; Wolmar 2000), there has been little research undertaken. Evidence comes from a few local studies and reports of inquiries set up following some of the major incidents. Kendrick's (1997) literature review for the Scottish Office is particularly helpful. Although abuse by staff in residential children's homes has hit the headlines, due to its appalling nature and persistence over many years, much of the available evidence has indicated that residents are most often at risk from *other young people* in the home (Barter 1997). Most of the accounts described below address the issue of peer violence in residential settings in the context of research on, or inquiries into, broader aspects of residential care.

Barter (1998) examined 36 NSPCC investigations into institutional abuse allegations made by 67 children against 50 abusers. A fifth of these involved abuse by other residents, mainly boys. Over a quarter of allegations of sexual abuse involved peers. Young people's accounts also provide evidence of the incidence and nature of peer violence. Morris and Wheatley (1994) investigated calls to a dedicated phone service by ChildLine for children in care. In the first six months of its operation, 250 calls were received; three-quarters of callers were girls. The most common problems related to bullying or other forms of violence from peers in the home. The behaviour ranged from teasing or being picked on, to physical attacks. Predominantly assailants were male. Most callers stated that they had informed staff but felt that their concerns had been ignored. Physical fights were usually unobserved by staff, who were reluctant to act on the basis of children's accounts alone.

Evidence presented to the major reviews of residential services, set up in response to a series of scandals, also indicated high levels of violence from young people. Members of the Children's Safeguards review team covering England and Wales held meetings with young people from 20 local authorities and reported that the danger most often identified was that from other children, especially bullying, physical abuse and theft (Utting 1997). Indeed, the report estimated that 'possibly half the total of abuse reported in institutions is peer abuse' (Utting 1997, p.99). Yet only one brief final paragraph out of 12 in the section on 'abusers' refers to children.

Research on young people going missing from residential homes indicates the extent to which running away is related to unhappiness with peers (Wade *et al.* 1998).

Sinclair and Gibbs' (1998) study gives a disconcerting account of the dynamics of everyday life in many establishments and of the unhappiness of residents. Nearly half (44%) of the 223 young people interviewed stated that they had been 'bullied' during their stay at the home. Younger residents were more likely to be victimised. However, for many, these experiences were a continuation of experiences prior to entry to residential care and not experienced solely in the care system.

Concentrating on sexual violence, Lunn (1990) reported that Nottinghamshire County Council had discovered that a worrying number of its children in residential homes were being sexually abused by other residents. In Sinclair and Gibbs' (1998) study, 23 per cent of females and 7 per cent of males reported that someone tried 'to take sexual advantage' of them, with peers rather than staff being responsible. As with bullying, those who had experienced sexual violence prior to care were more likely to be victimised in the residential setting. Farmer and Pollock's (1998) research into sexually abused and abusing children in substitute care discovered that children who had been abused at home were more likely to be placed in residential care, whereas those who had abused others mostly went to foster homes, where it was assumed they would be less of a risk. There were extensive gaps in information passed on to caregivers, insufficient attention was paid to whether or not the child would be a 'good match' with others in placement and it was not uncommon for abusers to share bedrooms with other children. Consequently, half the sexually abused children in the sample went on to abuse others, mostly involving peers in residential and foster placements.

The peer violence in children's residential care study

My own research was funded by the Economic and Social Research Council under its Violence Research Programme. The research team comprised the current author, David Berridge, Pat Cawson and Emma Renold (see Barter *et al.* 2004). The aim was not to measure the frequency of violent incidents, but to clarify the context within which particular types of violence occurred and their meaning to those involved. A qualitative methodology was used that combined a discussion of personal experiences through the use of semi-structured interviews, and more abstract discussions surrounding violence and its meaning through the use of vignettes (see Barter and Renold 2000). We also spent some time in each of the homes to enable the young people and staff to get to know us and for us to become accustomed to each environment. Young people's accounts of violence concerned both their current and previous residential placements.

The research took place in 14 English children's homes. The majority were run by local authorities; three, however, were from the private sector and two were managed by voluntary agencies. We interviewed 71 young people between the ages of 8 and 17 years. Slightly more boys (44) than girls (27) were interviewed and almost a quarter were from minority ethnic groups. Seventy-one staff were also interviewed, including residential social workers, seniors and managers.

Nature of violence

Four different forms of peer violence were derived from the young people's accounts:

- *Direct physical assault:* examples from young people's accounts included 'punching', 'grabbing hair', 'fist fights', 'leathering', 'beatings', 'slapping'.

- *Physical 'non-contact' attacks* which harmed young people emotionally rather than physically, such as destruction of personal belongings, invasion of personal space and intimidation via looks or gestures.

- *Verbal abuse,* generally name-calling concerning sexual reputations, family, appearance or ethnicity.

- *Unwelcome sexual behaviours,* experienced as both sexual and abusive by young people, including 'flashing', grabbing a girl's breast, inappropriate touching, unwanted sexual gestures and remarks and rape.

Young people described differential levels of impact. *Low-level* attacks were viewed as having little impact, they were infrequent, did not involve a severe use of force and were often a spontaneous response to an isolated event. *High-level* attacks were when force was severe, attacks were frequent and part of a wider power structure. Young people viewed the impact as significant, often couched in terms of 'fear' and 'vulnerability'.

Physical violence

> There's quite a lot of fighting in here, mostly showing off but sometimes kids do get hurt. (Male resident aged 12)

Three-quarters of young people experienced physical assaults, mainly as victims (40) but also as perpetrators (25). Half of the girls' experiences of violence, and a third of boys', were restricted to low-level physical violence; these generally occurred within friendship or sibling groups. Boys used this form of violence to publicly present a particular kind of 'macho' or 'hard' masculinity to their (male) peers. Such 'attacks' occurred only when staff were present, thus providing a safe arena in which boys could be seen as the 'aggressor' and thereby confirm their masculinity to others, in the full knowledge that staff would intervene to stop any injury to themselves or others. In contrast, girls often reported isolated and sporadic attacks in response to a specific trigger.

Fifty-two young people, proportionally more boys than girls, experienced high-level physical violence. Most incidents took place within, rather than between, groups of boys and girls. Incidents ranged from knife attacks to severe beatings resulting in broken bones and concussions. For a minority these attacks were isolated incidents, however, more commonly, the violence and intimidation was habitual, reflecting the wider power dynamics involved. According to the assailant, these attacks were often premediated, with the severest attacks happening in bedrooms and at night when staff surveillance was minimal. Nearly all perpetrators justified their violence as an appropriate response to an alleged provocation. In over half of incidents other residents were involved either as active contributors or passive bystanders.

Non-contact violence

> I've had my room trashed twice by them [other residents], all my stuff thrown out the window and ruined…like even my bedroom isn't mine in here. (Female resident, aged 13)

Non-contact violence was experienced by almost half of participants, generally as part of a wider cycle of peer violence; consequently, two-thirds viewed these attacks as high level. Most often, young people described non-contact violence as 'bullying'. The most frequently experienced incidents involved the destruction of personal belongings from the victims' bedrooms. As privacy and personal belongings are particularly important to girls (McRobbie 1990), they found these incidents especially hurtful. Other incidents included threats of physical injury, psychological control mechanisms which affected a young person's freedom or imposed an aggressor's will upon them or non-verbal forms of aggression.

Verbal violence

> It can really hurt what they say to you, especially if they say something bad about your mum, that really hurts. (Male resident, aged 11)

Maybe predictably, low-level verbal insults seemed to be a common, taken-for-granted aspect of residential life which went mainly unchallenged by staff. However, high-level verbal attacks contravened boundaries of acceptability. Girls most often relied on tarnishing the sexual reputation of their (female) victims to cause harm. Boys were more likely to insult (female) family members, especially through 'mother cussing'. This may be particularly upsetting for boys who may feel through male codes of honour that their role is to protect female family members. The impact of these predominant forms of verbal attacks should not be underestimated. Over a third of young people who suffered repeated attacks stated that the long-lasting emotional harm caused was more damaging than some forms of high-level physical attacks, echoing previous findings (Tomison and Tucci 1997).

Sexual violence

> This lad [another resident] came in one night stoned out of his head and thought he could do what he wanted and took advantage [sexual assault]…it was horrible. (Female resident, aged 14)

Overall, disclosures of peer sexual violence were the lowest of all forms of violence. Girls were three times more likely to report this than boys, and most saw it as being high level. Girls spoke to us about a range of sexually harmful behaviours they had experienced in their current or past placements up to and including one rape. Most perpetrators were male. All incidents involved some degree of coercion. The majority of attacks occurred in the victim's bedroom. Over half of young people had not informed staff, although they had told other young people. We were also made aware through staff accounts that some of the young participants, mostly males, who had experienced some form of sexual violence had decided not to tell us.

Wider cultural contexts

From young people's accounts three main contexts governing peer violence were identified within young people's peer cultures: peer group hierarchies, gender and racism.

Peer group hierarchies

Peer group hierarchies or 'pecking orders' were a central context in which young people experienced violence. The existence of pecking orders and 'top dog' networks has been highlighted in previous literature (Brannan, Jones and Murch 1993; Parkin and Green 1997). Within our study, nearly all homes had a resident hierarchy which was often linked with abuses of power, including violence. Young people viewed the hierarchy as an inevitable but not necessarily a natural aspect of residential life. Many of the 'lower-status' young people we spoke to described their experience of the hierarchy as one of intimidation and exploitation. Staff, in contrast, often saw it as benign, even helpful in controlling young people in their care by utilising the power that 'top dogs' had over other residents.

Peer group dynamics were seen as being most problematic when they were in flux: when a new resident had to find his or her position or when a resident from the top of the hierarchy left and his or her position thus became vacant. Workers stated they sometimes left young people to 'sort it out' themselves as long as it didn't 'get out of hand'. Unfortunately a great deal of the violence that occurred at these times was hidden from staff and strong disincentives were present in many homes to stop young people telling or 'grassing'.

Gender

Young people and staff felt that male physical violence was a normal, although uncontrolled, aspect of boys' behaviour and a natural expression of their developing masculinity. Similarly, girls saw sexual aggression from boys as a common, if unwelcome, part of male sexuality. Residents and staff often regarded sexually provocative behaviour from girls as a trigger for sexual assaults by boys, thus the victims were often blamed for the violence. Staff were aware of gender differences in patterns of aggression, although they both underestimated girls' involvement in physical violence and lessened its significance through narratives of 'cat fights' and 'bitching matches'.

Racism

The research found less racist behaviour in homes than might have been expected, given the accounts of racism in other contexts, for example schools (Barter 1999). Indeed both young people and staff agreed that racist insults were rare. Racism was one area where staff were more proactive within clear agency policies, and young people generally gave an anti-racist perspective, although certain 'outsider' groups, specifically South Asians, were at greater risk of racial victimisation. Such groups were not ascribed the 'street credentials' of wider youth cultures with which many of the young people engaged (Majors 1989; Sewell 1997).

Children's and young people's protective strategies

Most young people advocated retaliation as their main response to a perceived attack. High-level attacks generally were thought to justify targeted and planned retaliation. Nearly all accounts used language of revenge, prevention, protection of honour and similar justifications. In most homes, young people used peers rather than staff as a source of emotional support (Emond 2002). Peers were the first port of call in all incidents later disclosed to staff. Reasons given included feeling that staff would be unable to solve, or might even exacerbate the problem; lack of trust/empathy; and to avoid 'getting into trouble' themselves through violating non-disclosure cultures ('grassing'). In homes where young people evaluated their relationships with staff as being very positive, staff were more often approached for emotional support. In addition, within these homes young people perceived interventions as being more successful.

Staff understanding and response

Consistency of staff intervention differed both between and within homes. Responses to physical violence produced the most consistent accounts, indicating it was routine for staff to intervene in physical violence, up to and including restraint if conciliatory methods were unsuccessful. However, staff members were also confused and concerned about their ability physically to restrain young people when necessary (Berridge and Brodie 1998), although young people felt that restraint was used appropriately and we received no complaints regarding its use. Non-contact violence was unanimously considered the most difficult to identify and intercept, due to its hidden nature, rooted in the group's power dynamics. Staff described its covert nature as 'undertone', 'undercurrent' and 'backdoor' violence. Staff recognised that the indicators of such violence could be very subtle, 'a look', 'a stare' or 'simply the tone of voice'. Staff were often reluctant to talk about sexual violence, although managers appeared more confident. Workers felt unsure about what constituted 'inappropriate' sexual behaviour and how best to respond; some felt they had failed to challenge 'relationships' which they felt contained some degree of coercion. Many workers diminished the importance of verbal abuse, especially sexual insult, thinking it too ingrained in the young people's everyday language for them to have any significant impact for change. They did recognise that verbal violence based around 'mother cussing' had a significant effect, but primarily were preoccupied with children's physical safety. Only two homes routinely challenged such language reflecting their managers' and residential workers' high expectations of children's behaviour generally; in both homes all forms of violence were low. Similarly, work by Kendrick and Mair (2002) in a unit for sexually aggressive young men found that when swearing and sexualised language were systematically challenged a marked difference was observed in bullying levels.

The main method of securing young people's safety was through direct supervision. Restriction of young people's movements, for example to certain parts of the building, especially bedrooms, was a key mechanism to increase surveillance. Overall strategies appeared reactive rather then proactive. For example, in many homes, we found a preoccupation with negative sanctions for disruptive behaviour, but few systematic rewards for positive behaviour or achievements. Hardly any homes undertook any form of proactive group work with young people. Indeed, staff stated that they lacked the confidence and ability to undertake group work. This was despite the fact that we observed some of these same workers 'informally' discussing very sensitive matters with young people to significant effect. Over half of the homes had access to an independent advocacy service; however, most young people viewed this as helping with practical problems, such as placement difficulties, rather than being a source of emotional support and few had discussed issues of violence.

Confronting peer violence in residential settings – developing good practice

Reducing violence requires a planned, proactive approach. Clear and agreed definitions and descriptions of the unacceptable behaviour and its consequences are a prerequisite. Training needs to enable staff to recognise both the signs of peer violence and possible intervention techniques. Young people's experiences and insights need to inform and shape this process through direct consultation. Responses need to acknowledge the harm caused by verbal attacks, and how this provides the context for physical and sexual violence. Cultures that treat violence as a 'natural' or 'normal' aspect of peer relations, whether through peer group hierarchies, derogatory language or gender, need to be challenged.

The absence of strategic approaches to peer violence within children's homes is in marked contrast to the approach taken in education, at least in relation to bullying. School-based research has shown that the school ethos, attitudes of teachers in bullying situations and degree of supervision of free-time appear to have a major effect on the extent of bullying (see Oliver and Candappa 2003). The importance of whole-school policies has been stressed, which involves all parties: management, staff, students, parents and governors, creating an atmosphere of shared ownership.

Evidence from schools suggests that:

- Adopting an anti-bullying policy is not enough; policies need to be effectively implemented and sustained over a long period of time.

- To be effective, research has shown that anti-bullying policies need to be developed with managers, staff and young people as well as other significant parties (such as social workers and parents) (Sharp and Thompson 1994).

- Policies and practices need to be revisited frequently and evaluated in the light of changing circumstances (Smith and Sharp 1994).

- Initiatives need to be accompanied by regular and comprehensive staff training.

- New staff need to be properly inducted.

- A system of review needs to be incorporated.

- Effective monitoring and evaluation are central components in combating peer violence; however, specific residential monitoring methods need to be developed.

- Effective leadership and administrative support need to be provided, including the provision of adequate resources and acknowledgement that 'results' cannot be obtained immediately.

Identifying and adapting strategies that may work

As we have seen, peer violence is a complex phenomenon and one where a multilevel approach is more likely to be effective in the long term than isolated or narrowly focused initiatives. Rather than ask 'what works?', evidence indicates it is more realistic to ask 'what might work?' in a particular setting (Oliver and Candappa 2003). Most responses have been developed in schools and in relation to bullying. These cannot necessarily simply be transferred to other settings or, indeed, impact on other forms of peer violence. For example, although violence between young people in children's homes shows many similarities to that found in other contexts, its operation throughout all areas of young people's residential lives, particularly the likelihood of invasion of personal space and attacks at night, can make its impact much greater. Nevertheless, there is a good enough evidence base to make a start on identifying the most hopeful approaches for children's homes. A range of possible approaches that may be developed for the residential context are presented below.

- *Friendship support* – Enhancing friendship skills can act as an important protective factor (Besag 1989), and programmes that incorporate this approach, for example 'circle of friends', have shown promising results (Ginsberg, Gottman and Parker 1986).

- *Mentoring* – Mentoring schemes in which older, more confident non-aggressive young people are matched with younger and more isolated ones have been attempted.

- *Peer group initiatives* – Frost (1991) claims that peer group pressure offers the most effective deterrent to bullying. School-based responses have highlighted the importance of working with individuals and groups. Approaches have included peer support and mediation including peer counselling and 'listener' schemes, group education and discussion (Cowie and Sharp 1994; Department for Education and Skills 2002; Eslea and Smith 1998; Smith and Sharp 1994).

- *Confidential support* – The provision of confidential support and confidential reporting systems, independent from staff, has been associated with positive outcomes in some settings.

- *Positive reward system* – My research found a reliance on controlling behaviour through negative sanctions. However, homes that accompany this with a reward system for positive behaviour or achievements showed some promising results.

Residential managers, working alongside young people and staff, will need to explore how such initiatives can be used, as well as developing a range of strategies specific to the residential context. The building blocks of a more comprehensive, coherent and inclusive approach to addressing peer violence exist. Young people need to be systematically consulted to ensure we provide them with the best protection we can in a way that builds on their strengths and understandings. Ultimately, change is dependent on residential providers and staff having the impetus to look beyond their own adult-defined agendas and instead prioritise the safeguarding concerns of the children and young people in their care.

References

Barter, C. (1997) 'Who's to blame: Conceptualising institutional abuse by children.' *Early Child Development and Care 133*, 101–4.

Barter, C. (1998) *Investigating Institutional Abuse of Children: An Exploration of the NSPCC Experience*. London: NSPCC.

Barter, C. (1999) *Protecting Children From Racism and Racial Abuse: A Research Review*. London: NSPCC.

Barter, C. and Renold, E. (2000) 'I wanna tell you a story: The application of vignettes in qualitative research with young people.' *Social Research Methodology, Theory and Practice 3*, 4, 307–23.

Barter, C., Renold, E., Berridge, D. and Cawson, P. (2004) *Peer Violence in Children's Residential Care*. Hampshire: Palgrave.

Berridge, D. (2004) 'Nowhere to hide.' *Community Care*, 5–11 August, 37–8.

Berridge, D. and Brodie, I. (1998) *Children's Homes Revisited*. London: Jessica Kingsley Publishers.

Besag, V.E. (1989) *Bullies and Victims in Schools: A Guide To Understanding and Management*. Milton Keynes: Open University Press.

Brannan, C., Jones, J.R. and Murch, J.D. (1993) 'Lessons from a residential special school enquiry: Reflections on the Castle Hill Report.' *Child Abuse Review 2*, 4. 271–5.

Colton, M. (2002) 'Factors associated with abuse in residential child care institutions.' *Children and Society 16*, 1, 33–44.

Committee of Inquiry into Children's Homes and Hostels (1986) *Report of the Committee of Inquiry into Children's Homes and Hostels (Kincora Inquiry)*. London: Her Majesty's Stationery Office.

Cowie, H. and Sharp, S. (1994) 'Tackling Bullying Through the Curriculum.' In P.K. Smith and S. Sharp (eds) *School Bullying: Insights and Perspectives*. London: Routledge.

Department for Education and Skills (2002) *Bullying: Don't Suffer in Silence*. London: Department for Education and Skills.

Department of Health (1991) *The Children Act 1989 Guidance and Regulations*. Volume 4. London: HMSO.

Department of Health (1992) *Choosing with Care: The Report of the Committee of Inquiry into the Selection, Development and Management of Staff in Children's Homes.* London: Department of Health.

Department of Health (1998) *Quality Protects: Framework for Action.* London: Department of Health.

Department of Health (2002) *National Minimum Standards for Children's Homes.* London: Department of Health.

Emond, R. (2002) 'Understanding the resident group.' *Scottish Journal of Residential Child Care 1,* 1, 30–40.

Eslea, M. and Smith, P.K. (1998) 'The long-term effectiveness of anti-bullying work in primary schools.' *Education Research 40,* 2, 203–18.

Farmer, E. and Pollock, S. (1998) *Sexually Abused and Abusing Children in Substitute Care.* Chichester: Wiley.

Frost, L. (1991) 'A Primary School Approach: What Can Be Done About the Bully?' In M. Elliot (ed.) *Bullying: A Practical Guide to Coping for Schools.* Harlow: Longman.

Ginsberg, D., Gottman, J. and Parker, J. (1986) 'The Importance of Friendship.' In J.M. Gottman and J.G. Parker (eds) *Conversations of Friends.* Cambridge: Cambridge University Press.

Kendrick, A. (1997) 'Safeguarding Children Living Away from Home: A Literature Review.' In R. Kent (ed.) *Children's Safeguards Review.* Edinburgh: The Stationery Office.

Kendrick, A. and Mair, R. (2002) 'Developing Focused Care: A Residential Unit for Sexually Aggressive Young Men.' In M. Calder (ed.) *Young People who Sexually Abuse: Building the Evidence Base for Your Practice.* Lyme Regis: Russesll House Publishing.

Kent, R. (1997) *Children's Safeguards Review.* Edinburgh: Scottish Office.

Kirkwood, A. (1993) *The Leicestershire Inquiry 1992.* Leicester: Leicester County Council.

Lunn, T. (1990) 'Pioneers of abuse control.' *Social Work Today 22,* 3, 9.

Majors, R. (1989) 'Cool pose: The Proud Signature of Black Survival.' In M.S. Kimmel and M.A. Messner (eds) *Men's Lives.* New York: Macmillan.

McRobbie, A. (1990) *Feminism and Youth Culture from 'Jackie' to 'Just Seventeen'.* London: Macmillan.

Morris, S. and Wheatley, H. (1994) *Time to Listen: The Experience of Young People in Foster and Residential Care.* London: ChildLine.

Oliver, C. and Candappa, M. (2003) *Tackling Bullying: Listening to the Views of Children and Young People, Summary Report for Childline.* London: Department for Education and Skills.

Parkin, W. and Green, L. (1997) 'Cultures of abuse within residential child care.' *Early Child Development and Care 133,* 73–86.

Scottish Executive (2002) *National Care Standards: Care Homes for Children and Young People.* Edinburgh: The Stationery Office.

Sewell, T. (1997) *Black Masculinities and Schooling: How do Black Boys Survive Modern School?* Stoke on Trent: Trent Books.

Sharp, S. and Thompson, D. (1994) 'The Role of Whole School Policies in Tackling Bullying in Schools.' In P.K. Smith and S. Sharp (eds) *School Bullying: Insights and Perspectives.* London: Routledge.

Sinclair, I. and Gibbs, I. (1998) *Children's Homes: A Study in Diversity.* Chichester: Wiley.

Smith, P.K. and Sharp, S. (eds) (1994) *School Bullying: Insights and Perspectives.* London: Routledge.

Tomison, A.M. and Tucci, J. (1997) 'Emotional abuse: The hidden form of maltreatment.' *Issues in Child Abuse Prevention 8,* 16.

Utting, W. (1991) *Children in the Public Care.* London: HMSO.

Utting, W. (1997) *People Like Us: The Report of the Review of the Safeguards for Children Living Away from Home.* London: Department of Health.

Wade, J. and Biehal, N. with Stein, M. and Clayden, J. (1998) *Going Missing.* Chichester: Wiley.

Waterhouse, R. (2000) *Lost in Care: Report of the Tribunal of Inquiry into the Abuse of Children in Care in the Former County Council Areas of Gwynedd and Clwyd since 1994.* HC 201. London: Stationery Office.

Wolmar, C. (2000) *Forgotten Children: The Scandals in Britain's Children's Homes.* London: Vision.

CHAPTER 11

Hold On

Physical Restraint in Residential Child Care

Laura Steckley and Andrew Kendrick

Introduction

The physical restraint of children and young people in residential child care is a highly contentious issue. Historically, evidence of the concerns of children and young people about physical restraint has appeared in the context of abuse in residential care (Hart and Howell 2004; Kendrick 1997). The death of Gareth Myatt following a physical restraint in a secure training centre in England brought to the fore concerns about restraint-related fatalities which have been increasingly profiled in the USA (Milliken 1998; Nunno, Holden and Tollar 2006). On the other hand, residential staff frequently have to deal with violence, aggression and challenging behaviour (National Task Force on Violence Against Social Care Staff 2001).

Legislation related to physical restraint is very complex, involving general criminal law, health and safety regulations, human rights legislation, education law, social care regulations, and national standards (Hart and Howell 2004). In the UK, there have also been concerns about the lack of practice guidance, although in Scotland this has recently been addressed through the publication of *Holding Safely* (Davidson *et al.* 2005).

Although in other countries the use of mechanical and chemical restraints is widespread, in the UK almost all physical restraints are interventions 'in which staff hold a child to restrict his or her movement...' (Davidson *et al.* 2005, p. vii). This chapter draws together research on physical restraint that has informed a recent study that explores children, young people and staff members' experiences of physical restraint in residential child care in Scotland. However, it must be acknowledged that, given the very serious nature of this area of residential work, there is a dearth of research and a need to develop a much better evidence base.

Restraint as abuse and restraint-related injury and death

A recent consultation with looked-after children in Scotland found that, although they understood the reason for physical restraint, they also identified much more negative experiences including unwarranted restraints, excessive force, improper techniques, pain or injury, and feeling disliked (Paterson, Watson and Whiteford 2003; see also Moss, Sharpe and Fay 1990; Safe & Sound 1995; Who Cares? Scotland n.d.). Unwarranted and excessive use of force in physically restraining young people has also been identified in inquiries into abuse (Kirkwood 1993; Waterhouse 2000).

Children and young people have suffered injury through physical restraint, although there is a concerning lack of information about the extent of injuries or comparison of different techniques (Stark 1996). Hart and Howell (2006) provide evidence that approximately one in seven of the injuries in one young offenders institute were related to the use of physical restraint. One recent US study compared the frequency of injury during physical restraint using two different restraint systems – professional crisis management (PCM) and therapeutic crisis intervention (TCI) (Henderson *et al.* 2005). All restraint incidents in the programmes of one agency in the states of Pennsylvania and New York during 2003 were recorded and analysed. Two different systems were used in these two states. Children and adolescents experienced 5 critical injuries and 189 serious injuries in the 5580 PCM restraints, and 10 critical injuries and 85 serious injuries in the 1274 TCI restraints. Staff injuries occurred more frequently than injuries to children. 'The TCI restraint method was associated with a higher frequency of injuries compared with the PCM method' (Henderson *et al.* 2005, p.195).

Increasingly, concerns have mounted over the risk of death related to physical restraint. Deaths have been associated with physical restraint in areas of law enforcement (Leigh, Johnson and Ingram 1998), emergency medical services (Stratton *et al.* 2001), mental health services (Paterson *et al.* 2003; Mohr, Petti and Mohr 2003), health care (Rubin, Dube and Mitchell 1993) and learning disability services (Paterson *et al.* 2003). Restraint-related deaths have also occurred in residential child care, with most reported cases in the USA. An investigative series published in the US newspaper the *Hartford Courant* (Weiss 1998) brought this issue to public attention and prompted the Children's Health Act of 2000; this Act requires state regulation of child management interventions and mandates certain conditions for the use of physical restraint (Jones and Timbers 2003). A recent US review of all known restraint-related fatalities in residential child care between 1993 and 2003 found that 38 children died during or following a physical restraint (Nunno *et al.* 2006). In those cases where information was available, the child's documented behaviours did not warrant a physical restraint in terms of danger to self or others. The study acknowledged that, due to limited information, it was unable to give an estimate of 'risk of death' related to type of restraint or position (Nunno *et al.* 2006, p. 1324).

Until recently, there were no recorded cases of young people dying as a consequence of the use of physical restraint in residential care in the UK. In April 2004, however, 15-year-old Gareth Myatt lost consciousness while being restrained by staff in a secure training centre in Coventry, England, and died a short time later. His death provided the impetus for an independent inquiry into the use of physical restraint, solitary confinement and forcible strip-searching in secure residential establishments for children and young people (Carlile 2006). The inquiry found a lack of consistency in the use of physical restraint across the establishments investigated, and serious instances of misuse and abuse. Recommendations included curtailing the use of restraint as a punishment or to gain compliance, stopping the use of handcuffs and pain compliance, and giving high priority to reducing violence, resolving disputes and ensuring regular training.

Methods of behaviour management and physical restraint

There are a large number of behaviour management and training packages which involve the use of physical restraint, and these are used in a range of settings. Little information and limited research, however, is available on those systems used in residential child care. There are concerns regarding the combination of commercial interests with an area of practice that carries so much complexity and potential for misuse. There is also a lack of a regulatory framework and many people hold concerns around the absence of a body to accredit these methods specifically for residential child care. This leaves establishments in the predicament of having to assess for themselves the suitability of the method and trainers they choose without the benefit of research evidence or objective criteria (Allen 2001). In the UK, the British Institute for Learning Disabilities (BILD) has attempted to address this issue by developing a directory of physical interventions training organisations, a code of practice and an accreditation scheme for those organisations that demonstrate compliance with this code (Harris 2002; BILD website). Questions still remain, however, about the efficacy and comparative effectiveness of different behaviour management and training packages.

Training

A review of the training of carers in behaviour management strategies across different user groups identified a range of positive benefits. These included an increase in staff knowledge and confidence and a decrease in incidents of challenging behaviour, subsequent 'reactive strategies' and injuries (Allen 2001). Two studies undertaken in residential child care settings also found an increase in staff knowledge and confidence (Nunno, Holden and Leidy 2003; Perkins and Leadbetter 2002). Nunno *et al.* (2003) also noted a decrease in critical incidents. Killick and Allen (2005) studied training in managing aggressive and harmful behaviour in an adolescent in-patient psychiatric unit. They found that staff confidence increased through training, though this was not maintained long term. An increase in knowledge, however, was maintained over time.

Bell and Stark's (1998) study assessing the competence of trainers and practitioners in their use of specific techniques for physical restraint found considerable variation among trainers in assessing the competence of trainees due to the complexity and speed of restraint techniques. Suggestions for improved acquisition and retention of skills included training only one technique at a time, allowing time for trainees to learn a technique to saturation level, maintaining regular refresher training, and regularly assessing the competence of trainers and practitioners. The importance of refresher training has been highlighted in other studies (CWLA 2004; Day 2000).

Currently, there are no studies comparing the different training approaches (Allen 2001), and 'little is known about the critical independent variables involved in the provision of effective training' (Kaye and Allen 2002, p. 129). Additionally, training in behaviour management strategies must be located within a wider, ongoing training plan that is well grounded in an understanding of child development and enhances practitioners' capacity to manage and understand the impact of their own fear, anger and other anxieties on their interactions with young people (Braxton 1995). Training must also be contextualised in a much broader approach which addresses leadership, training needs of managers, unit ethos, staff supervision, care planning, risk assessment, monitoring of incidents, trauma-sensitive care, de-escalation, post-incident de-briefing, and involvement of families (CWLA 2004; Nunno *et al.* 2003; Paterson, Leadbetter and Miller 2005). Such wider issues have been addressed in a small number of studies in residential child care.

Reducing restraint

Jones and Timbers (2003) examined the implementation of a comprehensive, systematic, skill-based model of care and treatment in two residential child care establishments. They found that not only incidents involving physical restraint rapidly and significantly declined, problem behaviour decreased as well (whether or not physical restraint was required). Rather than focusing on the suppression or containment of harmful behaviour, as crisis intervention programmes must, the treatment model in this study is wider reaching. Its core elements include selection and training of front-line workers, round-the-clock availability of professional consultation, a treatment orientation that supports young people in acquiring skills and empowers them to make choices and exercise leadership, and consistent and ongoing evaluation of practice and performance. In addition to enabling and empowering young people as a primary aim, this treatment model also seeks to professionalise the care and treatment of troubled young people.

Colton (2004) developed an instrument aimed at assisting organisations to identify and assess their progress in addressing those factors which influence the reduction of the use of seclusion and restraint. He reviewed over 80 publications and Internet resources addressing the use and/or reduction of seclusion and restraint, and used a content analysis to identify common themes. The instrument, based on these themes and the elements that comprise them, was pre-tested by 20 reviewers and field-tested in the USA in five behavioural health-care facilities, one of which was a residential treatment facility for children and young people. The nine key themes informing the instrument include leadership, training/staff skills, staffing, physical environment, programmatic structure, responsive and timely treatment planning, processing after the event/debriefing, communication and consumer involvement, and systems evaluation and quality improvement.

The Child Welfare League of America's study (CWLA 2004) involved supporting and evaluating five residential child care establishments, or demonstration sites, over a three-year period. During this period, each establishment implemented a model training programme and endeavoured to shift its own organisational culture, towards the ultimate objective of reducing the use of restraint and seclusion. The sites had varying levels of success in reducing physical restraint. This was attributed to the sites' overriding focus on reducing the use of mechanical restraint (where applicable) and seclusion (used in all sites), and in some cases, the fact that sites had significantly reduced the use of physical restraints prior to the start of the study. While all sites were successful in reducing the use of seclusion, only one achieved a significant decrease in physical restraints. More usefully, the study identified several practices and strategies for reducing restraint and seclusion, which informed the Child Welfare League of America's related guidance document (Bullard, Fulmore and Johnson 2003). These resonate with (and were included in) the research by Colton (2004), and include leadership; organisational culture, agency policies, procedures and practices; staff training and professional development; treatment milieu; and continuous quality improvement.

As a result of the study, the Child Welfare League of America also makes four recommendations for the field of residential child care. First, establishments are strongly encouraged to use the tools available for supporting reduction efforts. On a more macro level, two recommendations involve the adoption of a single set of agreed definitions regarding restraint and seclusion, and the subsequent development of a national incidence data-tracking system for monitoring their use. Perhaps most importantly, funding agents are compelled to ensure establishments have adequate funding to undertake efforts at reduction. Many successful agencies in the study acknowledged having to shift resources away from other areas, including personnel costs and training budgets, to achieve their targets (CWLA 2004). As is becoming clear, reducing the use of physical restraint requires a comprehensive approach that addresses many, often interrelated, aspects of a residential child care establishment's functioning and practice, so to cut resources from other areas in order to enable efforts at reduction will probably undermine those very efforts.

The views of children, young people and staff

The experiences of children and young people related to physical restraint have not been thoroughly explored. We have seen that their concerns about restraint have been raised in relation to wider issues of abuse and negative practice. Little research, however, has focused on children's and young people's actual views of physical restraint.

Mohr, Mahon and Noone (1998) identified trauma as a key theme in a study of the memories and experiences of 19 previously hospitalised children. This trauma manifested in three forms: direct trauma, alienation from staff and vicarious trauma. Similarly, Day (2000) identified a wide range of negative emotions, including fear, vulnerability, embarrassment, powerlessness and a feeling of being punished. His review, however, covered seclusion and mechanical restraint, as well as physical restraint.

In the UK, and narrowing the focus to residential child care, research and consultations have also identified the negative reactions of children and young people. Hayden (1997) explored the views of young people as part of a study of physical restraint in one social services department in England. The young people described feeling angry, frightened, frustrated and scared. None stated that they experienced the restraint as reassuring. Although this study was based upon discussions with only four young people, other studies reflect these negative feelings.

This being said, the young people in these studies did indicate that sometimes young people might need to be restrained under certain circumstances, for example, peer violence or the destruction of the unit (Hayden 1997). They have demonstrated an understanding of the rationale for restraint, including its use as a last resort. Children and young people reported that staff need to be able to avoid problems building up to a dangerous level. They accepted that restraint is sometimes necessary, but only when someone is likely to get hurt or property is likely to get seriously damaged. They were clear that restraint should never involve pain and stressed the importance of staff training in how to restrain without hurting (Morgan 2005; Paterson *et al.* 2003).

Even less research has focused on the views and experiences of staff related to physical restraint. While there is general consensus amongst staff as to the necessity of physical restraint in certain circumstances and the principle of its use as a last resort, most also express anxiety, upset, fear and/or guilt surrounding its use (Bell 1997; Day 2000; Hayden 1997; Stone 2005). This research, however, does not appear to explore these experiences in any depth; given the complex, demanding and often dangerous nature of practice related to managing harmful or potentially harmful behaviour, this represents a significant gap in research, addressed to some extent by the study detailed below.

Experiences of physical restraint in residential child care in Scotland

This study aimed to explore the views and experiences of children, young people and staff members related to their experiences of restraint, and to give voice to these views to inform policy and practice (Steckley and Kendrick 2007; Steckley and Kendrick forthcoming). Thirty-seven children and young people and 41 staff members participated in the research. They came from 20 residential establishments which included children's homes, residential schools and secure accommodation across the local authority, voluntary and private sectors. Semi-structured interview schedules and vignettes were used to assist participants to discuss their views and experiences in as much depth as they felt comfortable. Because of the sensitive nature of the research, careful attention was paid to ethics and the research integrated safeguards for protecting confidentiality, addressing potential disclosures of abuse and protecting participants from undue distress.

Many of the findings in this study parallel the research that has explored the views of young people and staff. There was near unanimity regarding the necessity, in certain circumstances, of physical restraint and these circumstances were almost always linked with issues of safety and harm. Most staff discussed the importance of using less invasive interventions to diffuse potentially unsafe situations, and only turning to physical restraint as a last resort. Young people were also aware of the concept of last resort and indicated an awareness and appreciation of staff members' other efforts to help them to calm down. Some young people, however, expressed frustration that staff members were too quick to use restraint, and concern about unnecessary, rough or painful restraint was a dominant theme across the young people's interviews. Young people did not, however, describe a feeling of being punished as a result of being restrained, and on the few occasions when asked directly whether physical restraint is ever (or should ever) be used as punishment, all clearly stated 'no'. Both young people and staff expressed ambivalence about the use of restraints, with some young people even directly contradicting themselves over the course of the interview.

Also similar to other findings were the myriad of negative emotions experienced by young people and staff. All of the young people who discussed their own experiences of being restrained described at least some of those experiences negatively. Negative emotions identified included sadness, frustration, embarrassment, regret, hate or aggression towards staff, hate or aggression towards themselves, and anger. Anger was the overriding and most readily identifiable emotion expressed. All of the emotions identified by staff related to their experiences of restraint were also negative, and they included anxiety, upset, sadness, fear, frustration, discomfort for the young person, worry, doubt and guilt. A sense of guilt, failure or defeat over not being able to avoid the restraint was a dominant theme within staff discussions of their feelings related to restraint.

This study, however, also provided additional information about young people's experiences of physical restraint which diverged significantly from other studies. First, young people discussed their views about seeing another young person get restrained, and both positive and negative views were given. Second, a small minority of young people stated having no recollection of or feelings about being restrained, and, third, a significant minority of young people identified positive emotions linked to restraint. These included feeling glad that a restraint occurred because it helped to keep them safe or out of trouble, and feeling cared about. These positive experiences appeared to be clearly linked with young people's views about their relationships with staff members, another theme identified in this study and discussed below.

In regard to staff members' experiences of physical restraint, related dilemmas and complexities do not appear to be covered in any depth in the research literature. Those discussed by the participants in this study include the ambiguity of the seemingly simple notion of last resort, the multitude of factors that need to be considered in assessing situations involving imminent harm (sometimes under extreme pressure and in a very short amount of time), the complexities and lack of clarity surrounding issues of absconding and property damage, the impact of gender on related practice, and the potentially positive impacts of physical restraint as part of an overall caring response to imminently harmful behaviour.

The significance of relationships as the context within which young people and staff experience restraints, and the impact of restraints on their relationships are dominant themes identified in the study. While a strong body of related theoretical and practice literature is developing (Bullard *et al.* 2003; Colton 2004; Fisher 2003; Garfat 2003), in terms of in-depth research, this has been a previously unexplored aspect of young people and staff members' experiences of physical restraint. Given the importance of relationship as a vehicle through which young people can develop, heal and change, its impact on physical restraint and vice versa bears closer scrutiny.

In analysing the data from this study, conceptual themes are being identified which may help to better understand and respond more effectively to the situations that potentially warrant physical restraint, as well as episodes of physical restraint once they do occur. One such theme involves the notion of containment, which has often been referred to as a primary task in residential child care (Sprince 2002; Ward 1995; Woodhead 1999). This can simply be a literal referral to practical aspects of care, the physical environment and limits on behaviour, with the extreme end of the latter being physical restraint. The concept also involves a more complex process involving the interplay of relationships, activities and models of care coming together in a manner that safely absorbs and assists young people to develop the capacity to manage previously unbearable (or uncontainable) emotions. Physical restraint can also be located within this conceptual framework, and understanding the relationship between physical containment and therapeutic or relational containment, while difficult (Deacon 2004), might assist efforts to reduce its use.

The meaning young people and staff ascribe to physical restraint generally, and to their own experiences of physical restraint specifically, must have a strong impact on how restraint is used and experienced: its appropriateness, its effectiveness, the intentions behind its use, and the outcomes of the event. This is evident throughout the themes identified in the study. Notably, Garfat (2004) has begun the process of researching and developing useful theoretical frameworks for becoming aware of and more consciously influencing the construction of meaning within residential child care settings (see Steckley and Smart 2005). Attending to the processes through which staff and young people make sense of restraint would enhance the effectiveness of residential establishments' attempts to address most, if not all, of the themes highlighted by Colton

(2004) and the Child Welfare League of America (Bullard *et al.* 2003), increasing the likelihood of the reduction of the use of physical restraint.

Conclusion

One of the clear messages from the literature reviewed here is the seriousness and complexity of issues surrounding physical restraint, and the importance of understanding it within a much broader context. Simply viewing physical restraint as an issue residing with the behaviours of young people or the skills of staff does little to improve efforts to reduce or eliminate its use. Nor does it ensure that when it must be used, it is used properly and effectively. Research efforts aimed at improving practices related to physical restraint must be creative in addressing this multilayered complexity. They must also continue to take on board the views and experiences of those most directly affected, residential staff members and children and young people.

The study outlined above reveals a greater breadth and depth of views than before. While many of its findings parallel previous studies, some are new. Children, young people and staff continue to have negative experiences of physical restraint, with misuse in varying forms an ongoing, serious concern. By the same token, findings related to the potentially beneficial aspects of its use give insight into a better understanding of the complex phenomenon of physical restraint and how practice might be improved.

References

Allen, D. (2001) *Training Carers in Physical Interventions: Research towards Evidence Based Practice.* Kidderminster: British Institute of Learning Disabilities.

Bell, L. (1997) 'The physical restraint of young people.' *Child and Family Social Work 1,* 37–47.

Bell, L. and Stark, C. (1998) *Measuring Competence in Physical Restraint Skills in Residential Child Care.* Edinburgh: Scottish Office Central Research Unit.

BILD Website: www.bild.org.uk, accessed on 19 July 2007.

Braxton, E. (1995) 'Angry children, frightened staff: Implications for training and staff development.' *Residential Treatment for Children and Youth 13,* 1, 13–28.

Bullard, L., Fulmore, D. and Johnson, K. (2003) *Reducing the Use of Restraint and Seclusion: Promising Practices and Successful Strategies.* Washington, DC: Child Welfare League of America Press.

Carlile, A. (2006) *An Independent Inquiry into the Use of Physical Restraint, Solitary Confinement and Forcible Strip Searching of Children in Prisons, Secure Training Centres and Local Authority Secure Children's Homes.* London: The Howard League for Penal Reform.

Colton, D. (2004) *Checklist for Assessing Your Organization's Readiness for Reducing Seclusion and Restraint.* http://rccp.cornell.edu/pdfs/SR%20Checklist%201-Colton.pdf, accessed on 24 November 2006.

CWLA (2004) *Achieving Better Outcomes for Children and Families.* Washington, DC: Child Welfare League of America.

Davidson, J., McCullough, D., Steckley, L. and Warren, T. (2005) *Holding Safely: A Guide for Residential Child Care Practitioners and Managers about Physically Restraining Children and Young People.* Glasgow: Scottish Institute of Residential Child Care.

Day, D.M. (2000) *A Review of the Literature on Restraints and Seclusion with Children and Youth: Toward the Development of a Perspective in Practice.* Toronto: The Intersectoral/ Interministerial Steering Committee on Behaviour Management Interventions for Children and Youth in Residential and Hospital Settings, Toronto.

Deacon, J. (2004) 'Testing boundaries: the social context of physical and relational containment in a maximum secure psychiatric hospital.' *Journal of Social Work Practice* 18, 1, 81–97.

Fisher, J.A. (2003) 'Curtailing the use of restraint in psychiatric settings.' *Journal of Humanistic Psychology 43,* 2, 69–95.

Garfat, T. (2003) 'Committed to the relational.' *Relational Child and Youth Care Practice 16,* 3, 3–5.

Garfat, T. (2004) 'Meaning making and intervention in child and youth care practice.' *Scottish Journal of Residential Child Care 3,* 1, 9–16.

Harris, J. (2002) 'Training on Physical Interventions: Making Sense of the Market.' In D. Allen (ed.) *Ethical Approaches to Physical Interventions.* Kidderminster: British Institute of Learning Disabilities.

Hart, D. and Howell, S. (2004) *Report on the Use of Physical Intervention across Children's Services.* London: National Children's Bureau.

Hart, D. and Howell, S. (2006) *Report to the Youth Justice Board on the Use of Physical Intervention within the Juvenile Secure Estate.* London: Youth Justice Board.

Hayden, C. (1997) *Physical Restraint in Children's Residential Care: Social Services Research and Information Unit Report No.37.* Portsmouth: University of Portsmouth.

Henderson, L., Siddons, K., Wasser, T., Gunn, S. and Spisszak, E. (2005) 'Frequency of client and staff injury during physical restraint episodes: A comparison of 2 child restraint systems.' *Journal of Clinical Outcomes Management 12,* 4, 193–8.

Jones, R.J. and Timbers, G.D. (2003) 'Minimizing the need for physical restraint and seclusion in residential youth care through skill-based treatment programming.' *Families in Society: The Journal of Contemporary Human Services 84,* 1, 21–9.

Kaye, N. and Allen, D. (2002) 'Over the top? Reducing staff training in physical interventions.' *British Journal of Learning Disabilities 30,* 129–32.

Kendrick, A. (1997) 'Safeguarding Children Living Away from Home from Abuse: A Literature Review.' In R. Kent (ed.) *Children's Safeguards Review.* Edinburgh: The Stationery Office.

Killick, S. and Allen, D. (2005) 'Training staff in an adolescent inpatient psychiatric unit in positive approaches to managing aggressive and harmful behaviour: Does it improve confidence and knowledge?' *Child Care in Practice 11,* 3, 323–39.

Kirkwood, A. (1993) *The Leicestershire Inquiry 1992*. Leicester: Leicestershire County Council.

Leigh, A., Johnson, G. and Ingram, A. (1998) *Deaths in Police Custody: Learning the Lessons*. London: Home Office Police Research Group.

Milliken, D. (1998) 'Death by restraint.' *Canadian Medical Association Journal 158*, 12, 1611–12.

Mohr, W.K., Mahon, M.M. and Noone, M.J. (1998) 'A restraint on restraints: The need to reconsider the use of restrictive interventions.' *Archives of Psychiatric Nursing 12*, 2, 95–106.

Mohr, W.K., Petti, T. and Mohr, B. (2003) 'Adverse effects associated with physical restraint.' *Canadian Journal of Psychiatry 48*, 5, 330–7.

Morgan, R. (2005) *Children's Views on Restraint: The Views of Children and Young People in Residential Homes and Residential Special Schools*. www.rights4me.org/content/beheardreports/101/restraint_report.pdf, accessed on 1 August 2007.

Moss, M., Sharpe, S. and Fay, C. (1990) *Abuse in the Care System: A Pilot Study by the National Association of Young People in Care*. London: National Association of Young People in Care (NAYPIC).

National Task Force on Violence Against Social Care Staff (2001) *Report and National Action Plan*. www.dh.gov.uk/en/publicationsandstatistics/publications/publicationspolicyandguidance/DH_4010625, accessed on 19 July 2007.

Nunno, M., Holden, M.J. and Leidy, B. (2003) 'Evaluating and monitoring the impact of a crisis intervention system on a residential child care facility.' *Children and Youth Services Review 25*, 4, 295–315.

Nunno, M., Holden, M.J. and Tollar, A. (2006) 'Learning from tragedy: A survey of child and adolescent restraint fatalities.' *Child Abuse and Neglect 30*, 1333–42.

Paterson, B., Bradley, P., Stark, C., Saddler, D., Leadbetter, D. and Allen, D. (2003) 'Deaths associated with restraint use in health and social care in the UK: The results of a preliminary survey.' *Journal of Psychiatric and Mental Health Nursing 10*, 3–15.

Paterson, B., Leadbetter, D. and Miller, G. (2005) 'Beyond zero tolerance: A varied approach to workplace violence.' *British Journal of Nursing 14*, 15, 810–15.

Paterson, S., Watson, D. and Whiteford, J. (2003) *Let's Face It! Care 2003: Young People Tell Us How It Is*. Glasgow: Who Cares? Scotland.

Perkins, J. and Leadbetter, D. (2002) 'An evaluation of aggression management training in a special education setting.' *Emotional and Behavioural Difficulties 7*, 1, 19–34.

Rubin, B.S., Dube, A.H. and Mitchell, E.K. (1993) 'Asphyxial deaths due to physical restraint: A case series.' *Archives of Family Medicine 2*, 4, 405–8.

Safe & Sound (1995) *So Who Are We Meant to Trust Now? Responding to Abuse in Care: The Experiences of Young People*. London: NSPCC.

Sprince, J. (2002) 'Developing containment: Psychoanalytic consultancy to a therapeutic community for traumatized children.' *Journal of Child Psychotherapy 28*, 2, 147–61.

Stark, C. (1996) 'Medical Aspects of Physical Restraint.' In M. Lindsay (ed.) *Physical Restraint: Practice, Legal, Medical and Technical Considerations*. Glasgow: Centre for Residential Child Care.

Steckley, L. and Kendrick, A. (2007) 'Young People's Experiences of Physical Restraint in Residential Care: Subtlety and Complexity in Policy and Practice.' In M. Nunno, L. Bullard and D.M. Day (eds) *For Our Own Safety: Examining the Safety of High-risk Interventions for Children and Young People.* Washington, DC: Child Welfare League of America.

Steckley, L. and Kendrick, A. (forthcoming) 'Physical restraint in residential child care: The experiences of young people and residential workers.' *Childhood.*

Steckley, L. and Smart, M. (2005) 'Two days in Carberry.' *Scottish Journal of Residential Child Care 4*, 2, 53–63.

Stone, B. (2005) 'Care and control in a children's residential unit: Staff perspectives.' *Representing Children 18*, 1, 63–70.

Stratton, S.J., Rogers, C., Brickett, K. and Grunzinski, G. (2001) 'Factors associated with sudden death of individuals requiring restraint for excited delirium.' *The American Journal of Emergency Medicine 19*, 3, 187–91.

Ward, A. (1995) 'The impact of parental suicide on children and staff in residential care: A case study in the function of containment.' *Journal of Social Work Practice 9*, 1, 23–32.

Waterhouse, R. (2000) *Lost in Care: Report on the Tribunal of Inquiry into the Abuse of Children in Care in the Former County Council Areas of Gwynedd and Clwyd since 1974.* London: Stationery Office.

Weiss, E.M. (series ed.) (1998) 'Deadly restraint: An investigative report.' *The Hartford Courant*, 11–15 October.

Who Cares? Scotland (n.d.) *Feeling Safe? Report: The Views of Young People.* Glasgow: Who Cares? Scotland.

Woodhead, J. (1999) 'Containing care.' In A. Hardwick and J. Woodhead (eds) *Loving, Hating and Survival: A Handbook for All who Work With Troubled Children and Young People.* Aldershot: Ashgate Arena.

CHAPTER 12

Blurring the Boundaries

The Relationship between Secure Accommodation and 'Alternatives' in Scotland

Aileen Barclay and Lynne Hunter

Introduction

Secure accommodation straddles both child welfare and youth justice systems and its complexity is reflected in the wide range of young people who enter its door. A key challenge for secure accommodation, then, is to cater effectively for this diverse group of young people. For Harris and Timms (1993), ambiguity is an essential characteristic of secure care, captured in the subtitle of their book: 'Between hospital and prison or thereabouts'. Taking a historical perspective, they argue that secure care is not a coherent service for troubled children, but a means of catering for a range of young people deemed to require containment and fitting readily within no other setting.

In 2002, the Scottish Executive commissioned a three-year study involving a research team from the Universities of Stirling, Strathclyde and Glasgow, aimed at developing an understanding of the use and effectiveness of secure accommodation in Scotland (Walker *et al.* 2006). This chapter aims to highlight relevant research, policy and service developments and to discuss relevant findings and implications from the research.

Issues in secure accommodation

Secure accommodation caters for two populations: those requiring care for their own safety and those who present a risk to others. Traditionally the first group is viewed as needing care or 'treatment', while the second is seen as requiring control, reform or punishment. However, with adolescents these distinctions become blurred partly because 'juvenile offending' is widely attributed to faulty parenting or socialisation, but also in light of evidence that both groups have similar characteristics and needs (Goldson 2000; Social Work Services Inspectorate 2000). A number of commentators point out that the inherent ambiguity in the secure care task cannot be attributed solely to the requirement that it should cater for different kinds of needs. Equally important is the fact that attitudes to troublesome teenagers and how they are constructed within policy is not constant, in that their vulnerability is emphasised at some points and their criminality at others (Goldson 2002a; Harris and Timms 1993; Muncie and Hughes 2002).

Whilst we acknowledge the ambiguity of the task, in that secure accommodation is evidently expected to provide care and control, it is also expected to effect some behavioural change. Cognitive-behavioural approaches are generally credited as the most effective way of changing criminal behaviour, though their appropriateness in work with young offenders has been questioned (Pitts 2002). Bullock and colleagues note that very cognitive-based interventions are less effective with young people who are very difficult and disturbed (Bullock, Little and Millham 1998), a consideration with obvious relevance for secure provision, since many of the young people admitted have serious and long-standing emotional difficulties (for example, Social Work Services Inspectorate 2000). The extent to which long-standing difficulties can or should be addressed within secure care is contested, but there is considerable evidence that many residents require a caring and supportive environment (Social Work Services Inspectorate 2000; Walker, Hill and Triseliotis 2002). Kroll *et al.* (2002) found that boys aged 12–17 in secure care had high rates of mental health, social and educational needs. Admission to secure care was followed by a great reduction in need and there were improvements in aggressive behaviours, substance dependence, social relationships, self-care and, particularly, educational needs, largely due to being in secure care with high levels of supervision. Rates of depression and anxiety, however, remained high. A two-year follow-up found that they had maintained some of their initial gains.

The levels of many problems, however, remained high; substance abuse became significantly more common, and many reoffended. The research highlighted the need for much more input by mental health and related services (Harrington *et al.* 2005).

The different needs of boys and girls have also been highlighted, with O'Neill reporting particularly poor experiences and short-term outcomes for girls placed on welfare grounds, since the service is geared to cater predominantly for male offenders (O'Neill 2001). A number of studies have highlighted that though the secure care task is talked about in terms of tackling problems, its first and predominant function is to contain (Goldson 2002b; Kelly 1992).

The importance of understanding the interaction between young people's own characteristics and behaviour and the actions of professionals and service providers is well established in the literature. Bullock *et al.* (1998) highlight that the routes by which troubled children reach secure care are a product of child-related factors and decisions and actions taken by professionals. They differentiate between the life *route*, which refers to children and their families' actions, and *process*, which encompasses actions taken throughout the child's life by professionals in health, social work and education or by courts and children's panels. Harris and Timms (1993) observed that decisions about secure care placement itself were rarely based on theoretically sound professional assessment of young people's needs. Rather, key participants in the decision-making process developed 'narratives' which defined young people in certain ways, thus justifying their favoured course of action. Furthermore, they reported variation in local authorities' attitudes to secure accommodation and found that 'the most reliable predictor of high usage of secure accommodation was whether an agency was a "provider" authority' (Harris and Timms 1993, p. 99) and concluded 'either that the mere existence of secure accommodation provokes its usage *or* that the pressures which led to a unit's construction in the first place continue to influence that usage' (Harris and Timms 1993, pp. 99–100). This inconsistency in the secure accommodation process extends to the decision-making of professionals which Kelly found to be 'arbitrary and somewhat whimsical' (Kelly 1992, p. 203).

Goldson (2000) identifies a number of influences which increase the likelihood of secure placement on welfare grounds. First there is a tendency to locate the problem in the individual young person, whereas deficiencies in the welfare system might be equally relevant. For example, open residential units vary in their capacity to provide appropriate care, control and support for seriously troubled young people, yet their failures are seldom mentioned when young people become out of control. In addition, he cites evidence that class, gender and ethnic origin influence the route young people take through child welfare services. Agency priorities, geographical location and ease of access to secure placements or alternatives also determine which children find themselves in locked accommodation.

> Irrespective of the legal criteria therefore, a range of ancillary factors exercise significant influence over the placement of children in secure accommodation. In turn, this suggests that the processes determining such placements are influenced by factors other than the children's behaviour and considered professional judgement. (Goldson 2002b, p. 27)

This may result not only in young people being admitted to secure accommodation inappropriately, but also in denying access to those who need it the most. It is perhaps unsurprising, therefore, that as well as finding geographical variation in local authority practice to secure accommodation, the National Children's Bureau also reported that secure unit managers 'considered that 60 out of 193 children surveyed could have been safely accommodated in open accommodation' (National Children's Bureau 1995, pp. 4–5). In two early studies of secure care, Petrie (1980) and Kelly and Littlewood (1985) compared the backgrounds of boys in open residential schools and secure units and reported that the difference between those in the secure and open settings did not relate to the incidence of violent crime or aggressive behaviour in care but rather to a history of absconding and a failure to respond in open residential settings. More recently, O'Neill (2001) observed that many young people in secure accommodation are not significantly different from those accommodated in open settings. This message supports evidence which suggests that improving standards of care in open settings and creating more imaginative alternatives could avoid the need for some secure placements (National Children's Bureau 1995; O'Neill 2001). Indeed, the Walker *et al.* (2002) evaluation of a Community Alternative Placement Scheme (CAPS) showed that foster care can potentially provide an alternative to secure accommodation.

Secure accommodation in Scotland

The nature and role of the children's hearing system contributes to secure accommodation in Scotland being quite different from locked provision for children in other parts of the UK, one of the key differences being that it is wholly located within residential child care provision and that a high proportion of young people are admitted primarily on welfare grounds. Scotland operates a tripartite system in that a young person can only be placed in secure accommodation on the agreement of three independent parties: the children's hearing, the director of social work and the head of establishment. Children's panels, however, can only authorise a secure placement and not enforce it, one of the criticisms levied at children's hearings. A young person can only be admitted if the director of social work and the head of establishment also consider it to be in the child's best interests.

In recent years, between 200 and 250 young people have been admitted to secure care in Scotland each year, with about 90 in placement at any one time. A majority are boys but girls typically account for more than a quarter, most being placed for welfare reasons rather than for offending (Social Work Services Inspectorate 2000, 2002). Approximately two-thirds of young people in secure accommodation are placed there on the authority of a children's hearing. The remaining third of the secure care population are subject to a court order, either serving a sentence for a serious crime or on remand.

The report *A Secure Remedy* (Social Work Services Inspectorate 1996) was important in defining policy aims and setting the agenda for change in this field. It defined the optimum position as one in which a secure place would be available for all young people who required it, whilst no one would be admitted to a secure setting if they could be safely accommodated within an open setting. This recommendation prompted the growth of a range of community-based 'alternatives', including schemes offering enhanced or intensive community-based support and specialist foster care. By adding electronic tagging to an intensive support package, the Intensive Secure Monitoring System (ISMS), introduced early in 2005, aims to provide a direct alternative for young people facing secure placement.

The report itself and two subsequent surveys (Social Work Services Inspectorate 2000, 2002) confirmed that the secure population encompassed subgroups with quite distinctive problems and needs. Girls, sexually aggressive young people, those with long-standing, chronic problems and young people whose difficulties emerge in their teens were recognised as having different requirements, even if they also had certain basic needs in common.

Recent policy and service developments have focused on developing capacity, both through increasing overall provision and enhancing the service within each individual unit. In March 2003, plans to create an additional 29 secure places were announced, raising the total from 96 to 125. This also allowed for greater geographical spread and dedicated provision for girls. In addition to the secure places, there are to be 30 further close support places and extra funds for intensive community support.

Findings from the *Secure Accommodation in Scotland* research

The aims of the research were to provide a clearer understanding of the purpose and effectiveness of secure accommodation in meeting the needs of young people, their families and communities, and a framework to assist the decision-making process by children's hearings and social work departments.

There were six specific objectives including identifying the characteristics of young people who had experienced periods in secure care and describing the nature of this experience for them and their families, obtaining evidence on the impacts of secure care on young people, identifying which interventions promote the most effective outcomes for young people and assessing to what extent the 'containment' aspect was crucial to the success of these, and comparing the impact of secure care upon the young people and their families with the experiences of those with similar behavioural characteristics who received alternative services (including non-secure residential settings and specialist fostering placements).

The research methodology included obtaining information on 53 young people shortly after their admission to secure accommodation. Initial data were collected from records and interviews held with social workers, key workers and some young people. Updates on progress were obtained from social workers at two points, approximately 12 and 24 months after admission. Similar information was collated on 23 young people considered for secure accommodation but sustained in an open setting for at least six months. A review of subsequent placements was also conducted for all young people made subject to secure authorisation by a children's hearing over six months.

Interviews took place with senior and first-line social work managers, panel chairs and reporters on decision-making in relation to secure accommodation and views about its function and effectiveness. These semi-structured interviews incorporated vignettes where informants were asked to discuss case scenarios and their likely responses. Respondents were drawn from eight local authorities, reflecting a geographical mix and different patterns of using secure accommodation. Two rounds of interviews were held with a senior manager in each secure unit.

In this chapter, we will first provide a brief overview of the impact of secure accommodation on young people. We have then chosen to focus on the relationship surrounding the use of secure and alternative resources in responding to the needs of young people in crisis. In particular we will look at the interconnectedness of service provision, discuss the role of decision-making within the local authority context and explore the expectations and capacity of both. We will briefly touch upon the issue of the availability of secure places before finally highlighting some implications of the research on policy and practice.

The impact of secure accommodation

In this study, most young people (89%) had been admitted to secure accommodation because of concerns that they were putting themselves at risk and although 75 per cent had committed at least one offence, in very few instances had this in itself prompted the placement. At the point when the placement ended, social workers considered that all young people had benefited in that all were considered to have been kept safe and, with good personal care, to be healthier than they had been when admitted. Improvements in behaviour which had prompted the secure placement were noted in relation to 58 per cent of the young people. For the remainder, either the problematic behaviour was continuing or apparent changes were thought unlikely to be sustained. Placements were considered particularly ineffectual in addressing drug misuse. Social workers attributed lack of change in behaviour to a range of factors including a poor fit between young people's specific needs and programmes offered, issues being tackled outside their usual environment and difficulties being too entrenched to be addressed in a relatively short placement. At the point when the secure placement ended, the impact on the young person was assessed as having 'clear benefits' for 33 young people (62%) and 'some benefits alongside some drawbacks' for 20 young people (38%).

Approximately two years after admission outcomes were rated as good, medium or poor, based on the following variables: whether the young person was in a safe and stable placement, whether the young person was in work or education, whether the behaviour which resulted in his or her admission had been modified and the social worker's rating of the young person's general well-being compared with that on admission. Young people whose rating was positive on all four dimensions were considered to have had a good outcome. Where at least one was negative the rating was medium and where no aspects were positive, the outcome was considered to be poor. On this basis, outcomes were assessed as follows: 'good' – 14 (26%); 'medium' – 24 (45%); and 'poor' – 15 (28%).

The spread of ratings was similar across age, gender, placing local authorities, units held and placement prior to the secure admission. Good or poor outcomes could not be attributed to single factors, but rather emerged from how several elements of the situation came together. Not surprisingly there was a close correspondence between ratings of change in behaviour and well-being. Those whose problematic behaviour had increased were typically involved in drug use, often with associated offending.

Social workers often attributed good or poor outcomes to service provision following, rather than during, the secure placement. One of the transition practices associated with good outcomes was to gradually reduce the level of structure and supervision to which young people had become accustomed. This so called 'step-down' approach was thought to have applied to a total of 17 young people, none of whom had a poor outcome.

The interconnectedness of service provision

Two key findings emerged as the study progressed. The first concerned the relationship between secure accommodation and 'alternative' services. It had been assumed that it was relatively common practice for young people to be seriously considered for secure accommodation, but sustained in an open setting through the support of alternative services. In practice, this applied to far fewer young people than had been envisaged. Instead 'alternatives' to secure accommodation typically engaged with young people before they reached a point where secure accommodation was proposed, and/or supported them during and following the secure placement. Thus the services were complementary, rather than alternative options; nor could outcomes be attributed to one or the other intervention.

The second key finding was that the point at which young people would be introduced to 'alternative' services or considered for secure accommodation differed across local authorities. This meant that the use and effectiveness of secure accommodation had to be understood within the local context.

The role of decision-making within the local authority context

Consideration of decision-making showed that it did not involve assessing whether an objectively determined threshold had been reached, but was a dynamic process in which the response to each young person was shaped by key characteristics of the local context. The following key considerations influenced decision-making and use in each local authority:

- ease of access to secure placements

- availability of 'alternative' resources which offer intensive support

- views about the role of secure accommodation

- practice in and attitudes towards risk management.

Though each authority claimed to use secure accommodation as a 'last resort', thresholds across authorities were inevitably different because of local variation in availability of places and perceptions of placements' potential value or harm.

On this basis, and taking into account patterns of admissions, four different local authority approaches were identified:

1. Ready access to secure accommodation, coupled with relatively low access to alternatives (in this context, 'alternatives' include access to open residential provision which can manage young people with challenging behaviour) and a belief that, though a last resort, secure accommodation can be a positive option.

2. Ready access to secure accommodation, coupled with well-developed alternatives and a strong reluctance to place in secure accommodation.

3. Difficulty in accessing secure accommodation, coupled with a strong reluctance to place in secure accommodation and emphasis on developing open and community-based alternatives.

4. Medium difficulty in accessing secure accommodation, with a moderate willingness to use it and moderate commitment to developing alternatives.

Expectations and capacity of secure accommodation and alternative services

There was broad agreement amongst respondents that the primary role of secure accommodation was to keep young people safe and secure at a time of major crisis in their lives, while at the same time providing an opportunity for their emotional, educational and health needs to be assessed and help offered to reduce the difficulties which had resulted in the secure placement. Key functions were to:

- protect the young person and the public
- assess needs and allow young people to take stock of their situation
- engage with young people and effect change
- equip young people to move back into the community.

With respect to its capacity to fulfil these functions, there was broad agreement among respondents that secure accommodation was effective in keeping young people safe and providing space in which their needs could be assessed and links with a range of services established. Whilst increased capacity to address difficulties was widely acknowledged, this was still viewed as patchy and the institutional elements and the separation from ordinary life were thought to detract from the capacity to effect lasting change. Appropriate placements and support on leaving secure accommodation was viewed as key to any benefits being sustained.

With respect to expectations of services offering an 'alternative to secure accommodation', a number of respondents questioned whether there could ever be a direct 'alternative' since, if young people required physical security, nothing else should be offered:

> I struggle slightly with this question because of the range of projects that have been set up as an alternative. I don't know if it's right just to equate them because either children meet secure accommodation criteria or they don't. (Social work manager)

This position was typically associated with the view that whether or not secure accommodation was required could be decided by applying certain objective criteria to the behaviour of the young person concerned.

Others took the view that the point at which secure accommodation was required depended to some extent on the availability of other services which provided enough supervision and support to sustain the young person in an open setting. This second perspective was associated with a willingness to develop packages in response to the specific needs and behaviour of individual young people, while continuing to monitor whether these allowed the risks to be adequately managed. With this incremental approach, the need for physical security was checked out in practice. As a result, some non-secure packages were thought to have provided a direct 'alternative' to physical security:

> I suppose we wouldn't use them [alternatives] instead of security, in that if they require security, they require security, but what [our use of alternatives] does show is that very often people don't require security in terms of being locked away. (Social work manager)

Elements of this approach were evident in three local authorities, two of whom reported difficulty in accessing secure places when these were required. Thus their commitment to developing alternatives had at least in part resulted from necessity.

Asked what 'alternatives' to secure accommodation should offer, views varied as to whether services which diverted young people by intervening at an earlier stage or providing after care merited the title 'alternative to secure accommodation', but these were nevertheless considered very valuable and potentially able to avoid the need for a secure resource and/or reduce the time young people spent there.

Expectations of 'alternatives' were high. The most common expectation was that the level of contact with the young person should be at least daily and preferably with a 24-hour stand-by service. This intensity of service, coupled with developing a productive relationship with the young person and his or her family was viewed as central to making change. The capacity to work with families and in the young person's community was expected to increase the likelihood that changes in behaviour would be sustained. Thus alternatives were expected to reduce some of the drawbacks of a secure placement. In addition alternatives were expected to provide some of the perceived advantages of secure accommodation, for example keeping young people safe and facilitating their engagement with appropriate resources, especially education.

'Not enough beds?'

Despite widely reported difficulties in finding secure places, recruitment for this study had indicated that very few young people were being made subject to or seriously considered for secure authorisation, then sustained in an open setting. To clarify this, a survey was undertaken of all young people made subject to secure authorisation by a children's hearing between July and December 2003. This applied to 104 young people, 59 boys and 45 girls, of whom 79 (76%) had been placed in secure accommodation by the time the survey was completed.

The findings of this survey indicated that most young people who required a secure place had been placed within a week. They also suggested that lack of immediate availability had given some young people a chance to settle and so avoid admission. All of those to whom this applied had been sustained in an open residential setting, primarily local authority units. This supports the view that ready access to secure accommodation may result in some young people being admitted who could be supported in an open setting. It also highlighted that it was residential units, rather than specialist projects, which were most commonly providing a *direct* alternative at the point when a secure placement had been authorised. The research team's experience in recruiting the 'alternative' sample had demonstrated that specialist 'alternative' services more commonly engaged with young people prior to secure accommodation being seriously considered and so diverted them on to a different pathway.

These findings indicate that the relationship between secure accommodation and 'alternative' services is more complex than was initially envisaged. Secure accommodation is viewed as a service which is used when all others have proved ineffective, so the availability of intensive support in the community or residential care is as important as the young person's behaviour in defining the point at which a secure placement will be required. Since provision varies across local authorities, so will its use.

Some implications of the research

This recognition of the interconnections between secure and other services and the extent of local variation has implications for strategic planning at a national and local level. First, in addition to what alternative resources are available, the use of secure accommodation reflected the level of risk decision-makers are willing to tolerate. This study indicated that panel members were willing to tolerate a lower level of risk than social work professionals and could be sceptical about the protection offered by individual packages built round a young person. These arrangements were sometimes developed out of necessity, when no secure place was available, but whereas some social work managers viewed this as an opportunity to extend the capacity to provide security without locking young people away, some panel members viewed them as a poor substitute. In light of this, panel members wanting to enforce the implementation of secure authorisations may stifle the development of innovative practice. However, it is also important that social workers have a high enough level of training, experience and contact with young people and their families to be able to safely assess and manage risk.

Second, findings in relation to current capacity highlighted that there can never be a straightforward answer to how many secure beds are required. The influence of availability of other services on the need for secure placement has already been considered. As discussed, there was a discrepancy between the widely held view that it was difficult to find a bed when needed and the results of the survey of authorisations which indicated that most young people had been placed within a few days and that most young people who could not be placed no longer required the bed when one became available or they returned to a children's hearing. Had a place been available, these young people would have been admitted, suggesting that if capacity is increased, so will the number of admissions. Whether this is to be welcomed or not depends on what a secure placement can offer.

Conclusion

The study found that so called 'alternatives' to secure accommodation were seldom introduced at the point when secure authorisation was being seriously considered. More usually projects offering an 'alternative' were introduced at an earlier stage, thus preventing the need for secure accommodation from arising, or they provided after care support. So secure provision and 'alternatives' were complementary services rather that directly alternative options. The ways in which they complemented each other varied across local authorities, depending on both the availability of secure and other resources and prevailing attitudes about their use.

The research highlighted that the use and effectiveness of secure accommodation in Scotland is highly context specific. It was required when the current level of risk could not be safely managed in an open setting, so the point at which an admission was necessary and appropriate depended to a considerable extent on the capacity of local resources to manage young people in crisis. Correspondingly its effectiveness was dependent not just on what was offered within the secure setting, but on appropriate services being available when young people moved on.

References

Bullock, R., Little, M. and Millham, S. (1998) *Secure Care Outcomes: The Care Careers of Very Difficult Adolescents.* Aldershot: Ashgate.

Goldson, B. (2000) '"Children in need" or "young offenders"? Hardening ideology, organizational change and new challenges for social work with children in trouble.' *Child and Family Social Work 5*, 3, 255–65.

Goldson, B. (2002a) 'New Punitiveness.' In J. Muncie, G. Hughes and E. McLaughlin (eds) *Youth Justice: Critical Readings.* London: Sage.

Goldson, B. (2002b) *Vulnerable Inside: Children in Secure and Penal Settings.* London: The Children's Society.

Harrington, R.C., Kroll, L., Rothwell, J., McCarthy, K., Bradley, D. and Bailey, S. (2005) 'Psychosocial needs of boys in secure care for serious or persistent offending.' *Journal of Child Psychology and Psychiatry 46*, 8, 859–66.

Harris, R. and Timms, N. (1993) *Secure Accommodation in Child Care: Between Hospital and Prison or Thereabouts.* London: Routledge.

Kelly, B. (1992) *Children Inside: A Study of Secure Provision.* London: Routledge.

Kelly, B. and Littlewood, P. (1985) *Factors Underlying the Referrals and Committals Processes Relating to a Secure Unit for Young People* (II). Report to the Social Work Services Group. Glasgow: University of Glasgow Sociology Department.

Kroll, L., Rothwell, J., Bradley, D., Shah, P., Bailey, S. and Harrington, R.C. (2002) 'Mental health needs of boys in secure care for serious or persistent offending: A prospective, longitudinal study.' *The Lancet 359*, 1975–9.

Muncie, J. and Hughes, G. (2002) 'Modes of Youth Governance: Political Rationalities, Criminalisation and Resistance.' In J. Muncie, G. Hughes and E. McLaughlin (eds) *Youth Justice: Critical Readings.* London: Sage.

National Children's Bureau (1995) *Safe to Let Out? The Current and Future Use of Secure Accommodation for Children and Young People.* London: National Children's Bureau.

O'Neill, T. (2001) *Children in Secure Accommodation: A Gendered Exploration of Locked Institutional Care for Children in Trouble.* London: Jessica Kingsley Publishers.

Petrie, C. (1980) *The Nowhere Boys.* Farnborough: Saxon House.

Pitts, J. (2002) 'The End of an Era.' In J. Muncie, G. Hughes and E. McLaughlin (eds) *Youth Justice: Critical Readings.* London: Sage.

Social Work Services Inspectorate (1996) *A Secure Remedy.* Edinburgh: Social Work Services Inspectorate.

Social Work Services Inspectorate (2000) *Secure Care Survey Report.* Unpublished: Scottish Executive.

Social Work Services Inspectorate (2002) *Secure Care Survey Report.* Unpublished: Scottish Executive.

Walker, M., Barclay, A., Hill, M., Hunter, L., Kendrick, A., Malloch, M. and McIvor, G. (2006) *Secure Accommodation in Scotland: Its Role and Relationship with 'Alternative' Services.* Edinburgh: Scottish Executive.

Walker, M., Hill, M. and Triseliotis, J. (2002) *Testing the Limits of Foster Care: Fostering as an Alternative to Secure Accommodation.* London: BAAF.

PART FOUR

Context and Culture

CHAPTER 13

Children's Voices, Children's Rights

Ruth Emond

Introduction

> Attending to children's rights is of particular relevance where children are in public care, separated from their families, emotionally and socially vulnerable and subject to the discretionary decision making of social workers and 'professional' carers. (Smith 1997, p. 7)

Over the course of the last century, the notion of 'human rights', and in particular 'children's rights', has been hugely contested. These terms have moved quickly from being located in philosophical and legalistic discourses through academic and policy debates to become embedded in everyday discussions and conceptualisations of what it means to be a child. It may be argued that viewing children as having social and legal rights has sparked greater debate and frustration amongst adults than it has amongst children — even more so amongst those working with children in public care.

This chapter considers the ways in which concepts of rights and participation have impacted on the experiences of children in public care. It begins by outlining the debates surrounding children's rights and then moves to consider how the assertion of rights can in some ways be regarded as the recognition of children's voices. Finally, the chapter turns to the idea of participation. It looks critically at how this term can be used as a means of examining the extent to which the rights of children in care are exercised and their voices are heard.

What do we mean by 'children's rights'?

Understanding children's rights cannot be separated from understanding the changing construction of childhood. James, Jenks and Prout (1998), amongst others, have argued that the meaning given to childhood is socially, culturally and temporally specific; it changes over place and time. Thus the significant societal changes that have taken place over the last three centuries in the UK have seen our understandings of, and beliefs about, children alter dramatically. We no longer believe that children are born with 'original sin' requiring adults to instil 'goodness'; rather we have increasingly come to view children as active in their socialisation, navigating their way around adult controls and constraint, creating what might be seen as a dynamic of parenting (Mayall 2002).

This changing view of childhood has had much to do with historical shifts in society's structure and functioning, primarily in the form of industrialisation and the resulting move toward urban living. During this period, the state began to take an active role in the physical, emotional and spiritual 'development' of children, motivated not only by care but by a more fundamental anxiety relating to the threat children (and in particular working-class children) posed to society. This was not only a threat of individual harm from 'vagrants' or 'delinquents' but a concern relating to how these children would discharge their future roles as workers (Aries 1962; Parton 1987). Greater legislative control of all aspects of children's lives followed. Children began to be withdrawn from the world of work (where they were often working alongside adults) and were instead increasingly forced to participate in education (where they were educated alongside other children) (Abrams 1998). School provided a social arena where the core ideologies of the dominant middle classes could be imparted to children.

Therefore, throughout the nineteenth century, children began to be moved away from contributing both economically and practically to the family, and from being managed and controlled by family members. Rather they were to be educated, monitored and managed outside the family home. Childhood began to be regarded as a life stage in itself, a time of innocence and vulnerability that was globally applicable to all children regardless of class, ethnicity and culture. Indeed, Annetts (2005) has argued that how we understand and respond to children today has much to do with what could be regarded as the polluting and threatening nature of adulthood constructed in the nineteenth century. It is from this threat that children have been regarded as in need of protection.

Increasingly, the notion of protection has been articulated in the form of 'rights'. The idea of children having rights independently of adults is a relatively new concept developed over the course of the last century (Munro 2001). However, over the last three decades in particular, the concern with the protection of children has become an international movement culminating in the 1989 United Nations Convention on the Rights of the Child. Alderson (2000) states that the Convention Rights can be considered as comprising three types of rights for children:

- provision rights, such as to education or health care

- protection rights from neglect, abuse and discrimination

- participation or civil rights which adults who live in democracies take for granted.

Implicit in the Convention is the notion that children, due to their developmental distinctiveness as well as structural place in society, are different from adults and that this difference renders them vulnerable to the exploitation of the more powerful 'adult'.

The philosophy of the Convention underpins the most recent legislation affecting children and young people across the UK. Although the term 'rights' is rarely used in the legislation, the need for children to have access to resources which educate, nurture and protect them and to have a say in how these resources are selected and implemented runs through these Acts (see Children (Scotland) Act 1995).

However, the concept of human rights is complex in terms of definition and interpretation (Freeman 1983) and the concept of children's rights in particular has not been without its critics. Many have argued that the rights agenda has served to take the moral code of society and turned it into legalistic frameworks which become themselves the motivating factor for behaviour rather than the moral 'rightness' of the action itself (Smith 1997). In other words, we give children privacy, for example, because the law tells us to do so rather than because we see this as important or valuable to the child. Similarly, it has been suggested that increasing children's rights has disguised an increasing level of surveillance and regulation by the state. James and James have argued:

> In spite of the UN Convention therefore, and all of the political rhetoric about children and their right to be heard, it can be argued that this may, in effect, amount to little more than an artifice which conceals the real nature of the way

in which mechanisms for retaining and increasing the control over children are being sustained and even extended. (James and James 2001, pp. 225–6)

Similar critiques have come from those who challenge the bureaucratisation of care giving, parenting and protection of children. For example, Smith (1997) argues that the rights agenda has run in parallel with the changing nature of social work which, she argues, places emphasis on measuring outcomes and performance and requires workers to follow formalised sets of rules and procedures. She contests that this is done at the expense of the relationship and quotes Howe to support her point:

> In shifting their focus of attention from actors to acts, social workers have changed their theoretical outlook from one of promoting psychological under-standing to one of developing political rights. (Howe 1994, p. 528)

That children's rights appear to be visible, and arguably measurable, is the feature that their supporters view as their strength but by contrast is what critics view as rendering rights restrictive and clinical.

Children in public care

Children in public care can be considered as consumers or recipients of a range of universal as well as tailored services. They have been identified by adult professionals as in need of care and protection. Often they are considered to be those most at risk and at times, by contrast, the most risky. If 'modern childhood' is constructed as a time of innocence and vulnerability, these children represent either those whom society has deemed a threat to the innocence of others or those who have had their vulnerability exploited. In addition, by living separately from parents (who are regarded in the 'mainstream' as adults who act as advocates and protectors to children), children in care are regarded as being at greater risk of harm and exploitation. Care status itself brings with it stigma, social exclusion and labelling which in turn increases the challenges these children face (Kendrick 2005).

As such, the recognition of the rights of children in public care has become central to the policies and practices which seek to prevent further experiences of abuse or harm. In addition, institutional or indeed foster provision for children has been increasingly regarded as 'less good' than the care that children should experience from families. Taking all these factors together has resulted in a view that these children, even more than those children living with their family, need to have tangible rights, which can be respected and monitored (Willow 2000).

The UN Convention has 40 articles relating to those rights which should be achieved in respect of *all* children. However, Smith (1997) argues that there are certain rights which have particular resonance to children in public care. These include:

- that the state shall ensure that the child has such protection and care as necessary for his or her well-being (Article 3)

- the right of the child to preserve his or her identity (Article 8)

- the right of a child to express his or her views freely and to have them accorded due weight (Article 12)

- the right to privacy (Article 16)

- the right to protection from abuse (Article 19).

In a number of recent government enquiries (Kent 1997; Utting 1997) as well as research studies (see, for example, Colton 2002) abuses of these rights by residential care staff, foster carers, social services systems and personnel have been highlighted. This is despite a far greater level of surveillance of state systems surrounding child care and protection through inspection, registration and training of staff.

Alongside the rise in 'rights talk' has been the notion that children's voices should be heard. Indeed this is made explicit in Article 12 of the Convention. As such it has contributed to a number of political and policy measures including the setting up of specially appointed children's rights officers and supporting advocacy organisations (for example Who Cares? Scotland) as well as an increase in the number of research studies which have concerned themselves with collecting data from children and young people in public care and giving them prominence in subsequent reports and academic writing (Greene and Hogan 2005). It would appear that children have moved to a position where the law requires, and society asks, that they be seen *and* heard.

However, the complexity of the rights debate comes into sharp relief when it is applied to children in public care. The law has often struggled to manage the rights of the child with considerations relevant to his/her welfare (Parton 1994). Indeed Cantwell and Scott (1995) in their experience of working as court welfare officers argue that 'A child ultimately needs to know that others will take responsibility for caring for him or her' (Cantwell and Scott 1995,

p. 342). By asking children their views and placing emphasis on them, there is a danger, they argue, of the child being isolated from those that surround him or her. In such cases, the right of the child to express his or her views, on, for example, contact with parents or a return to their care, can supersede the child's right to the care and protection that is necessary for his or her well-being. The child can therefore be left not only with the *right* but also the *responsibility* of making the decision.

Etzioni (1993) argues that rather than be concerned with personal rights we should move to a position of community responsibility. Within this, the responsibility for individuals becomes a collective enterprise rather than an individualised legislative requirement. Interestingly, a recent child protection review in Scotland has in some ways attempted to straddle both of these positions. The title of the document, *It's Everyone's Job to Make Sure I'm Alright*, reflects this position and indeed it asserts that 'Every adult in Scotland has a role in ensuring all our children live safely and can reach their full potential' (Scottish Executive 2002, p. 1).

Children's participation in decision-making

As the previous section illustrated, changing constructions of childhood have led to children being increasingly seen as having rights (Hodgson 1999). Crucial changes have occurred in the monitoring and enforcement of children's rights and the active role that such rights give to children and young people. This has not followed a smooth trajectory in that all 'rights' have not become operationalised simultaneously. The right to participation in decision-making, for example, is a more recent development that is still only at the early stages of being implemented (Munro 2001). This aspect of the children's rights movement is underpinned by the notion that children's opinions and wishes are worth knowing. This in itself is quite a recent and not homogeneously held belief.

Perhaps a more commonly held belief is, as Sinclair (1996) suggests, that 'the right of children to participate is closely linked to their rights to protection' (Sinclair 1996, p. 91). Thus, in order for children to feel protected by society they need to be given a meaningful place in decision-making processes. However, this view of children's participation, as implicitly concerned with children's responsibility for, and agency in, their own well-being, has been questioned by a number of writers. Such a position, they argue, places the child not only at the centre of decision-making, but as responsible for that process. This can contribute to the sense of confusion and self-blame that some children carry in relation to their position as, for example, looked-after child, patient or pupil. Thus the rhetoric of participation can be quite different from the reality. A case in point would be the Scottish children's hearing system. This system, whereby lay people act as objective decision-makers about the care and protection of children, is underpinned by the notion that children and parents are fully involved in the proceedings of the children's hearings (Kendrick 2000).

In a previous study (Emond 2000), young people described their view of children's hearings as having a monitoring role and a forum whereby adults made decisions about their future lives. The children's hearing system was regarded as having little to do with 'care' or 'protection' and instead was seen as a body to which young people had to explain their misdemeanours. This perpetuated their belief that they had been placed in residential care as a result of their 'bad behaviour'. Thus while they were clear they were expected to participate, this participation was likened to being 'in the dock' rather than as being an active decision-maker.

As previously mentioned, the importance of consulting children and young people is a principle enshrined in the UN Convention on the Rights of the Child. Article 12 states the need to take into account children's wishes when making decisions about their welfare. It gives (to) a child who is:

> capable of forming his or her own views the right to express these views freely in all matters affecting the child, the views of the child being given due weight in accordance with the age and maturity of the child.

Implicit in the Convention therefore, is the notion that participation should be viewed as if on a continuum, the child's right being afforded based on his or her 'age, capability and maturity' as judged by the adults.

Studies conducted with 'looked-after' children and young people illustrate the extent to which children are increasingly being expected to participate in decision-making forums. Thomas and O'Kane (1999) report that children's participation in review meetings has steadily increased over the last two decades, from small numbers of older teenagers attending in the late 1980s to the more recent norm of the majority of children in mid primary school and above attending almost all of their reviews (although often not attending the whole meeting). An earlier study conducted by Kendrick and Mapstone (1991) illustrated the trend for older rather than young children being present at formal review meetings. Indeed, in their study, three-quarters of the children aged over 12 attended three-quarters of their reviews. Many regarded these meetings as crucial forums that allowed them to express their views:

> they are important because they give me the chance to say anything I want to say. It gives them the chance to ask me the things they want to know. (Young person) (Kendrick and Mapstone (1991), p. 165)

However, there were a number of children who reported a level of ambivalence about not only attending but the review process as a whole:

> I wouldn't mind if there weren't any reviews. It wouldn't put me up nor down. (Young person) (p. 172)

Decision-making also relates to the ways in which children's views are sought and respected in relation to their everyday lives. For example, research conducted with children and young people in residential care has illustrated the range of ways that they may be involved about decisions which affect their day-to-day lives: participating in the selection and appointment of care staff, house meetings, support groups for foster children, planning menus and going shopping (Berridge and Brodie 1998; Sinclair and Gibbs 1998). Children have also shown the ways in which they navigate around the decisions imposed on them by adults and their understanding of why such imposition takes place. For example, Emond's (2000) study of young people in residential care found there was a clear sense that, whilst adults controlled who was admitted to the unit, the young people could control the extent to which the new member was allowed to be admitted to their group. They were clear that adults made decisions about admission to care based on information which they were not party to. They did not appear to challenge the view that a child should be in care. However, they were of the view that whilst they couldn't control who they lived with they could control how they lived with them in terms of their inclusion and belonging within the resident group.

Barriers to participation

It may be argued that to legally require children's participation in decision-making about their current and future lives does not necessarily mean that this will influence the decisions made. As Annetts states:

Although the UN Convention on the rights of the child sought to give children a voice, the construction of children as not able and needing protection mitigates against their serious involvement in contributing to the making of decisions that affect them. (Annetts 2005, p. 32)

Clearly, children are not one homogeneous group. Their capabilities, wants and needs will be determined by their age, abilities, experiences and knowledge. However, that children's rights are seen as different from adults' rights appears to be centrally concerned with children's capacity to reason and to emotionally and cognitively process information to produce 'good' decisions. There remains a deep-seated tension between the protection agenda and the support for children's (protected) development. This is to some extent played out in the debates surrounding children's capacity to make decisions, their potential need for protection from such decisions and the subsequent role of adults. The result can be care and protection prevailing over children's rights as autonomous citizens (Cemlyn and Briskman 2003).

Children and young people themselves have identified factors in their external world which serve to inhibit their level of participation in decision-making. In a study conducted in England by Munro (2001), children stated the negative impact that frequent changes in social workers had on their experience of participation. This was made worse by lack of consultation over the location of reviews, the lack of preparation undertaken with them for these meetings and a lack of clarity concerning their purpose. She argues that both social workers and children felt that they were unable to be creative in their approach for fear of making mistakes. By contrast, children talked of the hugely positive benefit that 'good social workers' had on their experiences of reviews. These workers took time to build a relationship with the child, undertook to prepare the child and his or her parents for the structure and function of the review and how and what they might want to contribute.

Similar findings were produced in studies conducted in Scotland. For example, Hallet and Murray's (1998) extensive study of the children's hearing system identified a range of factors which children and young people regarded as inhibiting their participation in proceedings. Such barriers included feeling inhibited or frightened, and having to speak out in front of a large group of people and/or strangers. Again, many of these feelings appeared to stem from a more general lack of preparation for the hearing itself, much like the young people in Kendrick and Mapstone's study (1991).

It would appear that adults seek to retain the power to include or exclude children from participation and that many of these decisions are based not only on the impact that participation might have on the child but also how the child is likely to 'perform' (Thomas and O'Kane 1999). Such studies have also found that children are more likely to attend review meetings if their situation is seen as stable and/or if it is unlikely that no major decisions will be made. By their very nature, reviews and hearings for children in looked-after care have an emotive content. They are forums where the experiences that children and their parents have had are discussed and where plans are made for the future care of the child. In that respect children can find it even more difficult to present as controlled and 'mature'. That Article 12 suggests that the weight afforded to the views expressed by the child is dependent on 'age and maturity' allows for children's voices to be expressed only within particular parameters and even where this does occur, their voices may not necessarily be listened to. It is of note that children themselves have made the distinction between feeling listened to (which the majority did) and having influence (which was the case for less than a third of the sample group) (Thomas and O'Kane 1999).

Conclusion

Any discussion about children's rights is necessarily concerned with how children are viewed and understood. Over recent years we have been witness to a growing expectation that children have their views and experiences listened and responded to. Such a shift has occurred as a result of wider changes to society's construction of childhood, fundamentally as a time of innocence and purity. The growing recognition of children as 'able citizens' has added momentum to a movement which seeks, not only to protect children, but to actively involve them in this process.

This current state of childhood and the responses to it is in many ways highly sophisticated. It is a finely balanced position between recognising and respecting the abilities of children whilst at the same time viewing them as inherently vulnerable. It may be argued that the emphasis on hearing (and responding to) children's voices, giving them tangible and measurable rights, has been a global attempt at making these abstract ideas concrete. Perhaps as a way of managing the complexities of this position, children have increasingly been viewed as 'victims' or 'villians' (Harden and Scott 1998). Trinder (1997) argues that this process of classification is even more apparent amongst professionals working with children. Such children are 'classified as either subjects or objects, competent or incompetent, reliable or unreliable, harmed by decision making or harmed by exclusion, wanting to participate or not wanting to participate' (Trinder 1997, p. 301).

It is not just children who are unique and therefore hard to categorise, it is also the relationships that exist for them, between child and parent, child and teacher, child and friend etc. Rights theories are, argues Alderson (1994, as cited in Brownlie and Anderson 2006), too impersonal to explain all the varied complex relationships even between children and parents.

Crucially, it would appear that whilst children's rights may partially serve to ensure that all children are afforded the basics of shelter, food and water to grow and develop in safety, they do not in themselves provide the answer. Rights are legal obligations imposed on society by the state. They are not cultural changes in values, beliefs and practices by adults towards children. As King and Piper state, 'To see social relations in terms of "rights" is also to structure and understand the world in a very different way than to evaluate them, for example, according to the level of love or trust they contain' (King and Piper 1995, as cited in Smith 1997, p. 12).

Rights therefore may be seen as a product of a society which seeks to measure and monitor that which is intrinsically qualitative in nature: love, respect, security, trust, reliability and responsiveness.

References

Abrams, L. (1998) *The Orphan Country: Children of Scotland's Broken Homes from 1845 to the Present Day.* Edinburgh: John Donald Publishers Ltd.

Alderson, P. (2000) 'School students' views on School Councils and daily life at school.' *Children and Society 14*, 2, 121–34.

Annetts, J. (2005) 'Childhood and family life?' In J. Beech, O. Hand, M.A. Mulhern and J. Weston (eds) *The Individual and Community Life: A Compendium of Scottish Ethnology*, vol. 9. Edinburgh: John Donald in association with The European Ethnological Research Centre and The National Museums of Scotland.

Aries, P. (1962) *Centuries of Childhood: A Social History of Family Life.* New York: Alfred A. Knopf.

Berridge, D. and Brodie, I. (1998) *Children's Homes Revisited.* London: Jessica Kingsley Publishers.

Brownlie, J. and Anderson, S. (2006) '"Beyond anti-smacking": Re-thinking parent-child relations.' *Childhood 13*, 4, 479–498.

Cantwell, B. and Scott, S. (1995) 'Children's wishes, children's burdens.' *Journal of Social Welfare and Family Law 17*, 3, 337–53.

Cemlyn, S. and Briskman, L. (2003) 'Asylum, children's rights and social work.' *Child and Family Social Work 8*, 3, 163–78.

Colton, M. (2002) 'Factors associated with abuse in residential child care institutions.' *Children and Society 16*, 1, 33–44.

Emond, R. (2000) 'Survival of the Skilful: An Ethnographic Study of Two Groups of Young People in Residential Care.' Unpublished PhD, University of Stirling.

Etzioni, A. (1993) *The Spirit of Community: Rights, Responsibilities and the Communitarian Agenda.* New York: Crown Publishers.

Freeman, M. (1983) *The Rights and Wrongs of Children.* London: Pinter.

Greene, S. and Hogan, D. (eds) (2005) *Researching Children's Experience: Approaches and Methods.* London: Sage.

Hallet, C. and Murray, C. with Jamieson, J. and Veitch, B. (1998) *The Evaluation of Children's Hearings in Scotland: Deciding in Children's Interests*, vol 1. Edinburgh: Scottish Office Central Research Unit.

Harden, J. and Scott, S. (1998) 'Risk anxiety and the social construction of childhood.' Paper presented at the International Sociological Association World Congress, Montreal, July 1998.

Hodgson, D. (1999) 'Children's rights.' In D. Shemmings (ed.) *Involving Children in Family Support and Protection.* London: The Stationery Office.

Howe, D. (1994) 'Modernity, postmodernity and social work.' *British Journal of Social Work 25*, 5, 513–32.

James, A., Jenks, C. and Prout, A. (1998) *Theorizing Childhood.* Cambridge: Polity Press.

James, A.L. and James, A. (2001) 'Tightening the net: Children, community and control.' *British Journal of Sociology 52*, 2, 211–28.

Kendrick, A. (2000) 'The views of the child: Article 12 and the development of children's rights in Scotland.' Poster presentation to the 13th International Congress on Child Abuse and Neglect. Durban, 3–6 September 2000. http://personal.strath.ac.uk/andrew.kendrick/article12Kendrick.pdf, accessed on 30 April 2007.

Kendrick, A. (2005) 'Social exclusion and social inclusion: Themes and issues in residential child care.' In D. Crimmens and I. Milligan (eds) *Facing Forward: Residential Child Care in the 21st Century.* Lyme Regis: Russell House Publishing.

Kendrick, A. and Mapstone, E. (1991) 'Who decides? Child care reviews in two Scottish social work departments.' *Children and Society 5*, 2, 165–81.

Kent, R. (1997) *Children's Safeguards Review.* Edinburgh: Scottish Office.

Mayall, B. (2002) *Towards a Sociology for Childhood: Thinking from Children's Lives.* Buckingham: Open University Press.

Munro, E. (2001) 'Empowering looked after children.' *Child and Family Social Work 6*, 2, 129–37.

Parton, N. (1987) *Governing the Family: Child Care, Child Protection and the State.* London: Macmillan.

Parton, N. (1994) 'Problematics of government (post modernity) and social work.' *British Journal of Social Work 24*, 1, 10–32.

Scottish Executive (2002) *It's Everyone's Job to Make Sure I'm Alright: Report of the Child Protection Audit and Review.* Edinburgh: Scottish Executive.

Sinclair, I. and Gibbs, I. (1998) *Children's Homes: A Study in Diversity.* Chichester: Wiley.

Sinclair, R. (1996) 'Children's and young people's participation in decision-making: The legal framework in social services and education.' In M. Hill and J. Aldgate (eds) *Child Welfare Services: Developments in Law, Policy, Practice and Research.* London: Jessica Kingsley Publishers.

Smith, C. (1997) 'Children's rights: Have carers abandoned values?' *Children and Society 11*, 1, 3–15.

Thomas, N. and O'Kane, C. (1999) 'Experiences of decision-making in middle childhood: The example of children "looked after" by local authorities.' *Childhood 6*, 3, 369–88.

Trinder, L. (1997) 'Competing constructions of childhood: Children's rights and wishes in divorce.' *Journal of Social Welfare and Family Law 19*, 3, 291–305.

Utting, W. (1997) *People Like Us: The Report on the Review of Safeguards for Children Living Away from Home.* London: Stationery Office.

Willow, C. (2000) 'Safety in numbers? Promoting children's rights in public care.' In D. Crimmens and J. Pitts (eds) *Positive Residential Practice: Learning the Lessons of the 1990s.* Lyme Regis: Russell House Publishing.

CHAPTER 14

Therapeutic Approaches in Residential Child Care

Irene Stevens and Judy Furnivall

Introduction

It is perhaps an indictment of the state of residential child care that there are only some types of residential provision which are specifically *therapeutic* in terms of their practice. After all, residential child care establishments are dealing with some of the most damaged and vulnerable children and young people in society (Berridge and Brodie 1998; Department of Health 1998). Even more worryingly, the poor outcomes for children and young people who leave residential care are well documented, and a disproportionate number of adults in prisons, drug rehabilitation centres and psychiatric wards have been in care as children (Edwards *et al.* 2005; Social Work Services Inspectorate and Prisons Inspectorate 1998). For example, one study found that 'lifetime use of any drug among young people living in institutions was twice as high as in the household survey' (Edwards *et al.* 2005, p. 2). This has prompted central government and policy-makers to ask a question about how residential child care can be more explicitly therapeutic in its orientation.

Since the mid-1990s there has been a renewed interest in therapeutic approaches to residential care, and, more generally, in the ways that residential child care can provide a positive choice for children and young people. In 1997, the New Labour agenda placed social services under a degree of public and political criticism. However, the new government was prepared to increase resources and the residential sector in England was boosted by the innovative Quality Protects initiative which funded the development of policy, practice and research in areas such as the health and education of children in care (Department of Health 1999).

In recent times, residential child care does appear to be more securely located in terms of the policy agenda and has become the focus of a number of central government initiatives which have aimed to improve the quality of the sector. Endorsements about the value and place of residential care demonstrate that policy-makers have a degree of commitment to residential child care (Skinner 1992; Utting 1991). These reports implicitly suggest the need for therapeutic services. Similarly, reports into the abuse of children in residential settings highlight the need for a more purposeful approach to interventions while the child is in care. For example, recommendation 65(d) of the Waterhouse report, which examined allegations of abuse in Wales, stated that 'all residential placements should be designed to be developmental and therapeutic rather than merely custodial' (Waterhouse 2000, p. 856).

When examining therapeutic approaches to residential child care, it is important to have some discussion about what is meant by this. Kendrick and Fraser (1992) looked at a variety of definitions in their review of residential child care. They highlighted the diversity of residential care and outlined some definitions which might be associated with therapeutic approaches. Terms such as *therapeutic community* and *therapeutic milieu* suggest a totality of provision within the care setting, where all aspects of group living contribute to the well-being of the child or young person. Other settings where therapeutic interventions may be assumed to take place would be in *residential treatment centres* and in centres which operate *milieu therapy*. However, as Kendrick and Fraser point out, these terms are not used consistently. Residential care units which used one of these labels were likely to adhere to a particular theoretical orientation in their approach to work with children and that this theoretical approach 'fitted into a range which begins with psychoanalytic/psychodynamic theory and ends with behaviour modification/learning theory' (Kendrick and Fraser 1992, p. 7). As well as reflecting a particular theoretical perspective, therapeutic interventions can be applied in a holistic way, or as a discrete part of the total care package for the child. It will be argued in this chapter that a diverse range of therapeutic approaches to residential child care does indeed exist and that they can be used to meet the varied and complex needs presented by children and young people who come into residential care.

Holistic therapeutic approaches: Therapeutic communities

The therapeutic community is a specialised residential unit for children, which usually has education on site. It is organised on the basis of offering planned therapeutic help and support over a long term, usually at least three to four years. The theoretical base of the therapeutic community is explicitly psychodynamic. The existence of and effects of the unconscious mind are key concepts within the rationale of interventions for these establishments. As Brearley (1991) stated:

> Psychodynamic practice is seen as predominantly concerned with certain key relationships, namely, those between self and significant other people, past and present experience, and inner and outer reality. (Brearley 1991, p. 19)

Within a therapeutic community, all interactions within the unit are potentially therapeutic in nature. Staff are part of this equation, because they are viewed as participants within the community. The impact of staff dynamics upon an institution was explored most effectively by Menzies-Lyth (1988). When studying medical staff working on wards with seriously ill patients, she said that staff pool anxieties into a collective defence which may inhibit work. This defensive stance is an unconscious reaction to the stressful and highly traumatic activity of working with people who are ill. In a similar way, dealing with emotionally and behaviourally disturbed children is in itself highly traumatic and anxiety provoking. The psychodynamic rationale of the therapeutic community would suggest that staff have to deal with these unconscious defensive reactions in order to work effectively. Hence, the therapeutic community approach is holistic and not just confined to the therapeutic 'hour', group work, family work or unit meetings.

Therapeutic communities do not offer one blueprint for practice but follow many different approaches. Perhaps the one common element is that they are based on the need for staff to understand child development and the impact of early separation, deprivation and trauma. This can be demonstrated by examining the various types of therapeutic community which evolved in Britain over the twentieth century, as reported by Campling and Haigh (1999). During this time, the establishment of such communities was guided by the ideas of charismatic leaders driven by a sense that they could improve the lot of 'deprived' children and enhance their development through the application of particular ideas. The Caldecott Community, founded by Leila Randall, started as a residential community in London in 1917 and moved three times before it ended up in Kent in its final form in 1947. She wanted to help 'underprivileged' and 'deprived' children to reach their full potential using a combination of care, education and treatment. The influence of theoretical perspectives could be seen in the application of the ideas of Maria Montessori on the work of this community.

Summerhill School also demonstrated the importance of an overriding ideological approach. Within Summerhill, lessons were not compulsory and rules were decided at weekly meetings, by groups of adults and children, reflecting the notion of 'community'. Later times saw the explicit development of psychodynamic approaches. The Mulberry Bush School, set up by Barbara Docker-Drysdale in 1948, established strong links with the Tavistock Institute in London, and was clearly psychodynamic in orientation.

The first resource for children to name itself a therapeutic community was Peper Harow. Established in the early 1970s, it encouraged adolescents to re-experience their childhood so that the community could undo some of the damage done by their early childhood experiences. Under the leadership of its charismatic head, Melvyn Rose, it championed and widely publicised the therapeutic community approach and as such influenced work in a myriad of residential settings. Although the original Peper Harow closed, the Peper Harow Foundation continues to initiate new projects for children with emotional, social and behavioural difficulties.

The Peper Harow Foundation was also the impetus behind the establishment of the Charterhouse Group, a group of therapeutic communities for young people, in 1987. The founder members of the Charterhouse Group wished to ensure that an active voice for the continuation and development of a psychodynamic treatment approach for children and young people was heard. Member organisations adhere to therapeutic community and psychodynamic principles within their practice framework. The work of writers such as Winnicott (1965) continues to be very influential in the development of the therapeutic approaches used by these communities. Winnicott was interested in child development from its earliest stages, and in the role of *holding* children, both physically and emotionally. This idea of holding extended to groups of staff working within the communities, and this is generally facilitated through the use of external supervision. Tomlinson (2004), in relation to the work of the Cotswold Community, identified how the development of a 'thinking culture', where all staff were fully engaged in the process of intervention, was crucial to its approach.

The work of therapeutic communities for children and young people is under-researched. As Ward and his colleagues commented: 'In today's "evidence-based" terms its effectiveness is still technically unproven...' (Ward *et al.* 2003, p. 13). One piece of research into the work of a therapeutic community was the study by Little, in association with a young person called Siobhan Kelly (Little and Kelly 1995). This piece of research looked at the work of the Caldecott Community, and gave an in-depth description and analysis of the experience of one young woman. The experiences and words of Siobhan were interspersed with commentary from Little, which gave an excellent insight into the therapeutic community. Little examined outcomes for young people from the Caldecott Community and found that it provided as much stability as any other option. His figures indicated that children from 'fragmented families or exhibiting behavioural difficulties' were the most likely to do well, compared with children who were long-term victims of abuse (Little and Kelly 1995, p. 178). He also found that family involvement with children was also a good indicator of a successful outcome.

Discrete therapeutic approaches

Lifespace or opportunity-led work

Therapeutic approaches in residential child care are not necessarily about an all-encompassing philosophy, such as that practised within therapeutic communities. The therapeutic use of daily life events in residential settings has been highlighted in the literature, and perhaps constitutes a more naturalistic approach than therapeutic communities. Ward (2000) defined this as *opportunity-led work*. When describing opportunity-led work, he spoke of the difference between *reacting* and *responding*. For Ward, reacting to a situation in a residential setting was where the practitioner made a response to the immediate situation without thinking about this. This kind of hasty judgement could lead to the practitioner missing out on an opportunity to carry out a piece of work related to the situation. Responding is an action based on good judgement. It is a more considered response which leads to a potential for growth and change in the young person. For example, it may be part of a young person's care plan that he or she begins to address inappropriate behaviour caused by anger. One way to do this might be by having individual sessions with the key worker. However, Ward would suggest that a better way of dealing with this might be if the young person becomes angry because he or she is challenged, for example, about not carrying out chores. If the practitioner works with the young person while he or she is angry and helps him or her to work through these feelings in a more constructive way, this may be more beneficial. In this way, the work is *opportunity led* insofar as the residential practitioner works with whatever opportunities arise in the day-to-day life of the unit.

This type of intervention has similarities to working in the *lifespace*. Work in the lifespace recognises the potential for communication with young people that is provided by shared life experiences. Daily life events, which are shared by residential practitioners and young people in residential settings, are exploited by the team to help the young people gain an understanding of their life experiences. This approach is heavily influenced by existentialism as espoused by writers such as Buber and Marcel, cited in Creswell (1998). Existential practice concerns what Redl and Wineman (1957) refer to as the *act of presence* with the child. One worker put this well when she said that, 'I was the one who ate with him, I was the one who held him, I was the one who read him stories at night' (Sladde 2003, p. 6). Writers such as Brendtro and Ness (1983) and Anglin *et al.* (1990) comment upon how this existential understanding can become the foundation from which support is given to the young person to develop his or her strengths. A key aspect of working in the lifespace is the opportunity for the development of close working relationships between young people and staff. These relationships can be extremely positive. Lefrancois (1999) found that young people in residential care had greater opportunities to find someone with whom they could make a connection and build up a trusting relationship. This concurs with findings from young people themselves. For example, in one Scottish report a young person commented, 'If there's something you need to talk about, think of a staff you can trust and go and talk to that staff and that builds up the relationship between you and the staff which means you can trust each other' (Paterson, Watson and Whiteford 2003, p. 14).

Working in the lifespace, therefore, involves the *conscious* use of the everyday opportunities that present themselves in residential work, to engage meaningfully with children and young people about what is happening in their lives. As Smith (2005) pointed out, a child's seeming misbehaviour in the 'here and now' may reflect emotions or responses that have their roots in past experience. This approach requires that residential practitioners build up a knowledge and understanding of children's personal histories in order to make sense of their behaviours in the present. Workers also need to maintain an appropriate balance between understanding where particular behaviours might be coming from in terms of past experiences and presenting a safe and authoritative adult response in the 'here and now'. Garfat's work on *meaning-making* is also highly relevant to lifespace interventions (Garfat 1998, 2004). If an event occurs in a residential unit, both staff and young people involved in the event will create a meaning for the event based on their current circumstances, their past experiences and the environment and culture around them. If the workers understand the process of meaning-making for the young person, their helping interventions with them can be much more effective. Meaning-making involves not just taking a situation at face value. Here, we can see a link with Ward's concept of responding.

In order to implement effective lifespace interventions, workers need to be able to create a therapeutic *milieu* within the unit. The term 'milieu' is not particularly tangible, but could be referred to as the 'feel' of the unit. Anyone who has set foot in a residential unit picks up very quickly on its atmosphere. They can detect whether there is a tension, or a sense of calm. The 'feel' of a unit is fundamental to how it is perceived, and will have a profound impact on the experiences of the children and young people placed there. Residential practitioners need to identify the elements involved in shaping the milieu, in order that they can influence it for the benefit of children and young people. A range of variables will impact on the milieu. Some examples might be the physical design, the organisational culture or the composition of resident and staff group. The importance of physical environment is highlighted by Trieschman (1969) and Maier (1982). Maier suggests, quoting Redl and Wineman (1957), that the layout of a building should be arranged to ensure 'an area which smiles, with props that invite, and space which allows' (Maier 1982, p. 57). Research into the importance of interior design in residential units in Scotland also demonstrated the importance attached by staff and young people to pleasant surroundings in the unit (Docherty *et al.* 2006).

Lifespace work is purposeful and should contribute to the overall development of the child. Developmental group care has become a significant theme in residential child care and is synonymous with the work of Maier (1979). He identifies seven essential components of care: bodily comfort, differentiation, rhythmic interaction, predictability, dependability, personalised behavioural training and care for the caregiver. Maier, in common with other writers, discussed the centrality of relationships between practitioners and children as the key factor in encouraging development. Fulcher and Ainsworth (1981) emphasised the role of group care to child development and also highlighted the importance of relationships in contributing to continuous assessments and effective interventions in the lifespace.

Maier's work on the *core of care* (1979) introduced terms such as *rhythm* and *ritual* as ways of conceptualising how units operate. Rhythm is the process through which the worker and the young person find a comfortable way of being together. The idea of rhythm can also be applied at an organisational level, to convey the sense of order and predictability in the patterns of daily living in a home. Rituals are those practices that become embedded in a unit's way of working and which have a significance and special meaning to the staff and children who engage in them. Examples of the kind of rituals that can develop between workers and young people might be settling on bean bags to watch a television programme. Maier spoke of the individual and the organisational level in terms of unit functioning. Brown *et al.* (1998) also spoke of the importance of a high degree of congruence between policy, organisational, unit and individual goals. Their study into the structure and culture of units in England demonstrated that structure determines staff culture which determines child culture which determines outcomes for units and children. By structure they meant 'the orderly arrangement of social relationships within the home, governed by its societal, formal and belief goals' and by culture they meant 'the shared understandings of staff and residents' (Brown *et al.* 1998, p. 133). Once again, we can see how the idea of the 'feel' of the unit is defined.

Cognitive-behavioural approaches

Cognitive-behavioural approaches are based on the assertion that changes in behaviour can occur through the ways in which people understand, interpret and can alter their thinking in relation to events in their life. A variety of cognitive-behavioural approaches are now being incorporated into residential child care, with a clear therapeutic aim.

Sheldon (1995) provides a helpful definition of cognitive-behavioural approaches by saying that they seek to change behaviour:

by modifying the environmental contingencies that surround it; weakening previous conditioned associations which have resulted in maladaptive emotional reactions; offering clients more effective models of problem-solving and interpersonal behaviour, and seeking to change the ways in which stimuli are recognized and interpreted in the first place. (Sheldon 1995, p. 46)

Cognitive-behavioural approaches have their roots in behavioral psychology. Three theorists were particularly influential in their development. Skinner's work on behaviourism (1953) postulated that all behaviour is learned and can be understood in terms of reinforcers. Bandura's ideas (1977) built upon this but also emphasised that learning takes place in a social milieu and therefore cannot truly be understood unless account is taken of this. Ellis (1973) developed these ideas into cognitive-behavioural therapy. He said that maladaptive thoughts cause maladaptive feelings which in turn cause maladaptive behaviour. Hence, maladaptive behaviour can be transformed by asking questions which create cognitive conflict and force the person to alter his or her ideas.

Within residential child care, these interventions are routinely used in the field of learning disability, with behavioural analysis, clearly structured positive reinforcement, extinction of behaviour, and shaping using behavioural techniques. These are purely behavioural techniques, and the influence of Skinner can be clearly seen.

In mainstream residential child care, the use of cognitive-behavioural approaches is more piecemeal. Where they are used, particularly in secure accommodation, the tendency is toward using response control techniques, which are associated with the work of Bandura and Ellis. According to Sheldon (1995), there are four main types of response control techniques:

1. *Social skills training*: this is used where young people have a gap in their social skills. For example, they may not know the conventions for asking for something at the table while eating. They may snatch food, or demand something. A social skills training programme would involve the demonstration of competent behaviour. Discussion would take place to identify possible misinterpretations leading to problems. Rehearsal of new behaviour at the table would be put into place, and the new social skill should then be learned.

2. *Assertiveness training*: if a young person is either too passive or too aggressive, he or she may not know how to be assertive. This technique involves teaching the young person to distinguish between assertive, aggressive and submissive behaviour, and encourages role-play and discussion to practise the new behaviour.

3. *Self-control*: this involves young people becoming aware of situations that elicit maladaptive behaviour, particularly responses elicited by their anger. By becoming aware of these, they may avoid them. Alternatively, the techniques may encourage new associations in their mind with whatever provokes the behaviour, therefore changing the outcome. Finally, it may be about teaching young people to reward themselves for maintaining a newly learned and more adaptive piece of behaviour.

4. *Self-instruction*: this involves teaching the young person to develop an *internal dialogue* with him- or herself by making helpful self statements. The young person actively imagines a problem situation and interrupts this with 'new' instructions.

Stevens (2004), in her review of cognitive-behavioural interventions in residential child care, explored several issues in relation to the use of cognitive-behavioural approaches. She found that if staff have not had the training in assessment, child development or the theoretical basis of cognitive-behavioural interventions, they revert to their 'natural inclinations' and do not apply the interventions consistently. Alternatively, they may take their lead from the workplace staff culture, which was shown to be an important factor in the study on treatment outcomes by Gibbs and Sinclair (1999). These attitudes and values could affect the outcome of cognitive-behavioural approaches, for better or for worse.

Another issue concerned generalisation. There seemed to be a lingering question around the generalisation of cognitive skills, learned through cognitive-behavioural interventions, to the wider world. This has implications for the long-term goals of approaches. For example, in one of the few long-term follow-ups, Valliant (1993) indicated that eight out of ten adolescent boys had been imprisoned for offending behaviour a year after the interventions. Studies indicated that cognitive-behavioural approaches were more likely to be generalised to the outside world when integrated with other aspects of the young person's life such as peers (Duan and O'Brien 1998), parents (Sinclair and Gibbs 1998) or school (Thyer and Larkin 1999).

Sheldon (1995) emphasised this issue when looking at the use of cognitive-behavioural interventions in residential care. He stated that if a young person sees no distinction between behavioural change for *therapeutic* reasons and behavioural change for *institutional* reasons, the new behaviour or cognitive process may only exist within that setting and may not be carried on outside the setting.

Therapeutic approaches and children's rights

It could be argued that the use of particular therapeutic approaches may raise questions about children's rights, in relation to the need for free and informed consent when undergoing any intervention which may be seen as 'therapeutic'. The participation of children and young people and eliciting their views has been an important principle since the ratification of the United Nations Convention on the Rights of the Child (UNCRC). In particular, Article 12 of the UNCRC, which refers to the child's right to be heard, has been enshrined in the Children Act (1989) in England and the Children (Scotland) Act (1995). Encouraging the participation of children and young people in making decisions about their care presents a challenge to residential units. The power and role of discourses in society has been discussed widely in the work of the post-modernist philosophers such as Foucault. Harvey (1990) when commenting on Foucault's account of the relationship between knowledge, power and rhetoric said that:

> close scrutiny of the micro-politics of power relations in different localities, contexts and social situations leads him to conclude that there is an intimate relation between the systems of knowledge ('discourses') which codify techniques and practices for the exercise of social control and domination within particular contexts. (Harvey 1990, p. 45)

It is suggested that residential child care units are sites where these micro-political processes can be seen at work. The post-modernist philosophers also raise the issue of power, and whose voices are heard in discourses. Children in residential child care tend to be among the most powerless in social terms and the voices which are heard in relation to them are rarely informed by their actual views. For example, Sinclair (1998) in her review of the involvement of children in planning their care expressed concern at the absence of children's own words from reports and records. Children's views were reported in 'a very passive style' (Sinclair 1998, p. 138) by social workers, and their own words or direct quotes were rarely used. Given the relative powerlessness of young people in residential care, it is clear that residential staff and their parent organisations must be careful that they obtain permission from young people to work with them using such therapeutic approaches. It is also important that staff members and managers are clear and explicit about the reasons for the approaches being used.

Conclusion

The residential child care sector plays a significant role in the care of some of the most difficult and demanding children and young people. It has become clear that if such children are to be cared for safely *and* therapeutically then they need staff carefully selected and operating to high standards of professionalism. There needs to be a continuing emphasis on improving the therapeutic nature of residential care. Evidence of this new reality is found in the call made by Sir William Utting for new children's homes to be opened up in parts of England. He felt this was necessary in order to create *choice* of placement; a choice which he felt had been much diminished by the systematic closure of residential units over the previous 20 years. By encouraging diversity and an openness to explore different approaches, the residential child care sector may fulfil its potential.

References

Anglin, J., Carey, J., Denholm, R., Ferguson, V. and Pence, A.R. (1990) *Perspectives in Professional Child and Youth Care.* New York: Haworth Press.

Bandura, A. (1977) *Social Learning Theory.* London: Prentice-Hall.

Berridge, D. and Brodie, I. (1998) *Children's Homes Revisited.* London: Jessica Kingsley Publishers.

Brearley, J. (1991) 'Psychodynamic approach.' In J. Lishman (ed.) *Handbook of Theory for Practice Teachers in Social Work.* London: Jessica Kingsley Publishers.

Brendtro, L.K. and Ness, A.E. (1983) *Re-Educating Troubled Youth: Environments for Teaching and Treatments.* New York: Aldine Publishing.

Brown, E., Bullock, R., Hobson, C. and Little, M. (1998) *Making Residential Care Work: Structure and Culture in Children's Homes.* Aldershot: Ashgate Publishing.

Campling, P. and Haigh, R. (1999) *Therapeutic Communities: Past, Present and Future.* London: Jessica Kingsley Publishers.

Creswell, J.W. (1998) *Qualitative Inquiry and Research Design.* London: Sage.

Department of Health (1998) *Caring for Children Away from Home: Messages from Research.* Chichester: Wiley.

Department of Health (1999) *The Government's Objectives for Children's Social Services.* London: Department of Health.

Docherty, C., Kendrick, A., Lerpiniere, J. and Sloan, P. (2006) *Designing with Care: Interior Design and Residential Child Care.* Glasgow: Farm7 and Scottish Institute for Residential Child Care.

Duan, D.W. and O'Brien, S. (1998) 'Peer-mediated social skills training and generalisation in group homes.' *Behavioral Interventions 17*, 4, 235–47.

Edwards, K., Sumnall, H., McVeigh, J. and Bellis, M.A. (2005) *Drug Prevention in Vulnerable Young People.* Liverpool: National Collaborating Centre for Drug Prevention.

Ellis, A. (1973) *Humanistic Psychotherapy: The Rational-Emotive Approach.* New York: McGraw-Hill.

Fulcher, L. and Ainsworth, F. (1981) *Group Care for Children: Concepts and Issues.* London: Tavistock.

Garfat, T. (1998) 'The effective child and youth care intervention.' *Journal of Child and Youth Care 12*, 1–2, 1–178.

Garfat, T. (2004) 'Meaning making and intervention in child and youth care practice.' *Scottish Journal of Residential Child Care 3*, 1, 9–16.

Gibbs, I. and Sinclair, I. (1999) 'Treatment and treatment outcomes in children's homes.' *Child and Family Social Work 4*, 1, 1–8.

Harvey, D. (1990) *The Condition of Postmodernity.* Oxford: Blackwell.

Kendrick, A. and Fraser, S. (1992) *The Review of Residential Child Care in Scotland: A Literature Review.* Edinburgh: Scottish Office.

Lefrancois, G.R. (1999) *The Lifespan*, 6th edn. Belmont, CA: Wadsworth Publishing.

Little, M. and Kelly, S. (1995) *A Life without Problems? The Achievements of a Therapeutic Community.* Aldershot: Arena.

Maier, H. (1979) 'The core of care: Essential ingredients for the development of children at home and away from home.' *Child Care Quarterly 8*, 4, 161–73.

Maier, H. (1982) 'The space we create controls us.' *Residential Group Care and Treatment 1*, 51–9.

Menzies-Lyth, I. (1988) *Containing Anxiety in Institutions.* London: Free Association Books.

Paterson, S., Watson, D. and Whiteford, J. (2003) *Let's Face It! Young People Tell Us How It Is.* Glasgow: Who Cares? Scotland.

Redl, F. and Wineman, D. (1957) *Controls from Within: Techniques for Treatment of the Aggressive Child.* New York: Free Press.

Sheldon, B. (1995) *Cognitive-Behaviour Therapy: Research, Practice and Philosophy.* Routledge: London.

Sinclair, I. and Gibbs, I. (1998) *The Quality of Care in Children's Homes.* Report to the Department of Health. York: University of York.

Sinclair, R. (1998) 'Involving children in planning their care.' *Child and Family Social Work 3*, 2, 137–42.

Skinner, A. (1992) *Another Kind of Home.* Edinburgh: HMSO.

Skinner, B.F. (1953) *Science and Human Behaviour.* London: Collier Macmillan.

Sladde, L.R. (2003) 'On being a child and youth care worker.' *Child and Youth Care 21,* 8, 4–6.

Smith, M. (2005) *Working in the Lifespace.* In Residence, No. 2. Glasgow: Scottish Institute for Residential Child Care.

Social Work Services Inspectorate and the Prisons Inspectorate (1998) *Women Offenders: A Safer Way.* Edinburgh: The Stationery Office.

Stevens. I. (2004) 'Cognitive-behavioural interventions for adolescents in residential child care in Scotland: An examination of practice and lessons from research.' *Child and Family Social Work 9,* 3, 237–46.

Thyer, B.A. and Larkin, R. (1999) 'Evaluating cognitive-behavioral group counselling to improve elementary school students' self-esteem, self-control and class behavior.' *Behavioral Interventions 14,* 3, 147–61.

Tomlinson, P. (2004) *Therapeutic Approaches in Work with Traumatised Children and Young People: Theory and Practice.* London: Jessica Kingsley Publishers.

Trieschman, A.E. (1969) *The Other 23 Hours: Child Care Work with Emotionally Disturbed Children in a Therapeutic Milieu.* New York: Aldine.

Utting, W. (1991) *Children in the Public Care.* London: HMSO.

Valliant, P. (1993) 'Cognitive and behavioural therapy with adolescent males in a residential treatment centre.' *Journal of Child and Youth Care 8,* 3, 41–9.

Ward, A. (2000) 'Opportunity led work.' Paper presented at the 1st Annual Conference of the Scottish Institute for Residential Child Care, Glasgow, 4 June 2000.

Ward, A., Kasinski, K., Pooley, J. and Worthington, A. (eds) (2003) *Therapeutic Communities for Children and Young People.* London: Jessica Kingsley Publishers.

Waterhouse, R. (2000) *Lost in Care: Report of the Tribunal of Inquiry into the Abuse of Children in Care in the Former County Council Areas of Gwynedd and Clwyd since 1974.* London: The Stationery Office.

Winnicott, D.W. (1965) *The Maturational Process and the Facilitating Environment.* London: Hogarth Press.

CHAPTER 15

Staffing, Training and Recruitment

Outcomes for Young People in Residential Care in Three Countries

Claire Cameron and Janet Boddy

Introduction

Debates about safeguarding children in residential care (Kent 1997; Utting 1997) have drawn attention to the need for higher levels of qualification that is tailored to the specific residential care environment, highlighting questions about the nature of training for residential care work, the level at which training should be pitched and links between the preparedness of the workforce and the quality of care provided to young people. Government responses to these discussions have been to endorse social work training for managers and vocational qualifications for care workers (Department of Health 1998). Despite these policy drivers, the proportion of workers holding a qualification for residential care work – such as a Scottish or National Vocational Qualification (S/NVQ) Level 3 – remains low (Batty and Demopoulus 2005; Eborall 2003; Mainey 2003). In Scotland, there has been encouragement from government to incorporate European methods into professional training (Scottish Office 1998). More recently, the English government has also drawn attention to a European model of training – that of pedagogy – in discussions about new occupational models for work with children (Department for Education and Skills 2005a).

This chapter highlights key findings from a cross-national study that explored pedagogy and the work of pedagogues in children's residential settings, through a comparison of work in England, Denmark and Germany (see Petrie *et al.* 2006). In relation to staffing issues and to 'outcome' indicators for young people looked after, our findings show that residents in England are more likely to have difficulties than in Denmark or Germany. These cross-country differences may in part reflect wider variations, for example in populations of young people looked after, but more than that, the research indicated that the pedagogic approach – the integrity of a holistic, flexible knowledge base, supported by a degree-level qualification – was in itself associated with benefits for staff and young people looked after.

What is pedagogy?

In the English language, the term 'pedagogy' is usually familiar only in the context of referring to the science of teaching and learning in formal education settings (Mortimore 1999). In much of the rest of Europe, however, pedagogy has an additional meaning: it relates to overall support for children's development, and can be understood as 'education-in-its-broadest-sense' (Boddy, Cameron and Petrie 2005, p. 94). As such, pedagogy is about 'up-bringing' (*erziehung* in Germany, often cited as the birthplace of pedagogy in the nineteenth century).

Pedagogy in the continental European sense is a long-standing discipline and body of policy, research and practice relating to the overall support of a child's development or maintenance of his or her social, psychological and physical resources (Hansen 2004). Pedagogy is about the development of the whole child, and so learning, care, health, general well-being and development are viewed as inseparable. Within pedagogy, the nursery, classroom, out-of-school club or children's residential home are seen as 'life spaces'. In German, the term is *Lebenswelt* or 'living world', referring to sites for human relationships and the learning that accompanies social relations, springing from interaction. Each child is seen as a social being, connected to others but with his or her own distinctive experiences and knowledge. In particular, pedagogic theory emphasises the relationship between carer/worker and child: the practitioner sees her- or himself as a person in relationship with the child/young person, and, while together, the child and practitioner are seen as inhabiting the same life space, not existing in separate hierarchical domains. Moreover, the associative life of the group, whether composed of staff, young people or a mixture of the two, is highly valued.

Becoming a pedagogue

Across Europe, the education needed to become a pedagogue differs from the current UK systems of vocational qualifications in two key respects. First, pedagogy is a generalist education enabling graduates to work across sectors and age ranges, although there are opportunities for specialisation. Second, pedagogic education is not concerned with providing evidence of specific competencies, but is focused on developing knowledge and skills in four core areas: *theoretical work* in disciplines including pedagogy, law, psychology, sociology, health and education; *practice placements* which form a large component; *practical skills* such as drama, woodwork and environmental studies and *professional skills*, including communication, multidisciplinary working, teamwork and management skills.

In Denmark, pedagogues have degree-level training that qualifies them to work in a range of settings for children and young people, adults and older people. Training lasts for three and a half years full-time, of which one-third is practice placement. In Germany, the three main levels of pedagogic education each incorporate varying lengths of practice placements. The initial level is the most practice-oriented of the three, and is based on three or four years of full-time study, leading to qualification as an *erzieher*. The second level is a degree-level higher education diploma, akin to the Danish diploma, which takes four years of full-time study. Finally, the *Diplom-Sozialpädagoge* is equivalent to a Masters-level degree in the UK; this theoretically oriented qualification usually takes around seven years to complete.

By contrast to the pedagogic educational model, the current qualification for work in residential care in England is the NVQ 3 (equivalent to the English 'A' level) in 'Caring for Young People', awarded on the basis of demonstrated competencies in meeting given occupational standards. The award is usually workplace based and takes about 18 months to complete, although as learning takes place at the students' and assessors' pace, this can vary widely (Cameron, Carlisle and Moore 2003).

The study in context

In comparing work and life in residential care in Denmark, England and Germany, some contextual matters must first be acknowledged. Foremost, the populations of young people looked after differ across the countries, reflecting differences in policies about placement in residential care.

England has relatively few children looked after in public care, compared to Denmark or Germany. In 2003, 60,800 children were in local authority care in England (which has a national population of about 50 million), with just under ten per cent (5900) accommodated in residential settings (Department for Education and Skills 2005b). In Denmark, which has a population of 5.4 million, just over 14,000 children and young people were in placements outside of their homes in 2003 (Statbank Danmark 2003), and over 40 per cent (5934 children, about the same number as for the whole of England) were in residential placements. In Germany, with a population of 82.5 million, figures from 1998 showed that 59 per cent of young people in care (82,000) were placed in residential homes (Federal Statistical Office Germany 1998).

There are similarities across the three countries in much of the rhetoric of policy for children in public care, although there were differences in how policy objectives are implemented (Petrie *et al.* 2006). Policies emphasise that placements should be made as close to the young person's home as possible. In continental Europe, concern with the young person's social networks and 'living world' has led to diversification of placement models, including small local facilities and part-time residential settings (e.g. 'five-day settings', where residents return to their families of origin at the weekend). The English policy preference for foster care rather than residential placement has meant that residential care in this country tends to be used for young people who cannot be accommodated in foster care (Meltzer *et al.* 2003), while a decline in the number of children's homes in some areas has limited options for placement close to home.

Fundamentally, in Denmark and Germany, residential care is conceived as a positive placement choice for young people, an opportunity for therapeutic and developmental intervention. By contrast, the English approach has tended to conceptualise residential care as an emergency short-term option or a 'last resort' for young people.

Sample characteristics

Variations in policies and practice had an impact on sampling. Because the size of residential homes differed in each country, the number of establishments visited also varied, so that comparable numbers of young people could be interviewed in each country. In England, a sample of 100 young people was achieved by visiting 25 homes; in Denmark, 86 young people were interviewed in 12 establishments; and in Germany, 116 young people were interviewed in 19 residential homes.

Key sample characteristics are summarised in Table 15.1. In total, three groups of informants were interviewed: 55 residential home managers, 138 residential care staff (between two and four in each setting) and 302 resident young people (ranging from 2 to 12 per establishment). Managers also completed short questionnaires that included questions about the entire staff group (over 1000 across all 55 establishments), and recorded data from establishment records relating to young people resident in 2001 (information was missing from some establishments).

Staff characteristics

The gender, age and ethnicity of residential care workers were similar across the three countries. Between one-half and three-quarters of workers were female, ranging from 51 per cent in Denmark to 65 per cent in England and 77 per cent in Germany. This gender differential is less pronounced than in other forms of care work (Simon *et al*. 2003). The average age of the study residential care workers in all three countries was 39. There was some variation in the proportion of workers from minority ethnic, or, in the case of Denmark and Germany, 'non-national' backgrounds (from 27% in England to fewer than 10% in Germany and Denmark). This was mostly accounted for by a deliberate study aim of including the experiences of young people from minority backgrounds through sampling of residential homes in inner-city areas, where, in England, more workers from these backgrounds were likely to be employed.

Marked differences were evident in the extent to which staff held qualifications, and the level of qualifications. In comparing qualification levels across countries, it is necessary to understand what is available and expected in each country, and thus create comparative 'levels' of qualification (van Ewijk *et al*. 2002). Using van Ewijk's framework, the degree-level pedagogic qualification

Table 15.1 Characteristics of residential homes visited, as reported by managers			
Average N	*England (23 homes)*	*Germany (18 homes)*	*Denmark (12 homes)*
Young people			
Number resident in each living unit within the establishment	6.3	23.3	21.2
Aged 11 years or younger	0.13	5.9	5.7
Aged 12 to 15 years	4.7	8.7	9.9
Aged 16 and over	1.4	8.7	5.6
Rate of resident turnover in 2001	0.65	0.32	0.41
Staff			
Number of residential social workers/pedagogues	11.3	26.1	26.2
Total of all direct care staff (including, for example, teaching and nursing staff)	20.8	45.0	51.2
Staff-to-child ratio	3.7	2.1	2.5

in Denmark and Germany was classed as 'high level'; the German *erzeiher* qualification and English NVQ 3 were both designated 'mid-level'; NVQ 2 and
similar qualifications were classed as 'low level'.

Table 15.2 sets out the highest qualification reported by staff. Nearly all
(94%) the Danish pedagogues held a high-level qualification (some held social
work or psychology degrees rather than pedagogy), while this was the case for
half (51%) of the German workers and one-fifth (20%) of the English workers.
The German residential care workers were almost equally divided between
medium- and high-level qualifications, almost all in pedagogy. One-third of the
English workers held a medium-level qualification, including the NVQ 3, and a
further third either held no qualification or none that was relevant to their post,
indicating a diverse range of previous education prior to employment in
residential care. The English figures are broadly comparable with those found in
other studies (Brannen *et al.* 2007; McQuail 2001; TOPSS UK Partnership
2003), but most striking in the present context is the relative diversity of the
English workers' training. In Germany and Denmark, by contrast, pedagogy
provides a unifying theoretical and practice framework as preparation for work
in residential care.

**Table 15.2 Highest qualification for residential care,
reported by staff by country (numbers and percentages)**

	England N (%)	Germany N (%)	Denmark N (%)	Total N (%)
Low	4 (8)	0 (0)	0 (0)	4 (3)
Medium	18 (36)	22 (45)	1 (3)	41 (31)
High	10 (20)	25 (51)	30 (94)	65 (50)
Other child care qualification	0 (0)	1 (2)	0 (0)	1 (1)
No/no relevant qualification	18 (36)	1 (2)	1 (3)	20 (15)
Total	50 (100)	49 (100)	32 (100)	131 (100)

Recruitment and retention

Staff turnover was a major concern among English managers, with a permanent staff annual turnover rate of 27 per cent compared to 10 per cent across all public sector workers in England (Chartered Institute of Personnel and Development 2004); and compared with 18 per cent among German establishments and 10 per cent in the Danish homes. Almost all the English managers (22 of 25) said recruiting staff was difficult, compared to less than half of the German and none of the Danish managers. At the same time, half of the English managers found keeping staff difficult, compared to a tenth of those in Germany and none in Denmark.

These findings need to be considered in the context of staff views of their work. Across the three countries, over 90 per cent of staff interviewed said they were settled in their work, mostly because of commitment to the staff teams and to the children and young people. Two-thirds of the Danish informants also said they were committed to the ethos of the establishment compared to one-fifth of the English informants. The most commonly cited positive aspects of the work were as follows: in England, working with children's problems (82%); in Germany, relationships with children (90%); and in Denmark, both problems (90%) and relationships (92%) were seen as rewarding, as was working with colleagues (97%). Many fewer English and German informants mentioned working with colleagues as a positive aspect of the job (18% and 31% respectively).

Across all three countries, 'making a difference' to young people's lives was said to be an important source of reward for staff. For example, an English informant said a positive aspect of the work was 'when you get a really challenging child and who is aggressive and doesn't want to be told the rules and gradually you calm them and get them to almost enjoy living here and to integrate more'. The concept of 'being with' was expressed in particular by Danish pedagogues as rewarding. One pedagogue, for example, said she was rewarded through being 'together with the young people, maybe not for a long time, but that we are on their side and support them'.

However, between a third and a half of informants in each country had thought of leaving their present jobs, most of whom cited dissatisfaction with pay and conditions. A fifth (19%) of English and nearly a quarter (23%) of the German workers said the emotional and/or physical stress of the job was a reason for thinking of leaving, while this was less prevalent in Denmark (11%).

Overall, few staff were thinking of leaving because of the young people, indicative perhaps of an overarching commitment to this kind of work.

Difficulties with recruitment appeared to stem from the search for suitable people who would find the work meaningful, be qualified for the post and be willing to tolerate the working conditions. English managers predicted that this search would get progressively more difficult, citing a general shortage of qualified candidates, difficult working conditions (34%) and the low status of the work (18%) both within social work and as portrayed in the media. Heads agreed that a flexible approach to recruitment was required, such as a willingness to 'grow your own' staff through training programmes so they work 'to our ways', or offering support for job applicants to complete ongoing training. Recruiting suitable staff also relied on having a good local reputation, high staff ratios and a 'safe' place to work.

In both Germany and Denmark, the supply of pedagogically trained people available for work, as well as employment pressures in the wider economy, made recruiting staff largely unproblematic. Those German managers who faced recruitment difficulties (46%) related these to working conditions (70%), difficulties in obtaining properly qualified staff (30%), low status (18%) and pay (14%) and the availability of alternative attractive work (14%). However, some managers saw signs of problems ahead. Recruiting male staff, integrating new staff into established staff groups and conditions such as working shifts, relatively low salaries and high levels of work-related stress were all cited as emerging difficulties.

Difficulties in retaining staff in English establishments were primarily ascribed to two factors: the accommodation of young people with growing levels of need in residential care and what was seen as an increasingly off-putting working environment. Nine of the thirteen managers who had difficulties in retaining staff reported that violent behaviour among resident young people was becoming more commonplace. In the past, attending mainstream school and participating in organised activities were reported to have been the norm. This was said to have been replaced with a new set of norms: young people with criminal records, with rising levels of violence among residents, increasing numbers of assaults on staff, more absconding from the home and drug abuse, often related to other criminal activity.

English managers had devised a range of staff retention strategies to attend to this growing problem. These included structured entry to employment for workers, with probation and induction periods linking to qualifying training and an inclusive management ethos where the team feels valued, where there is a clear sense of direction and managers are available in a supportive capacity. Heads said they had to ensure they were seen as participatory, for instance doing weekend shifts, accompanying young people on outings and promoting group life, for example, by going out for meals as a group of staff and young people.

Taking an interest in the workers' wider lives was also seen as important, and wider policy measures were also seen by many English managers as helping to retain staff, by signalling wider interest in residential care. One manager spoke of 'having targets, goals and involvement in care of young people, and discussions which lead to better outcomes for them – and that encourages staff and increases satisfaction'. Targets for acquiring qualification awards highlighted the possibility for staff of making a career in children's services, rather than, as one manager put it, being seen as 'baby minders'. Managers of German establishments, who rarely had difficulty keeping staff once employed, attributed this success the value of the work (50%), with congenial conditions (58%); Danish managers emphasised that the staff liked working with the children (50%).

In summary, while there were some similarities in the characteristics of the residential care workforce in each of the three countries, their conditions of work were not the same. The extent to which the work is supported through educational qualifications differed markedly, with England having a workforce with much lower levels of qualifications. At the same time, English residential care managers encountered more difficulties with recruitment and retention, and higher staff turnover than their continental counterparts.

Young people in residential care

Turbulence among staff in the English homes was mirrored in the movement of young people in and out of the homes visited. English residential units were significantly smaller than those in Denmark and Germany, and less likely to accommodate children aged below 12 or over 15 years (Table 15.1), while having significantly higher turnover of young people – almost twice the rate reported in Germany. The average length of residence of young people interviewed in England was 11 months, compared with two years in Denmark and two and a half years in Germany. Half the English sample had been in their current placement for six months or less, and only 30 per cent for 12 months or more.

Some characteristics of the residents were similar across countries, such as the proportion who were nationals of their country, or had learning difficulties, or sensory or physical disabilities. The legal basis for placements, however, differed. Over 80 per cent of young people in Denmark and Germany were placed by voluntary agreement, compared with less than half in England. In addition, fewer than half of young people in the English homes had been placed within their local authority, compared with nearly three-quarters of those in Germany, and almost 90 per cent of Danish residents. This had a clear correspondence with contact with families, with fewer young people in England (75%) in contact with their families than was the case in Germany (93%) or Denmark (91%).

Staffing in relation to young people's 'life chances'

Interviews with managers and young people addressed a range of 'outcome indicators' in relation to health, education, employment and criminal offending. On all these indicators, English young people showed higher levels of disadvantage than their peers in Denmark and Germany:

- Twelve per cent of English under-16s were not attending school, compared with about two per cent of German and Danish residents in this age group.

- Among young people aged 16 and over, over half of English residents (55%) were not in education or employment, compared with around a quarter of German teenagers (23%) and five per cent of Danish young people.

- English managers reported almost four times the rate of pregnancies among residents under the age of 19 than was reported in Denmark, and more than twice that reported by German managers (average rate in English homes: 11.6%; Danish homes: 3.1%; German homes: 4.6%).

- The number of criminal offences committed by young people resident during the year 2001 was divided by the number of residents in 2001, to provide an index of the rate of offences per resident. In England, this figure was 1.73 offences per resident, compared with 0.092 in Germany and 0.158 in Denmark.

Such differences might to some extent be ascribed to characteristics of the care population in each country. In England at least, non-attendance of school and criminal behaviour can be factors in breakdown of foster placements and entry into residential care. And indeed, English young people in the homes participating in this study were more likely than their continental peers to have court ordered placements, or placements where criminal behaviour was a precipitating factor. Cross-country variations in the proportion of young people in education might reflect differences in provision of on-site educational services. Almost half of managers of Danish establishments stated that they provided education for residents, compared with a quarter of those in Germany and one in five English settings. Danish homes were also more likely to employ teachers, with an average of three teaching posts per establishment, compared with an average of 0.5 in Germany and England.

In considering why young people looked after in residential care in England do worse than those in other European countries, we must recognise that we are not comparing like with like. Poorer outcome indicators for English young people might reflect the fact that they are a behaviourally more challenging group, with greater disruption in terms of their placement history and their family circumstances. Our analysis – and any judgement about the value of social pedagogy – cannot ignore wider issues such as poverty, class and the welfare regimes of the countries in the research, all of which provide a context for young people's lives and opportunities, as well as for residential care provision. The differences observed in our sample, for example in the proportions out of education and employment, or experiencing teenage pregnancy, in part reflect this wider social context, which probably account for some of our findings.

Nevertheless, staff characteristics were the most important statistical predictors of outcome indicators such as engagement in education; the incidence of pregnancies under the age of 19; and rates of criminal offending. The different workforce characteristics observed in England, Germany and Denmark were also related to variation in child outcome indicators. For example, among under-16s, rates of non-school attendance were higher when more residential home staff had no qualifications ($r = 0.33$), and staff interviewed had worked for less time in the establishment ($r = -0.41$). For young people aged 16 or more, higher staff-to-child ratios were associated with a greater proportion of residents who were not in education or employment ($r =$

0.41). Lower rates of pregnancies among under-19s were reported in institutions where staff interviewed had higher rates of in-service training (r = -0.41) and intended to carry on in their current post for longer (r = -0.35).

This analysis describes associations between variables, not cause and effect. Nonetheless, it is striking that aspects of staff education and practice related directly to young people's well-being, such that a pedagogic approach was associated with lower levels of disadvantage. To make this observation is not to 'blame' residential care workers for the relative disadvantage of English young people, when compared with their Danish and German peers. Rather, the wider context in which English residential care workers are trained and conduct their practice must be taken into account. The differences we have described are not simply about workers' professionalism, or pedagogic education, although these are important, but are rooted in the policies, welfare regimes and cultural context of the countries studied.

Conclusion

Pedagogy, as understood in continental Europe, provides a coherent and well-established discourse underpinning policy and practice for all children, including those looked after. Policies for children and young people in public care in Denmark and Germany are explicitly pedagogic, and include legal requirements for a professionally educated workforce. While the professionalisation of the residential care workforce and the development of education is less advanced in England than in Denmark or Germany, a qualified workforce and the creation of a more coherent framework of qualifications for work with children are English government priorities. Policy documents such as *Every Child Matters* (Department for Education and Skills 2003) and the Children Act (2004) contain ideas and recommendations that accord with social pedagogic principles, such as 'educating through and for society and communities' (Hämäläinen 2003, p. 73). Just as the young person's developing independence and fulfilment of his or her potential are central to pedagogic work in continental European residential care, these principles are emphasised in the National Minimum Standards for Children's Homes (Department of Health 2002) in England and Wales, the Children Act (2004) and, similarly, in Scottish legislation, including the National Care Standards for Care Homes for Children and Young People (2002), and the Children (Scotland) Act (1995).

The question for England, and Scotland, is how such principled objectives can be met. In its response to the 2005 consultation on the children's workforce, the English government recognised that improvements in service quality would rely, in good part, on building a 'world-class' children's workforce, with established career pathways. It committed itself to developing, by 2010, an 'integrated qualifications framework'. In a parallel development, the green paper *Youth Matters* (Department for Education and Skills 2005c) endorsed the need for relationship-focused work with young people, as part of an 'integrated youth support service'. The professionalisation of the residential care workforce, through pedagogic education, and underpinned by pedagogic policies, could address these policy objectives. Most importantly, the analyses presented in this chapter suggest that a pedagogic approach is associated with substantially improved life chances for young people looked after in residential care.

Acknowledgements

This research was part of a project directed by Professor Pat Petrie, conducted by a team of researchers, including Antonia Simon and Valerie Wigfall, and overseas research associates including Inge Danielsen and Tim Tausendfreund. The study was funded by the Department for Education and Skills, to whom we offer our thanks. The views expressed here are those of the authors.

References

Batty, D. and Demopoulos, K. (2005) 'Care Home Workers' Training Target Missed.' *Guardian*, 24 February. www.guardian.co.uk/uk_news/story/0,,1424370,00.html, accessed on 3 May 2007.

Boddy, J., Cameron, C. and Petrie, P. (2005) 'The Professional Care Worker: The Social Pedagogue in Northern Europe.' In J. Boddy, C. Cameron and P. Moss (eds) *Care Work: Present and Future*. London: Routledge.

Brannen, J., Brockmann, M., Mooney, A. and Statham, J. (2007) *Coming to Care: The Work and Family Lives of Workers Caring for Vulnerable Children*. Bristol: Policy Press.

Cameron, C., Carlisle, J. and Moore, C. (2003) *Barriers to Lifelong Learning in the Care Workforce: A Study of NVQ Training for Social Care Workers in Cambridgeshire*. Cambridge: Cambridgeshire County Council/Learning and Skills Council.

Chartered Institute of Personnel and Development (2004) *Recruitment, Retention and Turnover 2004: A Survey of the UK and Ireland*. London. Available at: www.cipd.co.uk/subjects/recruitment/general/_recruitretnt04.htm, accessed on 3 May 2007.

Department for Education and Skills (2003) *Every Child Matters.* London: DfES. www.everychildmatters.gov.uk/_files/EBE7EEAC90382663E0D5BBF24C 99A7AC.pdf, accessed on 19 July 2007.

Department for Education and Skills (2005a) *Every Child Matters Children's Workforce Strategy: A Strategy to Build a World-Class Workforce for Children and Young People.* London: DfES. www.everychildmatters.gov.uk/files/ 7805B4A312A144238AED77508DCFED9B.pdf, accessed on 19 July 2007.

Department for Education and Skills (2005b) *Children Looked After in England (Including Adoptions and Care Leavers): 2003–2004.* Nottingham: DfES.

Department for Education and Skills (2005c) *Youth Matters.* Cm. 6629. Norwich: The Stationery Office.

Department of Health (1998) *The Government's Response to the Children's Safeguards Review.* Cnd 4105. London: The Stationery Office. www.archive.official-documents.co.uk/ document/cm41/4105/4105.htm, accessed on 3 May 2007.

Department of Health (2002) *National Minimum Standards for Children's Homes.* London: The Stationary Office.

Eborall, C. (2003) *The State of the Social Care Workforce,* vol. 1. Leeds: TOPSS England.

van Ewijk, H., Hens, H., Lammersen, G. and Moss, P. (2002) *Mapping of Care Services and the Care Workforce, Consolidated Report.* Utrecht: Nederlands Instituut voor Zorg en Welzijn. http://144.82.31.4/carework/reports/finalconsolidatedreportwp3.pdf, accessed on 3 May 2007.

Federal Statistical Office Germany (1998) *Fachserie 13, Reihe 6.1.2, Reihe, 6.1.4: Jugendhilfe – Erzieherische Hilfen außerhalb des Elternhauses.* Weisbaden: Statistisches Bundesamt.

Hämäläinen, J. (2003) 'The Concept of Social Pedagogy in the Field of Social Work.' *Journal of Social Work 3,* 1, 69–80.

Hansen, K.H. (2004) 'Danish Pedagogues: Well Educated Generalists Working with All Age Groups.' Paper given at Care Work in Europe Conference, London: 16 November.

Kent, R. (1997) *Children's Safeguards Review.* Edinburgh: Scottish Office.

Mainey, A. (2003) *Better Than You Think: Staff Morale, Qualifications and Retention in Residential Child Care.* London: National Children's Bureau.

McQuail, S. (2001) 'Working with Children: European Models of Pedagogy and Residential Care: Germany.' Unpublished report. London: Thomas Coram Research Unit, University of London Institute of Education.

Meltzer, H., Corbin, T., Gatward, R., Goodman, R. and Ford, T. (2003) *The Mental Health of Young People Looked After by Local Authorities in England.* London: The Stationery Office. www.statistics.gov.uk/downloads/theme_health/ChildrensMentalHlth.pdf, accessed on 3 May 2007.

Mortimore, P. (1999) *Understanding Pedagogy and its Impact on Learning.* London: Paul Chapman Publishing.

Petrie, P., Boddy, J., Cameron, C., Simon, A. and Wigfall, V. (2006) *Working with Children in Care: European Perspectives.* Maidenhead: Open University Press.

Scottish Executive (2002) *National Care Standards: Care Homes for Children and Young People.* Edinburgh: The Stationary Office.

Scottish Office (1998) *The Government's Response to the Kent Report on Children's Safeguards Review.* www.scotland.gov.uk/library/documents7/kent-ch0.htm, accessed on 3 May 2007.

Simon, A., Owen, C., Moss, P. and Cameron, C. (2003) *Mapping the Care Workforce: Supporting joined-up thinking: Secondary analysis of the Labour Force Survey for childcare and social care work.* London: Department of Health/Institute of Education.

Statbank Danmark (2003) *BIS2: Children and Young Persons Placed Outside of Own Home by Region, Place of Accommodation, Age and Sex.* Copenhagen: Statbank Danmark.

TOPSS UK Partnership 2003 (2003) *National Occupational Standards for Managers in Residential Child Care.* Leeds: TOPSS England. www.topssengland.net/files/119673_NOS_Booklet_MiRCC.pdf, accessed on 20 October 2005.

Utting, W. (1997) *People Like Us: The Report on the Review of Safeguards for Children Living Away from Home.* London: The Stationery Office.

CHAPTER 16

Leadership, Structure and Culture in Residential Child Care

Roger Bullock

Introduction

How can we separate the important from the unimportant in residential child care? Are the features that most people welcome as making life pleasant related to good outcomes for children and families or do they make no difference? Certainly some Spartan boarding schools and draughty colleges seem to produce endearment among their alumni, and young people often prefer to meet in scruffy locations than in gleaming facilities. Do we know what are the characteristics of effective residential care? Are these the same as for good quality provision?

When looking at a residential establishment for children, the immediate ports of call are the surface features, such as the style of leadership, the fabric and resources. Judgements about quality are often reached from first impressions, initial conversations with staff or the visible responses of the children. It is easy to assume that the most important aspects are either the people or the regime and that, if we can get these right, all will be well. But the research studies that have scrutinised the inner workings of child care settings reveal a more complicated situation.

Certainly, individuals, whether an efficient manager or an unruly adolescent, are important in affecting what happens in a residential context but they are not enough to explain everything. In their extensive surveys of children's homes, the research teams at York University (Hicks *et al.* 2003; Sinclair and Gibbs 1998; Whitaker, Archer and Hicks 1998) have found that managers successful in one context often run into difficulties elsewhere, and establishments vary widely in their capacity to meet young people's needs. Some features that common sense might associate with good provision were found to be relatively insignificant. The quality of buildings, the proportion of trained staff, the characteristics of the children, for example, are not sufficient *on their own* to produce good results.

So, while residential establishments have aspects that can be easily differentiated, such as buildings, staff roles or types of children, there is something extra – something more than the sum of the parts – that is important in determining what happens therein. Many writers used terms such as 'culture' or 'ethos' to describe this. These concepts may readily be dismissed as elusive or catch-all, too vague to be of analytic value, but it is precisely these feelings and messages that a visitor picks up. They may be long-standing, such as when there is a traditional way of doing things, or may be a product of stress or boredom. These cultures have been shown by research to be especially important because they directly affect staff behaviour, not just in terms of conformity or deviance but also in shaping attitudes.

The relationship between culture and structure

Researchers have explored this phenomenon from different angles. Five large-scale empirical studies have been undertaken in the last decade but they are all concerned with children's homes, establishments that nowadays are small with more staff than residents – producing a distinctive interaction style. The conclusions reached may or may not be applicable to larger residential settings such as schools or hospitals; we simply do not know. The five studies are *Working in Children's Homes: Challenges and Complexities* (Whitaker *et al.* 1998), *Children's Homes: A Study in Diversity* (Sinclair and Gibbs 1998), *Making Residential Care Work: Structure and Culture in Children's Homes* (Brown *et al.* 1998), *Leadership and Resources in Children's Homes* (Hicks *et al.* 2003) and *Managing Residential Child Care: A Managed Service* (Whipp, Kirkpatrick and Kitchener 2005). Each adopts a slightly different perspective on the 'what works?' question. For example, the first takes a relatively unusual starting point of the experiences of staff, the second analyses the factors that predict optimal outcomes, the third looks at the relationship between staff and child cultures and the fourth and fifth look at management issues.

The staff cultures described in the first book (Whitaker *et al.* 1998) had much in common in that they espoused the same overall goal of benefiting the young people, faced the same range of tasks and shared many of the same values. Yet each culture was unique with respect to the details of its beliefs and attitudes, rules of behaviour, procedures, routines and customs, degree of internal cohesiveness and the nature of the boundary between the home and the outside world. Hence, some staff groups were mutually supportive, some were conflict ridden, some were secure and competent, others were not.

The distinctive cultures that emerged in each case were influenced by the specific circumstances that staff faced, such as the:

- rate of turnover of the young people
- proportion of emergency placements
- mix of young people
- number of young people not in school
- stability of membership in the staff group
- composition of both young people and staff with respect to ethnicity and gender
- feelings of security among staff within their own organisation
- presence or absence of conflict with managers, and
- level of morale.

The second book (Sinclair and Gibbs 1998) looked at 48 children's homes in five local authorities to chart variations in the immediate and long-term outcomes of homes, and to explain these in terms of the characteristics of residents, structural features of the homes and regimes operated.

It was found that the wide variations in such outcomes as young people's offending behaviour and absconding were not explained by children's backgrounds. Moreover, difficult social environments in the homes were not related to previous difficult behaviour by residents or to levels of staff training.

Interviews with young people revealed that they appreciated homes more:

- if they were not bullied, sexually harassed or led into trouble
- if staff listened, the regime was benign and the other children friendly
- if they showed some tangible improvement, such as in education
- if their wish for family contact (but not necessarily to live with them) was respected.

In conclusion, Sinclair and Gibbs found that homes performed best if:

- they were small

- the head of the home felt that his or her role was clear, mutually compatible with external management, not disturbed by reorganisation and that he or she had autonomy

- staff agreed on how the home should be run.

When the outcomes for the children were assessed, it was found that individual misery was related to sexual harassment, bullying, missing family and friends, poor relations with other residents and lack of success in esteemed roles such as sport.

Regimes were connected to outcomes for children by virtue of the fact that young people adjusted better socially if the head of the home had a clear idea of the ways in which aims were to be achieved and staff turnover was not high.

The focus of the third study (Brown *et al.* 1998) is the relationship between the structure of homes and the staff and child cultures within them. It is well established that regimes have a considerable effect on children's behaviour while they are resident, and welfare-oriented approaches have consistently been found to produce the best results for children's health, education and personal social development. Staff and child cultures have long been known to influence outcomes even if the precise nature and direction of the association have been unclear. Until now, the principal conclusion from this evidence was that the best thing that managers could do was to ensure that cultures did not cohere in a negative way.

But the usefulness of these findings for managers and staff charged with making residential care work has been limited. Even homes seemingly well planned from the start have encountered problems. A list of correlations between structural variables and outcomes is difficult for managers to interpret, especially when the message is more a case of what should not happen than a clear indication of what needs to be done. Nor are global descriptions, such as the notion of a 'good home' or putting together a 'positive culture', of much value in the mêlée of daily living. As in life itself, everything in residential care can seem to be related to everything else, and emphasising single features can stifle rational discussion. How many times has the tautology 'a good home is one which has a good manager' or 'a good home is one which is a happy home' been heard?

Brown *et al.* (1998) define structure as 'the orderly arrangements of social relations and a continuing arrangement of kinds of people governed by a concept of proper behaviour in their relations with each other' (p. 58). Culture is defined 'as a quality discernible in response to a problem encountered by a group' (p. 16). The study sets out a linear model of cause and effect. It argues that, in children's homes at least, the structure of the home determines the staff culture, the staff culture determines the child culture which, in turn, determines outcome for homes and for children. While there is obviously some feedback in the process, the model is able to discount the possibility of the opposite situation where cultures determine structures. The study argues that it is the relationship between three types of goals – societal, formal and belief – that forms the basis of the structure of the home. Societal goals are those laid down or implied by law or public expectation; formal goals cover the local adaptation of these ideas by managers and their implementation in practice; belief goals reflect the underlying beliefs and values of managers and staff. If goals are out of balance or the relationship is contradictory, no amount of work on staff and child cultures will improve the situation.

A major contribution of these three studies is the focus on the homes themselves and the ways in which they change. Change, like all other components in the model, has good and bad effects, encouraging improvements in the better homes but exacerbating difficulties elsewhere. Change in itself is not sufficient to lift standards in the poorer establishments although, self-evidently, it is necessary to improve practice. Without knowing its effects or what it is supposed to achieve, much innovation is wasted. The difficulty is knowing where in the chain of effects to intervene. Is it best to empty a bad home and start again, or is more training or a new manager the answer?

A second contribution has been to show that, in children's homes at least, strong cultures are not necessarily bad. Indeed, staff can benefit from the insights and practical help offered by positive peer support and managers can use this strength, along with training and supervision, to further the work of the home. Child cultures are more difficult to manage but a strong culture can complement the work of staff provided children implicitly understand the goals of the establishment, comprehend the way their particular home implements these and perceive senior staff as people able to achieve something on their behalf. In such situations, there is no need to fragment the child culture. Thus, a hardy annual of residential care theory has been modified in the light of new evidence.

The relationship between leadership, structure and culture

If a salient feature of the studies discussed is the importance of 'culture' or 'ethos' for outcomes, whether for the home itself or for the young people who live there, it seems likely from the evidence that leadership is an important determinant of this. However, the findings on this were not conclusive and the processes that produced the effects little understood. To explore this possibility further, two pieces of research were undertaken. Hicks *et al.* (2003) conducted a survey of children's homes, looking specifically at leadership. Using information from 45 homes, 301 staff, 134 field social workers and 170 young people, they were able to tease out the qualities of management and the components essential for good outcomes. Similarly, Whipp *et al.* (2005) looked at leadership in terms of the external management of children's homes, an area frequently highlighted as deficient in inspections and abuse inquiries.

Both studies explored the concept of leadership in the context of overall management. Management, says Whipp and colleagues, implies 'a need to achieve some degree of control and co-ordination to meet goals' (Whipp *et al.* 2005, p. 16). Hicks and colleagues expand this with:

> in order to manage a children's home successfully, managers had to function as more than good administrators and supervisors of daily tasks operating from within fixed budgets. Children's homes managers have to keep their fingers on the pulses of their homes, build and develop their teams, and provide an example in terms of practice with young people. In short, the term manager denotes authority by referring to the most senior role in an executive hierarchy. Leadership, put simply, may be seen as denoting influence. (Hicks *et al.*, p. 113)

Both studies then seek to delineate the different tasks facing managers in residential child care. They stress that although managing a children's service in which residential provision plays a part is not the same as managing an individual establishment, both are riddled with contradictions and require more than overseeing a stable and predictable bureaucracy. In the former, the different demands of legislation and government guidance, politicians, finance officers and other parts of the wider children and family services have to be satisfied. In the latter a complex set of roles has to be performed.

Managers of homes are leaders in the sense that they have to supervise and develop a staff team offering therapeutic work, encourage relationships with children's schools and families and satisfy their superiors in central bureaucracies. In undertaking this work, there are balances to be struck, between energising staff but not disempowering them and being sensitive to the needs of individual children but setting boundaries and controls for the group. They also have to fulfil public and professional expectations to act as a role model to adolescents and sustain the work of the home through bad patches. Thus, four features of a residential setting have to be concordant if success is to be achieved. An effective establishment has to admit the right sort of children, has to operate a regime that best meets the needs of their residents, has to pursue good child care practice and has to be well run. Failure in any one of these areas will reduce success in others. So a manager who is a good administrator but little else is likely to fall short in three of the four areas.

After a review of the numerous theories of management and leadership (Burns 1978; Reed 1996), both research teams conclude that leadership is best understood in the context of a social role rather than a personal attribute or innate skill. This is because of the inescapable facts that good leaders in one situation frequently fail in others and similar results can be achieved by different management styles. The York team found a mixture of internal and external influences on leadership, any of which could affect performance. External factors included the status of the post, clarity of role and function, ability to spend time in the unit, autonomy and the quality of external support. Internal factors were experience with the team, ability to influence practice and an effective strategy for handling children's behaviour and ensuring their education. Successful leadership in terms of consistent and reflective practice rests on a combination of these factors.

The dominant leadership factor affecting outcomes was the concept of 'strategy' because this produced a chain of effects that generally worked for the good of the home. A clearly worked-out strategy for dealing with children's behaviour and education increased staff morale; they then felt they received clearer and better guidance with the result that the children behaved better. Young people also expressed more positive views about the social climate of the home and were seen by their social workers as functioning better. All of this was independent of the background characteristics of the residents.

With regard to effects on children's behaviour, a clear strategy robustly implemented also reduced the likelihood of young people being convicted of criminal offences and being excluded from school, but not of running away. The effects on children's wider well-being were more difficult to discern because of the influence of so many intervening variables. Young people's welfare was increased by a clear strategy but this only pertained while they were resident.

In leadership terms this meant managers having a clear, sanctioned and supported management role, a degree of autonomy and a self-perception as a leader of a team. But they also had to have clear strategies for implementing the practice they wanted and for ensuring that it was enshrined in guidance, induction and training. 'What seems to matter in children's homes is that the manager is accepted as embodying good practice from within a clear ethos, has positive strategies for working both with the behaviour of young people and in relation to their education, and is capable of enabling staff to reflect and deploy these' (Hicks *et al.* 2003, p. 173).

The perspective adopted by Whipp and colleagues was more focused on management, defined as a technical activity or process directed towards goals via control and coordination as methods. Twelve local authorities representative of national provision were selected for study and several aspects of management were explored. These were child care strategy and its implementation, the management of child placement, the line management of homes, managing and developing staff, monitoring and controlling the service, and the arrangements for acquiring placements external to the local authority.

The emerging picture was one of variability in all areas. While efforts were being made to improve the situation, all of this activity was taking place in an inauspicious context in which child care aims are complex and competing and have to be pursued in a professional bureaucracy displaying the same two features. Hence, 'the move to enhance management practices in the area of children's services have been uneven and uncontested. New forms of control have not been fully implemented. There has been little fundamental change in occupational cultures or in personnel management practices' (Whipp *et al.* 2005, p. 183).

The researchers proposed an optimal model for managing children's homes. It has three elements. The first is that it has an inclusive orientation to the problem of external management. This means encompassing not only the home and line manager but also all other stakeholders, such as residential staff, service managers and resource controllers, field workers, senior managers, support staff, other professionals, inspectors and elected members. The second element concentrates on how the process of management operates. The external management of homes comprises six core elements. They are strategic planning, placement decisions, line management, developing staff, monitoring and control and managing external placements. 'It is the choices made and actions taken in these areas which facilitate or constrain how external management operates at the level of practice within the distinctive context of children's services' (Whipp *et al.* 2005, p. 192). Finally:

> both the assumptions and practices of external management require explora-
> tion in terms of the extent to which they meet: the requirements and standards
> set not just by legislation, the DfES and relevant professional bodies but also in
> the light of recognised measures found across the management literature. In
> general, standards of management were found to vary in the homes studied
> with arrangements for monitoring performance and remedial intervention es-
> pecially poor. (Whipp *et al.* 2005, p. 192)

Coming from a business background, Whipp and colleagues seem surprised at the complexity of child care tasks and question the relevance of management models imported from commerce and industry, as envisaged in New Public Management Models. The potential benefits are clear – more efficient use of resources, stronger user consultation, improved monitoring of outcomes, clearer accountability and better value for money – but this approach implies a less centralised structure comprising independent quasi-business units subject to market forces. The authors argue that this might not be automatically applicable to children's services because of the inauspicious context described above. Indeed, the desired results might be achieved by other approaches, such as Matching Needs and Services exercises, better strategic planning, account-ability and information systems, more rigorous contracting and strengthening the relationship between needs, services and outcomes.

In drawing conclusions, the complications inherent in all discussions of leadership and management in residential child care surface to confound the arguments. The fundamental problem is that the 'clinical' interventions necessary to help children whose needs lead them to residential placements are by no means clear. The relationship between interventions and outcomes for children and families, especially if measured on child development criteria, are still relatively tenuous, even in therapeutic communities where treatment programmes are well articulated. While much has been written about good practice, it is mostly in terms of social care standards and administrative processes rather than the 'technology' used to help children and families. This dearth of validated interventions to meet particular needs means that views about the best ways of tackling the difficulties children present, such as hostile family relationships, challenging behaviour and the effects of poor parenting, are likely to be opinion as much as fact – hence the tendency to grant equal authority to people pontificating from shaky information as to researchers.

While it seems certain from the evidence presented that bad management exacerbates poor outcomes, in residential child care the opposite does not necessarily apply. Good management may not correlate with good outcomes, at least in terms of children's health and development, either because no proven 'technology' exists or because the contrast between the supportive care environment and life that follows in the outside world is so sharp. This is why the long-term results of much structural and process reform are often disappointing (Morpeth 2004).

So what authoritative findings can be drawn with regard to the relationship between leadership, structure and culture in residential establishments for children? The Department of Health's research review *Caring for Children Away from Home: Messages from Research* (Department of Health 1998), along with the more recent publications discussed, have highlighted the conditions auspicious for effective residential work. The scientific status of these findings is variable but there is sufficient evidence to show that outcomes for children and families and for homes themselves will be better if they are present. They cover a range of issues from the quality of information, creating good regimes, organisational features such as optimal size and staffing, and the structure of the wider children and family services in which homes function.

Optimal results will be obtained if:

- there is a strategic role for residential care in the wider children and family service

- expectations of residential care are realistic

- residential care is viewed as meeting some of the needs of the young people and families, along with other services, at particular stages of a child's development

- there is a care plan for the child that is based on his or her needs and harnesses services known to be the most likely to meet them

- societal, formal and belief goals are concordant.

The aspects of effective management and leadership for individual homes are that:

- the manager feels in control and supported

- he or she has a clear strategy to make the home child oriented

- he or she delivers interventions to children and families that are the most logical and evidence based to meet their needs
- he or she develops a staff team to implement these plans
- he or she can sustain the approach through difficult periods.

At a practice level, these aspects will be manifest in features of daily life in the home, such as:

- appropriate contact with family members
- involvement of children and, as appropriate, parents in decisions about their lives
- children being treated with respect
- children having the same access to education, health, employment and leisure as their peers
- children having access to the special services they may need
- a reduction in the aspects of behaviour that are known to be poor indicators for a child's development
- children being supported on leaving the home both in practical skills and in coping with potential loneliness and insecurity.

Although the concepts of management and leadership are now accepted parts of social work language, children's services professionals are still somewhat reluctant to accept their implications. They do not fit comfortably with a desire to help children who are developing individuals with their own aspirations and wishes. Management values smack too readily of ruthless efficiency at the expense of care, and of institutional practices that professionals have strived to leave behind. Similarly, unrestrained leadership calls to mind fraudulent zealots who have inflicted lunatic methods on defenceless subjects.

Yet as we seek to understand better the needs of children and families and react sensitively to them, we are faced with complexity and doubt. The fact is that without strong leadership and management, we shall never meet those needs, no matter how well meaning our efforts. But leadership and management are only means to ends. The task, whether planning a comprehensive children's service or making a care plan for a child, is to identify needs, set desired outcomes in different areas of children's lives and put in place the services most likely to achieve them. It is at that point that management and organisational issues come to the fore. Sadly, management is often the starting point for planning. It requires continuous effort to ensure that it supports rather than drives the needs-led and evidence-based services that are, and should always be, the stimulus of children's services work.

References

Brown, E., Bullock, R., Hobson, C. and Little, M. (1998) *Making Residential Care Work: Structure and Culture in Children's Homes.* Aldershot: Ashgate.

Burns, J. (1978) *Leadership.* New York: Harper and Row.

Department of Health (1998) *Caring for Children Away from Home: Messages from Research.* Chichester: Wiley.

Hicks, L., Gibbs, I., Byford, S. and Weatherley, H. (2003) *Leadership and Resources in Children's Homes.* York: The University of York, Social Work Research and Development Unit.

Morpeth, L. (2004) 'Organisation and Outcomes in Children's Services.' PhD thesis, University of Exeter.

Reed, M. (1996) 'Expert power and control in late modernity: An empirical review and theoretical synthesis.' *Organisation Studies XVII*, 473–598.

Sinclair, I. and Gibbs, I. (1998) *Children's Homes: A Study in Diversity.* Chichester: Wiley.

Whipp, R., Kirkpatrick, I. and Kitchener, M. (2005) *Managing Residential Child Care: A Managed Service.* Basingstoke, Palgrave MacMillan.

Whitaker, D., Archer, L. and Hicks, L. (1998) *Working in Children's Home: Challenges and Complexities.* Chichester: Wiley and Son.

Subject Index

Author Index